Industrial harmony in modern Japan

THE NISSAN INSTITUTE/ROUTLEDGE
JAPANESE STUDIES SERIES

Editorial Board:

J.A.A. Stockwin, Nissan Professor of Modern Japanese Studies, University of Oxford and Director, Nissan Institute of Japanese Studies

Teigo Yoshida, formerly Professor of the University of Tokyo, and now Professor, The University of the Sacred Heart, Tokyo

Frank Langdon, Professor, Institute of International Relations, University of British Columbia, Canada

Alan Rix, Professor of Japanese, The University of Queensland

Junji Banno, Professor, Institute of Social Science, University of Tokyo

Industrial harmony in modern Japan

The invention of a tradition

W. Dean Kinzley

London and New York

First published 1991
by Routledge
11 New Fetter Lane, London EC4P 4EE

Simultaneously published in the USA and Canada
by Routledge
a division of Routledge, Chapman and Hall, Inc.
29 West 35th Street, New York, NY 10001

Typeset by Columns
Printed and bound in Great Britain by
Biddles Ltd, Guildford and King's Lynn

British Library Cataloguing in Publication Data
Kinzley, W. Dean *1945–*
    Industrial harmony in modern Japan.
    1. Japan. Industrial relations
    I. Title
    331.0952
    ISBN 0–415–05167–3

Library of Congress Cataloging in Publication Data
Kinzley, William Dean.
    Industrial harmony in modern Japan : the invention of a tradition /
    W. Dean Kinzley.
    p.   cm.   (The Nissan Institute/Routledge Japanese studies series)
    Includes bibliographical references and index.
    ISBN 0–415–05167–3
    1. Industrial relations—Japan—History. 2. Corporate culture—
    Japan—History. I. Title II. Series.
    HD8724.K56   1991
    302.3'5'0952—dc20   90–8906
                                                                   CIP

for Alma

Contents

Note on Japanese names

Following Japanese practice, surnames precede given names in this book. The names of Westerners of Japanese ancestry or Japanese who have written in English are cited with their given name first. Long vowels are indicated by the use of macrons (e.g. Kyōchōkai, Ōsawa), but these are omitted in the case of a few well-known place names (e.g. Tōkyō, Ōsaka, Kyōto) when they appear in the text, in names of organizations or as places of publication.

General Editor's preface

With growing speed, as we move into the 1990s, Japan in her many aspects is becoming a subject of interest and concern. The successes of the Japanese economy and the resourcefulness of her people have long been appreciated abroad. What is new is an awareness of her increasing impact on the outside world. This tends to produce painful adjustment and uncomfortable reactions. It also often leads to stereotypes based on outdated or ill-informed ideas.

The Nissan Institute/Routledge Japanese Studies Series seeks to foster an informed and balanced – but not uncritical – understanding of Japan. One aim of the series is to show the depth and variety of Japanese institutions, practices and ideas. Another is, by using comparison, to see what lessons, positive and negative, can be drawn for other countries. There are many aspects of Japan which are little known outside that country but which deserve to be better understood.

Perhaps the most perplexing set of issues for students of twentieth-century Japan is that concerning tradition and modernity. Japanese experience appears to challenge unilinear theories of modernization, and to suggest that Japan's uniqueness lies in the creation of her own kind of modernity, sharply divergent from that to be found in Western countries, and based paradoxically upon a reaffirmation of Japanese native traditions of harmony, self-sacrifice and non-individualistic group striving in pursuit of a common cause.

This book is concerned with the ways in which labour–management relations were addressed in the period between the two world wars. Acute anxieties about the potential for social unrest implicit in the emergence of an industrial proletariat led to the formation of the Kyōchōkai, a body formed on conservative organicist principles. The Kyōchōkai promoted the principles of harmony between management and labour, an approach which ran counter to any idea of adversarial unionism. Yet as Dean Kinzley ably demonstrates, what was involved here was not merely the reassertion of tradition, but the creation of tradition, as conscious myth-making was called into play to maintain social cohesion and fulfil the aims of the Japanese state.

J.A.A. Stockwin
Director, Nissan Institute of Japanese Studies
University of Oxford

Acknowledgements

The debts any author incurs are numerous and manifold. This book is poor payment for the help and guidance provided me by many individuals and institutions. I must first thank Professor Kenneth B. Pyle of the University of Washington who supervised this study as a Ph.D. dissertation. This book has also benefited from comments by Gary Allinson, Gail Bernstein, Sheldon Garon and Andrew Gordon. In Japan, Professor Ishida Takeshi has given generously of his time and vast knowledge. Professor Nimura Kazuo guided me through the rich resources of the Ōhara Institute of Social Research. Also discussions with Professors Ikeda Makoto, Itō Takashi, Kimbara Samon and Tsuchiana Fumito unravelled many mysteries. In particular, I am grateful to Professor Banno Junji who has been a good friend and wise mentor.

Research, writing and revision were made possible with a Fulbright–Hays Fellowship and generous grants from the University of Washington, the Northeast Asia Area Council, the University of South Carolina Research and Productive Scholarship Fund, and the University of South Carolina Venture Fund.

The staffs of the East Asian libraries of the University of Washington, the University of California, Berkeley, and the Library of Congress; the Ōhara Institute of Social Research, and the libraries of Tokyo University's Institute of Social Science and Economics Department were all most helpful and without them this work would not have been possible.

Finally, my greatest debt is to my wife, Alma, for too many things to mention here. It is to her that this book is dedicated.

Introduction

Japan has become the object of a great deal of scrutiny. Its economic strength has finally put to rest the old notion that Japanese are little more than borrowers, clever mimics of Westerners. Instead, many in the West now look to Japan for guidance in solving their own nation's economic and social problems.[1] Its educational success, high rates of saving and low levels of crime have all been examined in the popular and scholarly media. Japan's emphasis on long-term growth, scrupulous market evaluation, and process engineering are all regarded as important components of its economic development. Nothing, however, has been more frequently considered than the nature of industrial organization itself, specifically Japan's now well-known system of labour–management relations. Those relations are linked with 'lifetime' employment, a participatory work environment and docile enterprise unions. What is most frequently noted in those relations is what appears to be a spirit of harmony between and among managers and workers. This sense of cooperation and shared purpose between groups which in the West are nominally antagonistic is often regarded as the central distinguishing feature of Japan's economic and social ideology. Many Japanese and Western observers view this 'culture of harmony' as the most distinctive, most unique aspect of modern Japan's economic organizations.[2]

It was once commonplace to argue that the organizational elements of Japanese industry were natural carry-overs from feudalistic relations and from the relations of the traditional patriarchal family. Venerable cultural values were used to explain the shape of modern institutional development.[3] Beginning with the work of Sumiya Mikio in the 1960s, however, scholars turned their attention instead to the structural and historical roots of Japan's employment practices. The 'Japanese employment system' came to be seen as the result of rational decision makers adjusting and readjusting organizational and institutional responses to tangible economic needs.[4] What this has meant is the rejection of culture as an explanatory variable. No one has been more insistent in repudiating the causal role of culture and societal values than Chalmers Johnson in his study on *MITI and the Japanese Miracle*.[5] The institutional studies of Japanese industrial and employment practices have done much to clarify our understanding of the Japanese workplace and its dynamics. They have lifted the veil of particularist exceptionalism that for so long covered Japanese institutional developments. What they do not explain, however, is the existence of the 'culture of harmony' as a normative economic value. This study addresses that question.

It is concerned with elite efforts from the Meiji period forward to fashion an industrial ideology that would domesticate capitalism. A basic argument of this book is that political and social elites set out to and succeeded in creating a Japanese-style economic ideology built upon their understanding of the Japanese past and its moral ideals rather than upon Western notions of economic and organizational theory. The impetus for this effort came from concerns over observable social and economic problems. Initially this meant the issue of poverty and the beginnings of factory organization. By the twentieth century the emergence of radical groups, the growth of labour union organization, the expansion of peasant activism and the development of radical feminism all seemed to augur the breakdown of the social order. To combat these dangerous conditions elites moved to define and put in place a new kind of modern industrial society, one that resonated with broadly accepted moral ideals and was couched in traditional moral language.

The principal actor in this effort was the semi-bureaucratic agency known as the Kyōchōkai (The Cooperation and Harmony Society) established in 1919. The Kyōchōkai took the lead in creating and articulating the new industrial ideology, the new tradition that its members hoped would redefine economic relationships. The organization and its spokesmen emphasized the primacy of moral community and the need for industrial harmony and cooperation. Theirs was an act of myth-making, creating normative ideals and forging a civil religion for the new modern industrial society. This effort did not begin with the Kyōchōkai. Chapter 1 discusses the Meiji roots of this work. Yet it was during the years following World War I that the greatest effort was made in this myth-making process. The Kyōchōkai was the most prominent player in it.

The invention of a new culture of harmony was tied to a substantial programme of social and economic reform. In the Meiji era this meant the establishment of relief regulations and moves toward the writing of a factory law. Later, reform programmes aimed at the passage of labour union legislation, factory law revision, health insurance legislation, severance pay regulations, and the like, dominated much of the interwar period's domestic political agenda. Beside playing a prominent role in the debate over these legislative issues, the Kyōchōkai was active in establishing worker education programmes, settlement houses and employment bureaux as well as frequently providing a forum for strike mediation. Two basic ideas underlay this reform effort. First, industrial and social reform were widely regarded as 'trends of the times'. The allied victory in the Great War not only solidified the allies' position as world powers but also seemed to suggest the rightness of their economic and social policies. Thus Anglo-American social policies and social reform programmes were considered appropriate and acceptable strategies for achieving economic growth and social stability. Second, the Kyōchōkai and other elites deemed reforms necessary to satisfy or at least accommodate popular demands. Leaders of the Kyōchōkai believed that a fundamental ideological reorientation would be unachievable if the more egregious inequities and serious social problems were not addressed. In short, reforms were necessary, at least in part, to create a more malleable, accepting populace.

This point suggests that interwar social reform and the effort to redefine Japan's modern economic society were not driven by liberal assumptions, however 'liberal' may be defined.[6] The desire to create a Japanese-style capitalism was rooted in very different soil. The emphasis on harmony and moral community was tied to ancient assumptions of Confucian moral economy. Reformers and ideologues of the Meiji era and beyond consciously used Confucian moral language and unconsciously embraced nativist ideals. They sought to recreate in the present an idealized past. This does *not* mean that the Kyōchōkai and other social policy reformers were nothing more than a collection of hidebound obscurantists. Quite the reverse. The morally based ideals of harmony and moral community were not pursued because no alternative could be imagined but, rather, because they represented the preferred alternative. They were seen to be viable constructs for coping with the dislocations of an emerging modern economy and were workable precisely because they were seen to have been part of the fabric of Japanese life in the past and could thus be so again. By imagining a living past through the language of traditional ideals, the Kyōchōkai led in the creation of an invented tradition, a culture of industrial harmony, a tradition with no substantial antecedents.

In one sense, therefore, this is a study of what Theodore Bestor has called 'traditionalism'.[7] In forging the new culture of harmony elites appropriated, manipulated and reconfigured ideas and cultural patterns from the past to meet new economic and social needs. The tradition was new but was fitted into the comfortable language and assumptions of the familiar. Thus attempts to distinguish between traditional and modern is to create a false dichotomy. In Japan, as elsewhere, tradition has been worked and reworked to explain, justify, or indigenize contemporary practices.[8]

But elite myth-making was not simply concerned with rendering the new familiar or acceptable. They aimed also at the establishment of a new civil religion for the emerging modern society.[9] The act of nation-building was marked by efforts to build a unified culture, a 'politically sanctified culture' that sought to eliminate differences and devalue that which was not deemed central.[10] This meant recasting not only political culture but the economic culture and its values as well. The rapid development of Japan during the Meiji era and beyond altered every aspect of life. The innumerable social problems that accompanied this transformation were widely regarded as moral problems as much as problems of institutional change. Poverty, labour unrest and radical ideology all seemed to signal an erosion of traditional morality. These problems, as a result, required moral solutions. Certainly, social reform too was necessary, but to be meaningful it had to be accompanied by and built upon a moral transvaluation. The new industrial ideology propagated by the Kyōchōkai sought to bring about this moral reformation. Industrial harmony and moral community were presented as normative values central to the very nature of Japanese-ness. They were not merely traditions but part of the fabric of national identity itself. As a result, this is also a study of one aspect of the larger Japanese obsession with national ethics training (*shūshin*) which aimed at the inculcation of the sanctified values of the new state. What it demonstrates, therefore, is that the emergence and evolution of the culture of harmony was a constituent element of the growth of prewar ultranationalism.

Chapter 1 discusses the Meiji roots of the culture of harmony. The emphasis on community in the Relief Regulation of 1874 and the concern with moral reformism in the debate over factory legislation in the 1890s laid important groundwork for the myth-making process. Chapter 2 discusses the forces leading to the creation of the Kyōchōkai, while Chapter 3 considers its creation of the ideology of harmonism. It also discusses the key ideas of the organization's founders and leaders during its first decade of existence. The social and institutional reforms pursued by the Kyōchōkai are the subject of Chapter 4. The final substantive chapter considers the changes in the organization, its ideology and programmes brought on by world depression and national crisis as Japan first prepared for and then found itself at war.

Through an examination of the Kyōchōkai and its creation of a new industrial ideology we get a more nuanced picture of Japan's industrial growth and the values that have supported it. At the same time, this is a story that illuminates the dynamic relationship between traditional and modern in the nation-building process and in so doing sheds light on the larger issue of development itself.

1 Society as moral community: the making of a myth

The forty-four year reign of the Meiji emperor, in whose name the modern Japanese state was created, was a period of tumultuous change. New national political institutions were established, a centrally controlled system of local governance was put in place, and a modern military system was created. Society was transformed by the elimination of the Tokugawa class system, the introduction of universal education, and by the imposition of a new land tax that routinized the relationship between cultivators and the state. Economic output grew sharply during this period. Growth was largely due to expansion of the traditional economy – textiles, mining, organized handicraft production and the like. Yet, accompanied by the development of rail and steamship lines, the introduction of the telegraph, the emergence of a national bank and the beginnings of a modern economic sector – steel, chemicals and machine tools – the growth of the Meiji economy was a dizzying spectacle. The Western romantic writer Lafcadio Hearn lamented the 'hideous rapidity' of Japan's modernization, a process which he saw eroding the fundamental character of Japanese life.[1] Most Japanese writers, however, were thrilled by what they saw. Fukuzawa Yukichi, the pre-eminent spokesman of modern Japan, for example, told a Keiō University audience of his joy for having been a part of the emergence of a strong, vibrant modern Japan that seemed to have 'materialized before our very eyes'.[2] For Fukuzawa and for many others the new, much changed Japan was a dream fulfilled.

But if the Meiji state brought forth new energy, new power and new opportunities, it also gave rise to undreamed-of problems. One of these was what came to be called, following European usage, the social problem (*shakai mondai*). The seeming contradiction between expanding industrial development and increasing social conflict alarmed political leaders and social elites alike. As in the advanced Western countries, the growing recognition of this problem brought forth calls for government intervention and policies aimed at social engineering. Regulations mandating poor relief and disease prevention, ordering the relationship between masters and apprentices, as well as controlling mass meetings and political organizing, proliferated in the period. With the new constitution, legislation broadening social welfare activity and state monitoring of factory life were introduced in the national Diet. Much of the research on Meiji social issues has focused on these regulatory or legislative efforts and upon the German-based social policy (*shakai seisaku*) that supported them. But the problems of Meiji society were seen not just as structural problems necessitating merely structural solutions. They were also seen to be moral problems: the erosion of the moral links between economic actors, the changing relationship of the individual and the community, and the need for a new social morality binding communities and the nation. The need to foster a sense of moral community was broadly felt and was embedded in the social policies of the Meiji period. Writing in 1909, the Home Ministry official Inoue Tomoichi emphasized the need to promote what he called a 'public-spirited social morality'.[3] His was not a new concern. Almost immediately following the Restoration, policies and programmes were initiated with this goal in mind. Fostering a myth of moral community and promoting a collectivist social morality were part and parcel of Meiji social policies. This chapter explores that effort.

SOCIAL RELIEF AND THE COMMUNITARIAN IDEAL

The social problem was discovered during the early 1890s by Japanese intellectuals looking at Europe and concerned with the social consequences of *laissez-faire* capitalism. The term social problem (or social question) became an important part of the popular discourse in that decade and grew ever more prominent in the twentieth century. But the social problem became an important issue before Japanese had a name for it. As in Europe it was poverty and the issue of poor relief that forced the new state to begin to grapple with the social meaning of modernity.

Poverty, of course, was not new nor were government programmes of relief distribution. Chronicles from the Nara and Heian periods document imperial generosity to victims of famine or natural disaster, and military leaders over the succeeding centuries undertook similar efforts.[4] Yet, as in early states everywhere, routine hardship was regarded as a normal, unvarying part of the human landscape. As a result, early relief activities were in no way regular or institutionalized, they were instead episodic, prompted only by severe distress. While peasants could claim no well-defined right to assistance, governments, aristocratic and military, did accept limited responsibility to demonstrate their benevolence in times of great need. Such gestures were an essential component of Confucian moral rule – evidence of the ruler's social conscience. The Tokugawa *bakufu* (Tokugawa era military government) accepted these basic assumptions of Confucian moral statecraft. But as in other areas of governance, in relief distribution the *bakufu* pursued a policy of what Michio Umegaki has called 'calculated indifference'.[5] Local domains were charged with the responsibility of relief distribution in the territories under their care. By the middle of the eighteenth century the *bakufu* in fact had mandated that all domains set aside funds for disaster and famine relief. Most did so and, more important, many were forced to distribute relief rice repeatedly to alleviate distress.[6] It would be wrong to suggest that domains provided relief assistance easily. Relief was a last resort and flowed only to those who repeatedly and persistently sought it.[7] Nevertheless, the creation and use of such programmes strengthened at least the rhetorical commitment to state benevolence. At the same time, the existence of relief programmes, however limited their scope, solidified popular expectations about the official role in the delivery of welfare assistance.

The final years of the Tokugawa regime and the early years of the new Meiji era brought hardship to many. The introduction of foreign goods into Japan in the 1860s and the treaty arrangements under which foreign trade was conducted weakened the domestic handicraft industry on which peasants depended so heavily. These conditions marked the beginning of an inflationary spiral that remained a serious problem until the Matsukata deflation of the 1880s. Coupled with the severe dislocations of the Restoration wars and the difficult transition to a new national state, these conditions meant at least temporary hardship for many and serious deprivation for many others.

Evidence of poverty was visible in rural and urban areas throughout the country. Inspection tours of the countryside by officials of the new imperial state revealed widespread destitution.[8] Reports of starvation and food riots during the winters of 1869 and 1870 were common. Large cities were not immune to the problem of poverty. In the city of Tokyo in 1869 40.1 per cent of the population was classified as 'poor' by the city government and 20.5 per cent more were classified as 'extremely poor'.[9] According to an Osaka survey the following year, the city contained nearly 57,000 persons (18 per cent of the population) identified as poor while, also in 1870, the smaller city of Kōfu identified 6,508 persons as poor.[10] These figures are not cited for their precision, the catagories are vague and methods of assignment are unclear (the differences between Tokyo and Osaka are striking in this regard). But the figures do provide useful impressionistic evidence about contemporary perceptions of the problem.

If the existence of poverty was not a new phenomenon in the Meiji period, neither was the response of the new imperial government; its leaders, after all, were political not social revolutionaries. This meant, first of all, a continued emphasis on an idealized benevolent paternalism. As early as March 1868 the government professed its despair about the problems of the poor and declared that 'mercy and benevolence should be shown to the dispossessed and disabled'.[11] The new emperor showed the way: during the imperial progress to the new capital in November the entourage dispersed relief to the impoverished all along the route. The emperor's role as benevolent moral monarch was frequently highlighted during the Meiji era with his well-documented assistance to charity hospitals and orphanages as well as his distribution of direct relief and his later contribution toward the establishment of the Relief Association (Saiseikai) in 1911. Although imperial benevolence was symbolically significant and politically important, the state regarded local governments as the principal actors in relief distribution just as the Tokugawa *bakufu* had. At the same time it was trumpeting benevolence and mercy a directive went out to local government offices making it clear that it was their responsibility 'to deal with disastrous situations and to construct relief programs'.[12] Several times during 1868 and 1869 nagging missives went out to the old domains and the new prefectures carved out of Tokugawa-held territories reminding them that they were charged with the establishment of social relief institutions. The creation of poor houses, orphanages, charity hospitals, as well as the distribution of direct disaster relief were pointed to as appropriate and necessary activities for local government.[13] While hoping to preserve the aura of Confucian moral monarchy with highly visible imperial bene-volence, therefore, the leaders of the new state also sought to maintain Tokugawa disinterest in more broadly based social relief.

Many local areas played the expected role. Many continued to provide tax remission and direct relief distribution from reserve granaries (at least they did until 1871 when the new prefectures were created). Several cities erected charity hospitals and outpatient clinics for the poor. Orphanages such as that established in 1869 in what is now Ōita Prefecture and poor houses like the one built by the city of Osaka in 1871 were important parts of local social welfare programmes.[14]

Despite cases of the continuation of local initiative in social welfare delivery, the reality was that many areas of the country lacked the necessary resources. Following the Restoration most of the domain governments found themselves in desperate economic straits and were essentially incapable of providing the basic social services that had traditionally been their responsibility and which the new imperial government expected them to continue providing. This was particularly true in the north where the Restoration wars went on the longest and were the most destructive. In the early months of 1870, for example, leaders of the Shinjō domain sent a petition to the new imperial government seeking assistance in providing relief. The petition pointed out that military destruction in the region made the need for relief great but had depleted the resources of the domain with which it could be provided. A follow-up petition in the autumn begged for a speedy consideration of their appeal since an early onset of winter was making an already bad situation worse.[15] Nearby Shichinohe made a similar appeal pointing out that throughout the domain there was 'much hunger and great suffering'. The Shichinohe petition had a sense of real urgency to it; the previous year food riots had broken out and the worry was that the situation would become worse since much of the seed and livestock that had remained had been eaten over the winter. Domain leaders specifically sought imperial benevolence to meet the obvious and pressing relief needs of their people.[16] Local economic problems were not, however, confined to the north. Before 1871 thirteen domains voluntarily dissolved themselves due to financial insolvency and twenty-eight more petitioned the government for the right to reallocate government income for use in meeting domain expenses.[17] In the same years twenty-four of the new prefectures carved out of Tokugawa-held territories sought central government assistance to meet local administrative and relief needs.[18] Local financial incapacity was a national problem. From Tōhoku in the north to Kyūshū in the south, old domains and newly formed local governments found themselves unable to provide the social services local residents and the central government expected of them.

The financial condition of the new imperial government was not much better. The unequal treaties, the burden of samurai stipends and the institutional instability of the post-Restoration years drained central government resources just as surely as they had depleted the coffers of local areas. Moreover, the leaders of the new state were committed to a basic restructuring of the economy which took priority in dispersal of the funds at its disposal. Thus reserve granaries of the dissolved domains were directed not to the provision of relief but toward building economic infrastructure.[19] However necessary the central government claimed relief distribution to be, it had neither the ability nor the will to pay for it.

The 1871 dissolution of the feudal domains and the establishment of a prefectural system only exacerbated the relief problem. These new bureaucratic levels had to rely on the same weak economic base that had proved inadequate for the earlier domains. Moreover, the new prefectures were not bound by the paternalistic requirements of the preceding feudal system. Some prefectures provided some forms of relief but avoided or could not afford others; other prefectures did little or nothing. As a result, the state began to take tentative steps toward coordinating social welfare activity. In 1871 the Dajōkan (Council of State) issued regulations mandating that specified levels of temporary assistance be given to the sick and the indigent and in the same year released a regulation directing that homeless orphans be provided food and shelter.[20] Yet the Home Ministry was forced to acknowledge that while it had been 'customary for each domain to administer various relief programmes prior to the creation of the new prefectures, since their establishment a sound regulatory program has yet to come into being'. This was, as standard bureaucratic parlance had it, 'an extremely regrettable situation'.[21]

Petitions for assistance and relief distribution continued to flow into the central government after the dissolution of the domains. At the same time, commoners sent their own appeals for relief to their local government offices. Early in 1873, for example, peasants in the new Shiga prefecture petitioned the prefectural government for distribution of aid funds collected by the earlier Hikone domain. Prefectural authorities in turn forwarded the petitions to the central government. Similar petitions were also sent from Chiba, Okayama and Kumamoto prefectures.[22] These petitions and the continuing concern over the wide variation of local relief initiatives prompted the imperial government to consider the creation of a coherent national relief policy. By mid-1874 the Dajōkan had drawn up a draft regulation,[23] and in December it issued the most important piece of social welfare legislation of the Meiji period, the Relief Regulation (Jukkyū kisoku).[24] Although several laws were on the books mandating disaster relief, care for orphans, and the like, the 1874 Relief Regulation constituted the legal basis of Japan's relief and social welfare programmes until the 1930s (despite numerous attempts at revision), when it was superceded by a new Relief Law (Kyūgo hō), passed in 1929.

Issuance of the Regulation did not mean that state leaders had come to accept central government responsibility for social welfare. Quite the reverse. Key figures in the national government and numerous important opinion leaders outside officialdom regarded comprehensive social welfare as a pernicious influence that ultimately sapped society's vitality. After his trip to Europe as a plenipotentiary in the Iwakura Mission, Ōkubo Toshimichi, for example, expressed his fears about the 'evils of relief'. His concern was a common one: institutionalized assistance to the poor encouraged laziness and undermined the incentive to engage in productive work.[25] Japan's first important newspaper, the *Tokyo nichi nichi shimbun* shared this concern. In March 1872, shortly after its creation, an editorial denounced the poor as being little more than lazy idlers and suggested that they would 'come to depend' upon government assistance if a broad-based relief programme was established.[26] The paper's hostile tone typified the broadly held view of poverty as a personal failure. Iwakura Tomomi, in this regard, was most explicit: 'the masses of so-called poor people', he said, 'do not work because they are lazy; they bring on their own impoverishment'.[27] Fukuzawa Yukichi, the pre-eminent popularizer of modernization agreed. The status of doctors, government officials, important businessmen, and landholders, he argued, was 'entirely the result of . . . the powers which education brings'. Therefore a person who studies diligently 'becomes noble and rich, while his opposite becomes base and poor'.[28] Such statements are evidence of the liberal, Malthusian critique of social welfare that permeated the new state system. Although obliged to erect a national programme of social welfare in the Relief Regulation of 1874, these sentiments served to legitimize an extremely restrictive definition of the deserving poor.

Befitting its role as paternalist benefactor the Regulation mandated that the state was responsible for providing direct aid to

specified groups of impoverished people. 'Extremely poor individuals unable to work as a result of disabilities' were eligible for
assistance as were persons over 70 'unable to work due to illness or
infirmity'. Similarly, poor people incapable of working because of
debilitating illness, and foundlings and orphans under 15 were
eligible to receive state assistance. The Home Ministry, which was
responsible for administering the Regulation took even greater care
in defining its applicability. In a notice sent to local officials in July
1875 the Ministry emphasized that under the Relief Regulation

> support should be given, as in the past, to those individuals
> incapable of working as a result of the infirmities of old age, or
> because of youth, disability, or serious illness. . . . But, the
> provision of *assistance must be limited to only those who are
> completely dispossessed and completely without recourse to other
> forms of aid.*[29]

Local officials had to guard particularly, the Ministry warned,
against people applying for relief simply to avoid work (*kinrō
chozai*).[30] It is hardly surprising that the restrictions on relief
eligibility written into the Relief Regulation and strengthened by the
agency responsible for its administration yielded only very limited
social relief distribution by the Meiji state. Annual relief outlays
amounted to less than 1 per cent of government expenditures
through 1890, a figure which, according to one estimate, was less
than that of most years of the Tokugawa period to say nothing of
contemporary Western countries.[31]

The narrow application of the 1874 Regulation was a consequence, first of all, of financial weakness. The new imperial state
had hoped to continue the previous policy of disinterest in local
relief distribution. It quickly became evident, however, that local
government was unable to bear the cost of relief; the frequency of
petitions for assistance both before and after dissolution of the
feudal domains seemed to make that clear. The central government
could not take up the slack. The universally accepted strategy of
becoming a rich nation with a strong army (*fukoku kyōhei*) meant
the state could not divert resources needed for development to the
dispersal of relief. Nor was it willing to, and this unwillingness
meant embracing a liberal critique of social welfare and the
rejection of any kind of new redistributive function for the national
government beyond the limited benevolence required of the moral
ruler.

Yet neither the Regulation itself nor public justifications for it touched upon these issues. Rather, the Regulation emphasized the social welfare role of the moral community. Under this new relief regime families and communities were to bear primary responsibility for providing aid and assistance to their members. The distribution of relief, the Regulation's preamble explained, must be 'based on a spirit of friendship and mutuality between people'. Mutual aid and communal solidarity were to be the animating foundation of poor relief. The administrative agency for the new relief system, the Home Ministry, likewise emphasized what it saw as the traditional 'customs of cooperative relief' and the importance of friendship and neighbourliness.[32] Prominent figures outside the government like Fukuzawa, Katō Hiroyuki and Fukuchi Gen'ichirō also trumpeted the virtues of communality. Fukuchi, for example, in a signed editorial published shortly after the release of the Regulation, argued that 'poor relief needs to be established with methods based on mutual friendship and cooperation between people'. This task, he felt, was the limit of government responsibility in social welfare.[33] The emphasis on mutual aid by state officials and opinion leaders and its insertion into the legal basis of the Meiji social welfare system inevitably meant a restrictive definition of the deserving poor and the construction of narrow parameters of relief eligibility. Aged indigents and orphaned children deserved aid; impoverished individuals with identifiable family members did not. Isolated and disabled indigents warranted assistance, able-bodied beggars did not. Thus the ideal of the moral community served to limit state financial responsibility for social welfare – a basic interest of policy makers.

The weaknesses in the Relief Regulation and the relatively small amounts of assistance actually distributed under its auspices have led to the view that the Regulation was little more than a continuation of feudal policies. Ogawa Masaaki's observation that the Regulation represented the imposition 'of *hambatsu*, feudal ideas, not the emergence of some kind of new relief policy' is a fairly typical view.[34] The centrality of moral community in state social welfare, however, constituted a significant departure from past practice. First, implicit in the Regulation was a new, distinctly modern conception of poverty. The perception of poverty as a product of personal failings was a repudiation of earlier assumptions in which poverty was a natural phenomenon to which all could be subject. This new approach was in keeping with the utilitarian thrust of the new state itself. The embrace of political and economic rationalism implied human control over political and economic phenomena. Poverty could not be a residual category in such a formulation, it could not be a natural and inevitable human condition; it must have proximate, identifiable causes: poor people themselves. Second, by emphasizing mutual aid, Meiji relief policy removed local authorities from the centre of the aid distribution system. Local governments were essentially relieved of their Tokugawa era responsibilities for social welfare. To be sure, some forms of institutionalized relief were still necessary – orphanages, medical assistance for the dispossessed, and the like. But the primary responsibility for direct relief for which Shinjō, Kumamoto and other domains had sought central government help no longer existed. Local self-sufficiency and community self-help were invoked as a substitute.

What this redirection meant, finally, was that the Relief Regulation shifted the moral fulcrum of relief policy. Under the Regulation mutual assistance and local self-help, not paternalism, became the moral core of Japan's new welfare regime. Paternalistic relief efforts by central and local government became substantially symbolic while the distribution of the bulk of relief had to depend on the 'voluntary charity' (*nin'i no jikei*) of the community.[35] The individual and the community were invested with the moral responsibility to provide the assistance that had once been the province of the government. While the moral monarch (i.e. the state) retained his symbolic role as compassionate father, the community became the *de facto* moral centre of the Meiji social welfare system.

Local self-sufficiency had long been extolled as an ideal for Japanese communities. The new social welfare system appropriated and expanded this ideal. By shifting the moral centre of relief to the local community the Relief Regulation legitimized and gave prominence to familial sentiments and elevated those sentiments to agents of public policy. The moral community had become enshrined as a social ideal with the task of overcoming social problems.

THE FACTORY AS MORAL COMMUNITY

Poverty and how it needed to be dealt with remained important concerns throughout the Meiji period. Abe Isoo, writing in 1901, remained convinced that the poor problem (*hinmin mondai*) was at the core of what had by that time come to be called the 'social

problem'.[36] Nevertheless, the quickening pace of industrial growth
and the expanding awareness of Western labour problems hastened
a redirection of state social policies. While fear of the social
implications of poverty remained strong, those fears were absorbed
into a more broadly defined 'social problem' centred on the place of
labour in modern society. The poor became the working poor and
social relief was folded into social policy.[37] The organization of
factory life and the relationship of workers one to the other as well
as with managers took priority. From the middle of the Meiji period
forward elites both within and without the government sought to
address these new, seemingly pressing issues.

By any measure economic growth during the Meiji period was
impressive. Precise figures are unavailable, but a conservative
estimate would be that between 1883 and the onset of World War I
total production expanded by 100 per cent.[38] Every sector of the
economy experienced growth in this period. The spectacle of this
growth, coupled with the image of Meiji as a time of great change,
tends to mask the fact that most economic growth in the period was
in the area of traditional industry. Small-scale cottage production of
traditional goods continued to dominate Meiji output. Even in the
cotton industry, one of the first industries to move toward modern
production, 87 per cent of the looms as late as 1910 were still hand
powered.[39] Other traditional industries such as soy sauce brewing or
silk production were only partially mechanized and continued to
rely heavily on traditional skills and forms of organization. A variety
of new products such as pencils or matches were also produced
along the lines of traditional industries in a highly labour-intensive
putting-out style of household production.

Modern industrial production grew up alongside the traditional
economy. Reacting to Western power, the new Meiji state led the
building of communication, transport and defence industries.
Government dockyards, machine industries and arms producers
were technological leaders throughout the Meiji period. During the
1870s the government also built model factories to produce goods as
varied as silk and ceramics or paper and cement. By 1883 large-scale
privately owned cotton mills began to be erected in various parts of
the country. Steps such as these were important but they were
nothing more than a beginning. Prior to 1895 Japan's economy was
still overwhelmingly agricultural, and exports were almost exclusively agricultural and mineral products. Despite the steps taken
toward industrial development, factories were in the main small and
few in number. Industrial production had only just begun.

The Sino-Japanese War and the Russo-Japanese War spurred growth in the modern sector. Factory output as a percentage of total production grew sharply as did the number of individuals employed full time as factory workers. Yet much of this expansion was still in traditional light industry, primarily textiles. According to the first factory census of 1909, 61 per cent of the total manufacturing workforce was employed in the textile industry.[40] The census also showed that a mere 8 per cent of Japan's workers were employed in the heavy machinery and tool industries. In the years immediately following the Restoration foreign textiles dominated Japan's domestic market, but by the turn of the century Japanese cotton was pre-eminent in the home market, and textiles accounted for nearly 60 per cent of the nation's export revenue.[41]

In all industries, both before and after 1895, the labour force was characterized by high mobility and fluidity. Nearly 80 per cent of industrial workers in 1900 had been on the job less than three years.[42] The young girls who dominated textile production were short-term workers by contract. In general their salary – save some pocket money – was paid to the parents of the girls as a kind of loan. These girls were not so much a modern working class as they were temporary indentured servants on loan to the mills from their impoverished families.[43] The male workers in early heavy industry too were highly mobile. Most had been artisans trained for their new factory jobs. These men continued to adhere to the old artisanal tradition of travelling (moving from job to job) to gain experience and upgrade their skills.[44] The young textile girls still had strong ties to the rural community and the traditional economy from which they had come and to which they expected to return. The male workers in heavy industry had no such links. But for both, factory life was, if for very different reasons, an alien experience.

Despite claims that Japanese factories operate socially as extensions of traditional rural relationships, it is clear that factory life in the Meiji period represented a novel form of social organization and a distinctly new form of working life. Work in the textile mills involved longer hours than the girls had encountered on the farms. Girls were effectively tied to their machines in monotonous unchanging work. In the cotton mills the air was filled with cotton lint and the noise was unceasing. In the silk filatures, mechanization increased the speed and number of reels each girl had to work, but drawing the fine threads out of the cocoons still had to be done by hand with ever greater speed and precision. By the mid-1880s several of the largest cotton mills went to around-the-clock operation with girls working alternating day–night shifts every other week. Prison-like dormitories kept the girls available for work as well as reducing their ability to flee the mills altogether. Conditions for male factory workers were not as onerous, neither were they village-like. Particularly in private factories, routinized labour, long hours and isolation in slum tenements surrounding the factories meant for males no less than the textile girls a profound distance from the social rhythms of rural life.

The economic changes of the Meiji period were substantially the result of the new imperial state's commitment to industrial development. The awareness that Western power rested on a base of superior technological capability and industrial productivity motivated state leaders to create an economic policy which, it was hoped, would lead to the creation of national wealth equal to that of the West. Economic success of this kind was essential since, as the senior government leader Ōkubo Toshimichi put it, 'a country's strength depends on the wealth or poverty of its people'. The central issue, Ōkubo continued, was that the prosperity of the nation's people 'is closely related to the amount of production'.[45] To spur growth the state acted both as entrepreneur and cheerleader. Industrial development was actively encouraged by government employment of foreign engineers, building model plants, and by dispatching students abroad to learn about Western industrial technology and organization. But encouragement and support by themselves were not enough. Merchants and commercial activity had extremely low status in Tokugawa era orthodoxy and business continued to be tainted in the new Meiji state. Many, therefore, saw it as essential that in order to promote modern economic growth the social place of economic activity had to be redefined. Enlightenment thinkers such as Fukuzawa sought to legitimize an elevated place for business and businessmen in terms of Natural Law. But most businessmen themselves relied on a different formula. Rather than basing their claim on the natural rights of the individual, businessmen emphasized their patriotism and commitment to communal values.[46] The well-known entrepreneur Shibusawa Eiichi was the prototype of this approach.

Shibusawa was the son of a prosperous farmer in what is now Saitama prefecture.[47] As a youth in Bakumatsu Japan he had embraced a vigorous anti-foreignism and was a participant in a variety of anti-*bakufu* activities. After a trip to Europe in 1867 he joined the Finance Ministry of the new imperial state, where he was a key figure in tax reform efforts. In 1873 Shibusawa left the government to begin his career as businessman and entrepreneur. Like most men of his generation he frequently pointed to patriotism as the motivating force behind all his actions. More important for present purposes was his unceasing advancement of a new commercial morality.

Shibusawa's moral idealism rested on a self-conscious embrace of Confucian social ethics and moral humanism. While it is tempting to point to his Confucian educational background to explain his reliance on Confucianism, it is significant that in 1914 Shibusawa himself stated that it was only in 1873, with his resignation from the Finance Ministry, that he came to see the relevance of Confucian teachings for the practice of modern business. He said that it was only at that time that he 'came to believe it was possible to seek profit and conduct business on the basis of the precepts outlined in the *Analects*'.[48] He believed that the orthodox view which placed merchants at the bottom of the social order was a fundamental misunderstanding of the humanistic values of Confucianism. Indeed, the contempt with which business and businessmen had been, and too often still were, regarded was a result of a variety of 'wilful falsehoods' embedded in the Sung (Neo-Confucian) tradition.[49] Rather than having placed commercial activity in a moral nether world, Shibusawa argued that Confucius himself had stressed the potential moral and social parity of all members of society – peasants, artisans and merchants. By separating morality and productiveness Neo-Confucianism made the creation of a social reward system for economic activity impossible. The intent of Confucius, however, had been not to emasculate economic organization but to ennoble work and effort. Profit that was 'unlawfully' obtained was to be scorned, but wealth and profit won by the dint of hard work and study were deserved and worthy.[50] For Shibusawa, therefore, the original Confucian humanistic ideals had important instrumental value. The moral parity of economic tasks implicit in that tradition had the capacity to elevate the social place of business and businessmen. By so doing, he believed, Confucian ethical morality could act to foster the economic growth of the nation.

Shibusawa's economic ideology was not, however, aimed solely at improving the social status of business. His views also gave industry a powerful moral purpose and refashioned the workplace into a coherent moral community. Businessmen were nothing less than the moral equals of all others and it was thus incumbent on them to behave morally. Businessmen, he said, 'must be nothing less than moral exemplars'.[51] They must not only be, but must prove themselves to be, worthy of respect. They must recognize that profit motivations untempered by moral considerations weaken the social order. Morality must be part of any complete economic calculus. 'If acquisitiveness and moral justice are not intimately bound together, if they are separated one from the other, it cannot but break down the social foundations on which we rely.'[52] He therefore urged that businessmen be 'mindful of the moral realm while seeking material progress and work earnestly for advancement in both areas'.[53] Where Neo-Confucianism had, in Shibusawa's view, separated morality and productiveness, he sought to reverse the process – to reunite moral virtue and economic activity. This effort was embedded in a philosophy he called the unity of the Analects and the abacus (*Rongo sorobanshugi*).[54]

The content of the moral system Shibusawa advocated was defined in code words, value-laden terms drawn from Confucianism. He repeatedly emphasized that business behaviour had to be grounded in the universalist ideals of benevolence (*seigi*) and humanity (*jindō*). It was essential that business be practised and organized, he said, on the basis of benevolent administration (*jinsei*). Like the samurai leaders before them, businessmen bore a paternalist responsibility to protect and nurture workers in their charge. At the same time managers and workers were to be part of a collective, unified organism dedicated to a common purpose and common destiny: the well-being of the state. Thus, ideally the workplace was seen to be characterized by a moral and status equality unrelated to functional differentiation. Shibusawa, therefore, was advocating a modern economic form of organization built on a Mencian moral universe that contained both a hierarchical paternalistic axis and one that was horizontal and egalitarian.

Shibusawa's was only one, if the most prominent, voice advocating a new business morality in the Meiji period. Kimbara Meizen, famous for his work in flood control projects and forestry, frequently talked of the fundamental humanity and equality linking all members of a firm.[55] From early in his career the textile executive Mutō Sanji asserted that a spirit of cooperation and harmony had to be brought into being in all Japanese companies and organizations.[56] With extraordinary regularity individual businessmen declared that an embracing humanistic moral order had to be part of modern Japan's economic ideology. Various business organizations were established specifically to further those ideals.

The Ryūmonsha, for example, established in 1885, was founded for the purpose of promoting Shibusawa's commercial ideals.[57] Other more general bodies such as the Kōgyō Kyōkai, begun in 1893, were created to foster the mutual welfare of managers and workers and to promote factory unity.[58] The appeal to communitarian values while certainly not universal among businessmen was extremely broad. Coupled with their emphasis on the patriotic role of commercial activity, business's embrace of a deeply humanistic social morality helped at least partially to resituate business in the popular imagination. This is not to say that the pre-Meiji stain on commercial activity was completely erased. Far from it. Yet businessmen could and did achieve high distinction in the new Japan, and like Shibusawa himself, many businessmen came to play very prominent social and political roles in the twentieth century.

Beyond justifying business activity, the commercial ideals of Shibusawa and others served to elevate the workplace to the status of an organic moral community. As a new form of social organization, factory life cut workers off from the fixed order that characterized the villages from which most of them had come. By advancing Confucian social ethics as the defining values of economic life and by emphasizing a communal morality, modern business was rendered into a moral universe parallel to the village. The workplace came to be defined in terms of a friendly, family-like relationship of its members. Managers and workers were seen to be bound together in a seamless web of moral relationships and moral responsibilities. Far from being a natural extension of traditional social relationships, Shibusawa and others forged this communal factory ideal to meet specific, practical needs of the new society. Confucian social morality had for Shibusawa and others tangible, instrumental value. By incorporating that morality and by manipulating traditional symbols, Shibusawa helped to forge an idealized humanistic vision in which the factory itself became an organic community. This moral construct achieved mythic status during the extended debates over Factory Law legislation in the late nineteenth and early years of the twentieth century.

At their most basic level these debates were concerned with the nature of modern factory life and with the relationship of members of the factory community. Officials in the Ministry of Agriculture and Commerce (Nōshōmushō) began studying and collecting examples of Western factory laws by 1882. The work began, in part, for reasons which had become familiar; factory laws were part of the fabric of modern life and Japan like the earlier developing Western countries should consider their implementation. As Ministry official Oka Minoru later put it, 'as well as introducing industry into the country, it was necessary for the Government also to establish those institutions which must inevitably accompany industry'.[59] Among the envisioned changes was the creation of a regulatory environment for ordering factory life.

But factory legislation was not simply a historicist issue, not simply a question of abstract future problems. As early as 1874 government ministries began to express concern about health and safety problems for workers, themes that persisted throughout the debates over factory legislation.[60] In addition to health issues in industry, officials believed they saw a second problem that demanded immediate attention. The well-known *Views on Promoting Industry* (*Kōgyō iken*) published by the Ministry of Agriculture and Commerce in 1884 worried that the 'natural friendship and intimacy' between master and apprentice that characterized earlier periods was breaking down. The glue that cemented close relationships was evaporating in the new factories. Since, the report continued, 'the well-being and continuity of industrial production is in worker's hands, such circumstances can only be disadvantageous to industry and to industrialists'.[61] Therefore it was necessary, according to the Ministry report, that laws be put in place that not only protected workers but also fostered a closer, more respectful relationship between managers and workers.

During the 1880s and early 1890s the government produced a succession of regulations and legislative drafts substantially concerned with regulating factory health and safety standards and controlling child and female labour. Following the Sino-Japanese War and the industrial growth that accompanied it, efforts to implement a comprehensive factory law began in earnest. Beginning in 1896 debate over this effort was carried out in a variety of public forums. Many have seen this debate as a contest between conservative business interests and progressive bureaucrats, officials committed to a Western-derived social protection agenda. This view tends to delineate the differences between the two sides in overly stark terms. What it misses is the assumptions both shared. One of those was that bureaucrats no less than businessmen were concerned first of all with economic development and growth. From the Restoration forward all key elite groups shared a commitment to economic growth as part of a general national programme. Even as it advocated protective legislation for workers, the 1884 report on promoting industry emphasized that protection must be understood in terms of improving the nation's economic position and expanding output. As Sheldon Garon has observed, 'the business of Meiji Japan was business'.[62]

Moreover, bureaucrats and businessmen shared the same moral language. Each eulogized harmony and cooperation between managers and workers. Bureaucratic supporters of the Factory Law no less than their capitalist opponents shared a belief in the worthfulness and reality of a mythic conception of the workplace as a moral community.

Business spokesmen at the various consultations on the Factory Law stressed that protective legislation was unnecessary precisely because, in their view, the 'beautiful customs' (*bifū*) of friendship and harmony continued to be the norm in factory relations. Baron Watanabe Kunitake in 1907 expressed the opposition viewpoint well. European employers, he said, 'regard workers as little different than horses or oxen'. In Japan, however, where there is mutual respect and friendship in the workplace, 'there is no significant animosity between employers and workers and conflict is not yet visible'.[63] Business opponents of the Factory Law argued that time-honoured social values continued to animate Japanese factory relations and mitigate the acrimony that was so apparent in Western factories. A Factory Law, therefore, could only cause mischief by mandating legalistic intrusion into what remained close personal relationships between managers and workers.

Watanabe's observation that 'conflict is not *yet* visible' suggests that business opponents were hedging their bets. Conflict *might* emerge, but the strength of Japan's communal tradition just *might* prevent it; the burden of proof was on Factory Law supporters. Indeed, at the meetings of the Higher Councils on Agriculture, Commerce and Industry convened in 1896 and 1898 to discuss the Factory Law, several opponents took the position that the data showing that social problems existed in industry was wholly inadequate. They emphasized that far more research was necessary on the issue before it could be convincingly shown that such a law was or would be necessary.[64]

Supporters took two, somewhat contradictory, lines in challenging this position. The first is what Ronald Dore has called the historicist argument.[65] Industrial development and technical change brought predictable, knowable social consequences; the Western experience made it clear what they were: ill-treatment of workers, increasing health problems among workers, an erosion of personal relations between managers and workers, growing class conflict and social disorder. The advanced nations also demonstrated that regulation and monitoring of the workplace lessened these problems. By implementing a factory law in advance of the emergence of such problems, late developing nations such as Japan had the capacity to forestall the worst effects of industrial growth. As the Treasury official Soeda Juichi observed in 1896, a Factory Law was not slavish mimicry of the West but a recognition of the fact that under Japan's industrial development as 'identical conditions come into being identical results will be produced'.[66] In speaking to the Tokyo Chamber of Commerce in 1902 the official Kubota Shizutarō was quick to point out that the problem was not simply at one or several specific plants nor was it the result of employer venality. Rather, he said, as factories grow larger in size and become more numerous the appearance of 'natural abuses' (*shizen no heigai*) was a predictable outcome.[67] Therefore, 'along with the growth of large-scale industry the implementation of a Factory Law becomes unavoidable'.[68] Ultimately, the objective of the Factory Law was 'to preserve social peace and stability amidst industrial development and the emergence of an industrial society through reform'.[69] The point was that it was still possible to head off the worst social effects of industrial development if only the state would act to institute reform legislation such as the Factory Law. The economist Kanai En stressed that all Japanese would come to 'bitterly regret' not doing so and doing it quickly.[70]

While Factory Law supporters argued for reform legislation as a prophylactic against serious conflict, they also stressed that even as they spoke all was not as it should be. Beside the health issues mentioned above, what was most worrisome was the seeming loss of 'natural friendship and intimacy' in emerging industry. In his statement to the Third Higher Council in 1898 Kanai En observed that labour–management relations had worsened in the preceding eight years and the pace of change seemed to be quickening. By the time of the Higher Councils, indeed, all who favoured passage of a Factory Law took the position that close family-style relations had either disappeared under the pressure of large-scale industry or were on the verge of doing so. Retired bureaucrat Shimura Gentarō stated that family-style relations in large-scale industry are simply not a credible idea. 'Can one really speak of family-style relations,' he said, 'when one does not know one's family members by sight.'[71] Soeda Juichi acknowledged that while there were some employers who 'demonstrate the human feelings of the Japanese people, and who act out of a spirit of benevolence and generosity to their inferiors, it must be said that many of Japan's workers are treated atrociously'.[72] Kanai made the point most clearly:[73]

> To be sure Japanese employers do not treat their workers with the cruelty of their counterparts in foreign countries. Nevertheless, while the treatment may not be cruel it is far from good. The individual relations which existed between master and servant in the past no longer obtain. With the coming of factory organization such as we see today there is an estrangement between managers and workers. While they may not be cruel, managers no longer see their workers as individuals and know nothing of what they eat, where they sleep, or what they do.

The erosion of sympathetic bonds between employers and workers in the modern economy meant that it was necessary that a regulatory environment be established to moderate the worst excesses of factory life and to lessen the tensions that threatened economic and social stability.

What this does not mean, however, is that Factory Law supporters rejected the ideal of close, friendly relations in the modern factory. Never did they reject the moral values implicit in what employers saw as family-style relations, either in the past or for the future. Those who reported the loss of intimacy in the factory did not do so happily; it was simply a sad fact. The hope of regulation was that by eliminating the excesses of individualistic capitalism factory harmony and cooperation would be restored.

A familialistic bond might be impossible in a large factory, but mutual respect, cooperation and harmony were all achievable. The operating premise was that factory problems had to be considered with the realization that 'the interests of capitalists and workers were identical'.[74] Soeda Juichi, for example, repeatedly alluded to the mutuality of interests among employers and workers. The purpose of a Factory Law was the restoration of harmony (*chōwa suru*) between these two equally necessary components of the nation's economy.[75] Factory legislation was not simply to protect workers from rapacious businessmen but was aimed at bringing about the harmonious development (*chōwa hattatsu*) of both managers and workers.[76] Supporters of factory regulation routinely invoked the time-honoured Confucian ideals of humanity (*ninjō*) and benevolence (*jiai*) as moral ideals that remained valid. To Oka Minoru humanity, charity and love were noble and satisfying, but in the new world of large-scale industry these eternal values had to 'operate in tandem with rigorous factory regulation'.[77] In 1910 the

Minister of Agriculture and Commerce, Ōura Kanetake, therefore stressed that factory legislation was crucial to the general welfare of the nation. By creating conditions conducive to 'the preservation of harmony between employers and workers', he said, the Factory Law 'would encourage long-term industrial development and would foster a spirit of national progress'.[78]

Passage of a Factory Law was therefore, at least in part, a moral imperative. Supporters did not reject the communitarian rhetoric of employers but rather charged that it was being honoured in the breach; employers were failing to live up to their own professed ideals. Factory legislation would force them to do so. The social policy radical Takano Iwasaburō said that in as much as the relationship between managers and workers is a human relationship 'it is one that can be, and I hope will be, infused with moral warm-heartedness [*tokugiteki onjō*]'.[79] To rebuild a 'moral relationship based on mutual trust'[80] was the imperative of the new industrialized Japan. Passage of a Factory Law was the way to start.

To be sure, at the forefront of the debate on the Factory Law were the specific conditions of factory life and the factory economy. Problems of health and safety, housing, working hours, child labour, capital shortage, international competitiveness, and the like, were all important topics of discussion. While supporters and opponents clashed vigorously on each of these issues, there was a startling convergence of moral language and moral concern. Harmony, cooperation, friendship and intimacy were either thought to be real and tangible or, alternatively, legitimate aspirations built on ancient, internalized values such as humanity, benevolence and love. The appropriateness of these ideals did not diminish because large-scale industry made them difficult to actualize. What was needed, in the view of Factory Law supporters, was a reconfiguring of those ideals to fit new economic realities.

For Factory Law supporters and opponents alike community, harmony and mutuality remained touchstones mobilized now in the name of industrial progress. Just as Shibusawa's commercial ideals proferred a vision of an organic factory community in service to the state, the Factory Law was offered, in part, as a legislative vehicle designed to reach the same end. Public policy therefore, in a sense, came to be directed toward the rejuvenation of a paradise lost, the recreation of moral community in the modern world. By emphasizing a 'moral relationship' characterized by harmony and mutuality, the debates over the Factory Law sanctified the ideal of factory as moral community. Their high visibility and the prominence of those involved elevated those ideals to a kind of economic and intellectual orthodoxy. The ideal of the factory as an organic moral community had entered the realm of national mythology.

SOCIAL PROBLEMS AND SOCIAL POLICY

The debate over the Factory Law did not take place in an intellectual vacuum. During the late 1880s and 1890s Japanese began to retreat from the experimentation of the first two Meiji decades. The movement toward constitutionalism focused attention on national values and the nature of national identity while the earlier cosmopolitanism of Japanese elites was tempered by a new acceptance of Japanese exceptionalism. The Rescript on Education of 1890 signalled a rediscovery of a unique cultural heritage while it provided legitimacy to the notion of Japan as a family-state (*kazoku-kokka*) imbued with particularistic, time-honoured ideals and traditions.[81]

During the same period the 'social problem' emerged as a clearly identifiable intellectual construct. It was 'discovered' by those intellectuals looking at Europe and concerned with the consequences of *laissez-faire* capitalism that they saw in the observations. One of the first to alert his countrymen to the situation was Sakai Yūzaburō. In a report sent from Paris in 1890, Sakai said that during the nineteenth century 'with the progress of material culture and the development of machines and factories, the gulf separating rich and poor grows daily wider. As a result, conflict between capital and labor grows steadily more intense.' Those problems, he said, were an 'unavoidable' result of modern industrial development and they must be addressed quickly and capably if the nation's future is not to be jeopardized.[82] The contradiction between rising industrialization and increasing poverty and social conflict Sakai called, following European usage, the social problem (*shakai mondai*).

From 1890 no issue so dominated intellectual discourse as the social problem. Following the Sino-Japanese War *shakai mondai* was one of the most fashionable phrases of the day. Articles with titles such as 'Japan's Social Problem', 'Education and the Social Problem' or 'The Social Problem and Religious Ideas' abounded in newspapers and periodicals.[83] Newspapers such as the *Mainichi shimbun*, *Yorozu chōhō* and the *Niroku shimpō* as well as the recently developed general interest magazines such as *Taiyō*, *Chūō kōron* and *Sekai no Nihon* all served to bring an awareness of the social problem before an ever-expanding audience. Study societies also emerged in the postwar years. The first and most important such group was the Society for the Study of Social Problems (Shakai mondai kenkyūkai) inaugurated in March 1897.[84] The society had over two hundred members including Tarui Tōkichi, Taguchi Ukichi, Miyake Setsurei, Katayama Sen and Kōtoku Shūsui. At its monthly meetings papers were presented on social issues, the subjects of which were as varied as the group's membership, from labour questions to the issue of education for the mentally retarded.

While the term the 'social problem' was applied to an almost unlimited range of issues there was one that elicited the greatest and most persistent concern: the problem of labour. When Sakai 'discovered' the social problem in Europe what he was seeing and describing was the new, emerging relationship between European management and labour. In Europe, as in Japan, the earliest response to modern development had been the concern over poverty or 'pauperism'. From the middle of the nineteenth century, however, the defining issue and the principal focus of the 'social problem' was discussion of the 'labour problem', namely the attempt to determine the proper place for industrial workers in the new society. It was this concern which Japanese noted and which helped alert them to the issue of labour in modern society.

German ideas which so influenced constitutional thinking in Japan also influenced and justified legislative and regulatory responses to the social problem. This was particularly true after 1890 and with the growing familiarity with German social policy ideas. In Bismarck's Germany a group of young economists and intellectuals organized themselves into the *Verein für Sozialpolitik* which challenged *laissez-faire* economic principles. They advocated state social reform as a means of overcoming the inequalities inherent in unadulterated capitalist economic organization. Social policy ideas were introduced into Japan in 1888 and quickly became a potent justification for rejecting economic individualism.[85]

Japanese advocates of social policy (*shakai seisaku*) argued that individuals and society represented a part of a single, unitary organic whole in which each depended upon the other for continued development. Men were social beings for whom both society and the state were essential. To deny this relationship and posit that men were independent was fallacious. Proponents of *laissez-faire* principles such as Taguchi Ukichi denied the state a role in the operation of the economy. But that independence of individuals was seen by social policy advocates to have simply resulted in poverty and social instability, leading them to 'insist that it is the duty of the state to remedy the misery of the workers'.[86] The leading proponent of social policy, Kanai En, observed in 1892 that the enactment of factory laws in England, the home of Manchesterism, demonstrated vividly the bankruptcy of *laissez-faire* and free-trade principles and led him to advocate the 'new principle of social policy'.[87]

To promote social policy ideas and study their implications for Japanese society and policy, Kanai along with Kuwata Kumazō, Takano Iwasaburō and other leading economists and social scientists formed the Social Policy Association (Shakai seisaku gakkai) in 1896. The Association expressed its concern that the rapid pace of industrial development was breaking down the harmony and stability of Japanese life. In particular, the organization feared that 'the seeds of conflict between capitalists and workers' had been planted and it was thus necessary to pursue a course of social reformism in order to prevent their growth. It affirmed its support for capitalism and hoped to defend social harmony within the context of that system 'by guarding against class strife through a combination of private action and state power' to bring about necessary reforms of the system.[88]

Adolf Wagner, one of the leading members of the *Verein für Sozialpolitik*, observed that the organization and its members constituted less a particular school of thought than a general direction of ideas.[89] That direction had evolved as a part of a broad counter-enlightenment movement which had grown to prominence in the nineteenth century, particularly in Germany. The principal objectives were to eliminate the amoral and acultural ideas of *laissez-faire* economics and to restore social harmony through programmes of reform instituted by a socially conscious monarch and his ministers. Despite unanimity on these general goals, sharp differences existed in approach in the specific programmes individuals favoured. This was no less true for the Japanese Social Policy Association. It embodied a general opposition to a wholly unregulated economy and was concerned with maintaining social consensus and harmony in the midst of industrial development. Despite this general agreement, the Association expressed no consensus on specific issues and ideas. Its members were highly heterogeneous and cannot be regarded as a distinct school of thought. Yet the reformist impulse which dominated social policy thought was instrumental in shaping government responses to the rise of the social problem in the 1890s and continued thereafter to guide and justify government intervention in the workings of the economy and society.

While derived from Western social science and certainly reformist in character, it is important to note that social policy ideas were, in one important sense, consistent with the positions taken by state and business leaders since the 1870s. That is, they embraced social harmony as the primary objective of reform. The emphasis was on men in society, men as part of larger community. Social policy, in effect, reinforced the communitarian impulse that had animated concerns over social problems since 1874. Moreover, as a coherent intellectual system, social policy provided clear, modern legitimacy to what had formerly been only vague, traditionalist sentiments. Yoking those communitarian sentiments to the supportive social policy theory created a powerful platform which informed state social action into the twentieth century.

Social problems had bedevilled the leaders of the new imperial state almost from its inception. The nation's rapid transformation brought new urgency to old problems while creating new ones. Poverty, economic organization and labour–management relations challenged the creativity and resourcefulness of the nation's leaders. To be sure, those issues required structural readjustment and institutional fine-tuning. But what concerned elites at least as much, if not more, was that these issues also represented moral problems – problems of human interaction. As such they required moral solutions. Just as state ideologists sought to blend Confucian morality and nativist mythology to sanctify new definitions of civic virtue, those concerned with social problems sought to refurbish the present with an idealized past. Traditionalist ideals of community and harmony were given new meaning for the new society. The moral community came to be seen as the normative ideal of the new world of factories, factory legislation and social welfare just as they were thought to be descriptive terms for the old world of the rural village. In seeking to solve specific problems of the new society a new social orthodoxy characterized by a profound organicist conservatism was created. The elevation of moral community to social ideal would, it was hoped, address existing problems while preventing even worse ones in the future.

Events of the twentieth century derailed these hopes.

2 Founding of the Kyōchōkai

The emergence of industrial labour was the focus of much of Japan's social policy thinking in the years after 1890. Yet, despite the fears of Factory Law supporters and social policy advocates, labour organization was in its infancy in the final years of the Meiji period and organized labour unrest was virtually unknown. Although historians have paid much attention to the early Japanese labour unions, the fact is that no more than 3,000 workers had joined such organizations, and more importantly most workers had no contact whatsoever with labour unions.[1] Those unions that did exist shared with political and social elites an interest in factory harmony and gradualist reform. The steep recession beginning in 1897 weakened union organization still further. With the failure to pass a Factory Law in 1898 and with the passage of the Peace Police Law in 1900 the already weak union movement collapsed.

But the 'social problem' had by no means been solved, a fact which became clear by 1918. World War I brought fundamental changes in the structure of Japan's economy and society. Japan was no longer simply becoming industrialized, it had become an industrial society. With this development the social problem came to be perceived by elites as having re-emerged in a new, more virulent form requiring new responses. Weak hopes of preventing social conflict and industrial unrest were dashed by the re-emergence and growth of an independent labour movement. Although in the period after World War I the number of workers belonging to unions remained relatively small, government bureaucrats and many political party leaders regarded union growth and increasing labour unrest with alarm. The task before them, they believed, was to integrate the new working class into the existing order. World War I pushed Japanese leaders for the first time to attempt to articulate a well-defined industrial ideology for the new society, one which addressed the new labour issue. The Kyōchōkai was to be at the heart of this effort. This chapter discusses the pressures and the debates leading to its creation in 1919.

THE IMPACT OF WORLD WAR I

To Henry James the coming of World War I was 'a nightmare from which there is no waking save by sleep'. He saw the cataclysm unfolding in Europe as a betrayal of the civilization that had gone before, a disaster which made a lie of his life and the world he had known. James's funereal view, written in a letter just five days after the declaration of war, anticipated the nearly universal view held by 1918 that an era, a civilization, had irretrievably passed away and a new one, of which the 'Great War' was the baneful symbol, had commenced.

For Japan, the World War I years were the threshold separating an industrializing, potentially modern state, from one which by 1919 had joined the ranks of the great powers and become one of a handful of industrial nations. Like Europe, Japan too had begun a new age. As one of the allied nations with only a very minor role in the fighting, Japan profited handsomely from the war, both from war-related exports and from its position of being able to take over Asian markets lost by other belligerents. This advantageous position brought with it a nearly 40 per cent increase in GNP and allowed Japan to experience an era of 'abnormal prosperity' during the wartime years.[2] For the first time Japan became an overall creditor nation during the war. From debts of 1.1 billion yen in 1914 the country amassed 2.77 billion yen in credits by the beginning of 1920.[3] Also, for the first time, labour in agriculture and forestry began to decline both absolutely and relative to manufacturing sectors.[4] As a result, urban population and the urban labour force grew substantially during the war, a process begun in the 1890s and accelerated during the favourable climate of the wartime years.

Within the manufacturing sector itself, prompted by export demand, there was a perceptible shift from light to heavy industry. Between 1909 and 1920 the total workforce in the textile industry nearly doubled from 486,508 to 854,623 workers. At the same time, however, the number of workers in metal and machine industries increased more than four times from 63,821 to 265,137 workers.[5] Along with this shift there was a commensurate decline in the

Table 1 Industrial strikes, 1914–19

	Strikes	Participants
1914	50	7,904
1915	64	7,852
1916	108	8,413
1917	398	57,309
1918	417	66,457
1919	497	63,137

percentage of temporary female workers in favour of permanent male workers.

With the growth and diversification of the manufacturing sector, Japan was able to increase its real output in mining and manufacturing by nearly 50 per cent during the war.[6] With the sharp rise in output went correspondingly high profits for export-oriented and war material industries.[7] In the Kawasaki shipyards, for instance, there was a 217.7 per cent return on paid-up capital for the second half of 1917 and more than 160 per cent for the whole of 1918 while dividends paid by the company rose from 8 per cent in 1914 to 40 per cent in 1918.[8]

The wartime boom distorted the country's financial and economic infrastructure as well as precipitating a severe rate of inflation, a decline in real wages and an average increase in the number of working hours for factory workers.[9] Such conditions inevitably gave rise to the not unjustifiable view that all segments of society were not sharing equally in the profits derived from wartime prosperity. It is at least partially for this reason that labour unrest and the number of strikes grew markedly during the wartime years. As shown in Table 1, between 1914 and 1917 the number of strikes and strikers increased more than seven times. Moreover, by the later years of the war the principal strike demand was for wage increases reflecting real wage declines or at least strikers' perception that their relative share was declining.[10]

World War I, therefore, was a mixed blessing for Japan. It gave the country the great power status it had so long sought and strengthened its position as an important imperial power as a result of its acquisition of the former German territories in China. The war also helped strengthen the economy by solidifying the industrial base and removing its near exclusive reliance on agriculture and textiles. It led to the creation of an expanded urban labour pool and a growing reservoir of skilled labour. At the same time, however, the overheated wartime economy reinforced the perception that an unfair gulf existed between capital and labour both in terms of economic position and social status. Moreover, by altering the composition of the factory workforce the war helped establish the preconditions for the emergence of a vigorous labour movement. These developments portended great difficulties for a government concerned with social harmony.

The war also had important intellectual repercussions. The imminence of victory by the allied democracies in 1918 provided the increasingly vocal liberal movement with more ammunition to fire against the government. Many had for some time believed that the emergence of democratic participatory government represented the 'trend of the times'. The events in Europe seemed to confirm that belief. Critics such as Yoshino Sakuzō, Ozaki Yukio and others stepped up their assault on the government as the outcome of the war became clear. Demands for party government, expanded suffrage, the abrogation of the Peace Police Law and passage of a labour union law increased in both frequency and intensity. Government leaders were less impressed. But they too recognized that the allied victory coupled with the enunciation of Wilson's idealist principles would have a significant impact on domestic policy and social action. Many army leaders, for example, believed that the collapse of the German and Russian armies at the end of the war and their complicity in the socialist revolutions in their respective countries argued against the rigidity and strict class orientation that those armies had practised. The British and American armies with their easy camaraderie and respect between ranks by contrast, they believed, constituted more meaningful models for the times.[11] Democratic ideas, it was recognized by those within and outside the government, were 'sweeping the world'.[12] Although leaders tended to see the Fourteen Points and Wilsonian democracy as little more than moral posturing,[13] they acknowledged that their implication for postwar Japan would be profound.

The re-emergence of the 'social problem' was abetted by the outbreak of the Russian Revolution in 1917. The overthrow of the Romanov dynasty in March and the later Bolshevik seizure of power electrified Japanese intellectuals of all political stripes. Revolution, Arahata Kanson later recalled, became a 'bewitching term' invoked constantly in speeches, writings and slogans.[14] Although keenly interested in events in Russia, Japanese, including radicals, were very poorly informed about the revolutionary developments and were, as a result, 'completely bewildered' by the nature of the revolution that was unfolding.[15] The Japanese response to the 1917 Revolution was, as Gail Bernstein has shown, a case of 'selective perception' in which individuals saw the revolution as a victory of their own ideas. Thus it was variously interpreted as a triumph of democratic ideas, a working-class revolution, the victory of anarchists or even a pacifist coup. In this way the Revolution had a profound impact on Japan's liberal critics, the labour movement, as well as a variety of radical groups.[16] This process of idealization had major consequences. By strengthening the belief that 'world trends' pointed toward democracy or revolution the Russian Revolution widened the perceptual gap between government critics and government leaders and intensified the sense of confrontation between them.

The outbreak of the Revolution had a particularly pronounced effect on the labour movement. From 1912 to 1917 the Yūaikai, Japan's earliest successful union had been virtually alone in the organized labour movement. It had been formed in August 1912 as a workers' mutual aid society but after 1917 Suzuki Bunji, the Yūaikai's founder and president, was under increasing pressure to take a more militant stance.[17] Internal pressure as well as the introduction of former radical students into the union helped push it toward an increasingly radical posture as the decade wore on. Moreover, there was a dramatic increase in the number of unions in Japan during this period. The burgeoning of the labour movement, both in the number of unions and unionized workers; the increasingly militant stance of the movement; and the rising wave of strikes over the wartime years made it clear that the labour and social problem had reached a new level of intensity.

Despite this, however, labour and social problems were not considered central issues by government and political leaders until the early autumn of 1918. They were shocked out of their complacency by the ominous Rice Riots that began in a fishing village in Toyama prefecture in August of that year. Before finally being brought under control by government troops more than two months later, the riots had spread to thirty prefectures and the nation's leading cities. The riots had been ignited by a protest against rice prices. As they spread, engulfing an ever larger number of participants, they took on the generalized character of the violent smashings (*uchikowashi*) of the previous century. Indeed, Ōshio Heihachirō, hero of the great 1837 Osaka riots, was often depicted as the inspiration of the 1918 riots.[18] Government leaders had been aware that democratic ideas were spreading and gaining increased potency. But the Rice Riots at last made clear to all the power of popular mass movements with the result that radicals and reformers became even more convinced that an era of change was upon them. Official interest in labour and social problems too was reawakened.

Symptomatic of the heightened concern over labour and social issues was the perceptible shift in editorial content of the bell-wether *Ōsaka asahi shimbun*. In six months preceding the Rice Riots the paper published only two editorials concerning the 'labour problem'. During the two-month period from January to March 1919, however, nine separate editorials on this issue appeared on the paper's pages.[19] During the same period the influential *Tōyō keizai shimpō* argued on its editorial page that finding 'a solution to the labor problem is the gravest issue facing the postwar world' and over the following months expressed repeatedly its concern about the growing intensity of social unrest.[20]

Within the government the bureaucrat Den Kenjirō spoke of the 'unprecedented challenges' facing postwar Japan. Meeting with aging *genro* Yamagata Aritomo in December 1918, Den along with Hirata Tōsuke, Kiyoura Keigo, Gotō Shimpei and others discussed the 'great problem' which had arisen in politics, economics and social organization. He said that the growing activism of the masses of people both at home and abroad was a condition fraught with peril and demanded careful study and vigilant attention.[21] 'Democracy,' grumbled Tanaka Giichi, had become the 'fashionable term' of the day and had to be invoked in all situations.[22] The growth of the labour movement, the vigour of the student movement, and the re-emergence of a highly variegated radical movement became matters of increased interest after the explosive Rice Riots.

Generalized social problems had been a concern of elites from the earliest years of the Meiji era. The intellectual construct referred to as the 'social problem' by Sakai Yūzaburō and others, the coming of which had so long been predicted, was at last a reality. As early as 1890, with a constitution in place, Shimada Saburō believed that Japan was 'leaving the day of politics and entering the day of the social problem'.[23] In the wake of World War I, the Russian Revolution and the Rice Riots it became clear that the social problem had not supplanted political questions; it had become the political question. Writing several years later the Marxist intellectual Kawakami Hajime wrote that 'in the early years of the Meiji era the central political problem was the issue of popular rights'. Today, however, he said, 'the real political issue is, to put it simply, the social problem'.[24]

NEW APPROACHES TO WORLD TRENDS

One of the first indications that the government had begun to regard social and labour problems with serious concern was the creation in June 1918 of the Relief Activities Research Committee (Kyūsai jigyō chōsakai). Authorized by Imperial Ordinance (*chokurei*) number 263 on 24 June, the Relief Committee was the first official institutional response of the Taishō period to social and labour problems. The committee was under the overall supervision of the Home Ministry (Naimushō) and chaired by its vice-minister. Beside the chairman, the committee was to include twenty members from the government, business, and scholarly worlds. The mandate of the committee was clear; it was to study existing social conditions and propose programmes to alleviate the conditions causing social and labour unrest and seek to establish the means of preventing future problems.[25]

On 3 July 1918 the committee had its first general meeting. Home Minister Mizuno Rentarō pointed out in his opening address that World War I had brought with it unsettling material and intellectual problems. He warned that Japan 'will not escape still greater social problems in the future' unless research is undertaken and institutions established to counteract them. There had been in the past, Mizuno observed, many research programmes and consultative bodies that had had great potential for providing solutions to social problems. However, they had accomplished little or nothing. It was incumbent on this new committee, therefore, to consider practical and achievable means of solving social problems. Committee members, he said were conversant with the real dilemmas confronting the nation, the economy and society. As a result, they should be able to, indeed they must, avoid the 'desk-top research' that characterized much of the previous work. Their work must not be built upon 'impossible abstractions or vacillating empty theories' but rather on their collective knowledge of actual conditions. Only by so doing could the committee develop and propose approaches and programmes capable of yielding tangible results.

Of the committee's twenty members, eight were important bureaucrats from the Agriculture and Commerce Ministry or the

Home Ministry. These officials included Oka Minoru as well as the head of the Police Bureau (Keiho kyoku) Kawamura Takeji and Soeda Keiichirō, head of the Home Ministry's Local Affairs Bureau (Chihō kyoku). Of the remaining twelve committee members seven were key leaders of the Social Policy Association including Kambe Masao, Kubota Shizutarō, Kuwata Kumazō and Yahagi Eizō. From its inception the Social Policy Association had had a close relationship with the government. Its members had participated in the debates over the Factory Law and had frequently consulted with and advised various ministries on social issues. What the composition of the Relief Committee suggests, however, is that by 1918 there had been a fusion of government agencies and the Social Policy Association; the Association had, in effect, become a government organ.

Despite the obvious effort to pack the Committee with members who shared the basic assumptions of society as moral community, there was a major clash between committee members over the direction of committee activities. The focal point of dissension was the Social Policy Association charter member and Tokyo University economics professor Takano Iwasaburō. Takano had organized and conducted the justly famous research project on Tsukiji working class society and for the previous decade had been an active proponent of labour unions and supporter of workers' rights of organization.[26] His principal interest, made to the Committee in an appeal of 5 July, therefore, was that the labour question be made the first priority.[27]

Takano's appeal was ignored. In the formal committee agenda announced the next day, labour problems, and more particularly labour union issues, occupied relatively low places.[28] The agenda was divided into eight primary categories including activities to improve living conditions, poor relief work, child protection and health related activities. Labour protection activities were listed number six with 'labor unions and mediation systems' as a minor subcategory. Despite its low billing, the labour question was the most hotly debated issue throughout the life of the Committee. On 8 January 1919 Takano urged the Committee to recommend and work to encourage the 'natural development of labor unions'. He also favoured the abrogation of Article 17 of the Peace Police Law.[29] The Committee's final report on labour questions issued on 3 March 1919 represented a compromise. The report offered the following five proposals for minimizing the tension between labour and management:

1 Labour unions should be permitted to follow their 'natural course of development'.
2 There should be established within the government an agency to supervise research on labour questions and to administer labour protection programmes.
3 The government should conduct investigations into and establish as soon as possible labour insurance programmes, mediation, profit sharing and related systems.
4 The government should aid in 'the establishment of an appropriate popular organ the purpose of which would be to promote cooperation and harmony [*kyōdō yūwa*] between labor and capital'.
5 Clause two of Article 17 of the Peace Police Law (concerning agitators) should be rescinded.[30]

The communitarian assumptions of the Committee and the programmes it proposed were widely attacked by radical and reformist critics. A widespread complaint was that the Committee lumped what had by that time come to be seen as two separate problems: the problem of relief and the question of labour.[31] In the view of Morito Tatsuo the conflation of relief activities and social policy suggested that the government objective in creating the Relief Committee was to establish programmes and policies aimed at perpetuating existing social injustice.[32] Moreover, the Committee seemed to demonstrate government unwillingness to recognize workers as a legitimate social class with distinct interests in the economic and social process.[33] Home Ministry officials acknowledged their conflation of relief work and social policy. As one middle ranking official wrote:

Relief work is generally considered as that which comforts the helpless and aids the sick and disabled. But, in the Home Ministry, what we call relief work is not so narrowly defined. Indeed the major part of the activities discussed under what is called social policy fall within the scope of relief work.[34]

From the time of the creation of the Social Policy Association there had been considerable overlap in the concepts of social policy and social relief. Association members such as Kuwata, Kubota and bureaucrats such as Gotō Shimpei had been active in promoting relief programmes in the name of social stability and national strength. Because the dividing line between the poor and the working classes was hazy in the late nineteenth century such an overlap did not constitute a major objection. By the late 1910s, however, workers had come to be widely seen as a distinct social class deserving of dignity as workers, not merely lumped into a broad undifferentiated lower class. This dilemma of where to fit labour in the social order was a problem which beset the Association throughout the 1910s and was ultimately the issue that broke it apart.

The creation and work of the Relief Committee marked a major watershed in modern Japanese history. Its proposals and the debate they generated, highlighted a new perception of social relationships, specifically the place of labour in the new society. The controversies that swirled around the committee and its proposals focused attention on the working class and its emergence as an important and distinct social entity. Recognizing this fact, the Committee's work was the first official acknowledgement of labour union legislation as a social and political issue.[35] By insisting on the need to establish an independent government agency to study and administer labour related programmes, Committee proposals foreshadowed the creation of the Social Bureau (Shakai kyoku) in 1922. At the same time, in its advocacy of a 'popular institution . . . . to promote cooperation and harmony between capital and labor' the Committee pointed toward the creation of the Kyōchōkai in the final month of 1919.

Committee proposals were advanced in a wholly new political climate. On 29 September 1918 Hara Kei, 'the Great Commoner' became the Prime Minster of Japan's first cabinet headed by the leader of the majority party in the Diet. The picture of the former Prime Minister, Terauchi Masatake, in his army uniform standing next to Hara dressed in a frockcoat prompted the radical intellectual Yamakawa Hitoshi to see that moment as the transition from Japanese militarism to democracy.[36] There was great public enthusiasm for what appeared to be the beginning of truly democratic government in Japan. Hara himself, however, was frequently criticized for his opportunism, and even members of his own party, the Seiyūkai, objected to what they saw as his parroting the ageing *genro* Yamagata's political line.[37] Reservations over Hara's political 'realism' continued throughout the tenure of his cabinet.[38] A consequence of that realism, however, was an important shift in the nuance of the government response to labour problems.

Prior to and during World War I successive governments had taken a hard line toward labour unions and labour activism.

Operating under what one scholar has called the 'Peace Police Law System' unions and worker groups were seen as completely antithetical to the existing economic and social character of Japan.[39] As the number of strikes rose during the later wartime period unions were under increasing pressure from government and business. The number of arrests of strikers and the number of unions forcibly dissolved increased markedly in 1917 and 1918.[40] Even the extremely moderate Yūaikai, which Katayama Sen derisively called the 'yellowest labor movement in Japan',[41] felt its very existence to be threatened, forcing Suzuki to work feverishly to disassociate his union from the rising wave of strikes and to disclaim Yūaikai responsibility for them.

During the tenure of the Hara cabinet, however, an important shift in attitudes toward workers, labour unions and social problems in general took place. The events in Europe, the creation of the International Labour Organization (ILO) and increasing activism at home convinced the new government that repression of the labour movement was no longer a practicable strategy for maintaining social stability. Throughout his career Prime Minister Hara had emphasized the importance of acting in accord with 'world trends' or the 'trends of the times'. This belief had early led him to the view that popular influence on government activity would steadily expand and force government leaders to accommodate the rising masses.[42] Hara understood that by 1918 the social and labour movements could only be dealt with in light of the new democratic world trends.

The point man of the new cabinet's efforts to deal with those problems was the Home Minister, Tokonami Takejirō. Graduated from Tokyo University in 1890, Tokonami joined the Home Ministry in 1895 after a five-year stint in the Finance Ministry. He rose quickly up the Ministry's administrative ladder and in 1906 he became the chief of the important Local Affairs Bureau (Chihō kyoku) during Hara's first term as Home Minister in the Saionji Cabinet. In 1913 he joined the Seiyūkai and by 1916 was favoured by some members for the presidency of the party.[43] But Tokonami remained a loyal Hara follower and was rewarded with the position of Home Minister in the Hara government. Stretching over the Hara and Takahashi cabinets, Tokonami's tenure as Home Minster was longer than any other holder of that office during the Meiji and Taishō periods. It was also one of the most important and influential periods in Home Ministry history. Under Tokonami the Home Ministry expanded its areas of concern and gained increasing authority in government administration. Most important, the Home

Ministry came to exercise greater authority in the area of labour issues, gradually usurping the role of the Agriculture and Commerce Ministry which had formerly been responsible for all industrial questions. As the Home Ministry's semi-official history put it 'Tokonami, more than any other Home Minister, laid the groundwork for modern administration'.[44]

Hara said that he had originally selected Tokonami for headship of the Local Affairs Bureau because Tokonami 'supported progressive policies',[45] by which he presumably meant that Tokonami supported 'realistic policies' and was aware of the importance of being in tune with political trends. Like his chief, Tokonami recognized early the need to deal with rising popular influence in government. In 1910 he argued that the growing power of public opinion was a natural trend (*shizen no ikioi*). Therefore, he said, government officials 'should recognize the strength of public opinion and seek to foster moderate views'.[46] In 1918, in his first official address to local officials as Home Minister, Tokonami stated that 'world trends have undergone a major transformation. The ideological and economic changes that have come with the restoration of peace hold great significance for the welfare of Japan.'[47] No longer was 'public opinion' an imminent problem; wartime changes had created a situation in which public demands had to be reckoned with.

Yet the solutions he advocated were of a piece with those advanced by reformers in the 1890s and which he himself had offered in 1910:

> To assure the healthy development of the state we must encourage a spirit of cooperative harmony among all parts of the nation.[48]

That is, the primary emphasis of the Home Ministry and the new Hara government continued to be didactic, stressing the inculcation of values and ideals conducive to stability and social peace.

Tokonami's overall approach and attitude toward social problems was mirrored in the final report of the Relief Committee; the bulk of the work was conducted under Tokonami's Home Ministry. That is, first of all, it was essential that the administrative machinery devoted to labour and industrial issues be expanded while, at the same time, it was necessary that there be some kind of institutional recognition of labour unions and the removal of the impediments to their growth. But this recognition, he believed, had to be accompanied by efforts to inculcate the values of social cooperation

and harmony. Tokonami, therefore, was advocating the abandon-
ment of what he saw as the 'conventional measures' for dealing with
social problems: legal curbs and police repression. Instead problems
had to be attacked on the economic and ideological as well as legal
fronts. This was particularly true for the labour problem, which he
believed to be at a 'crossroads'. If it was to move in the direction of
cooperation rather than conflict it was necessary to act immediately
to create an institution for the purpose of instilling the values of
harmony and cooperation.[49] It was this belief that gave rise to the
Kyōchōkai.

ESTABLISHING THE KYŌCHŌKAI

Shortly after assuming the position of Home Minister, Tokonami
sought out the prominent industrialist Shibusawa Eiichi. In their
meeting they discussed the labour problem, which they both agreed
was an issue of the utmost seriousness and one which required
immediate attention. They agreed further that a useful step in
dealing with the labour problem would be the creation of some kind
of group or organization which could act as a mediator between
capital and labour.[50] This meeting represented their first tentative
steps toward the creation of the Kyōchōkai.

Shibusawa was a valuable ally in Tokonami's effort to defuse
labour unrest. As both an entrepreneur and humanitarian his
reputation was enormous. He had been persuaded to lend the
weight of his name and reputation to numerous business and social
welfare programmes. But the question of labour–management
relations was an area he considered especially crucial. In 1916
Shibusawa gave up active work in business. Following his retirement
he said that there were three different areas to which he would
devote his not inconsiderable energies: (1) the promotion of
commercial morality (*shogyō dōtoku*), (2) improving labour–
management relations, and (3) narrowing the gap between rich and
poor.[51] The support of Shibusawa gave Tokonami's effort to
mitigate the labour problem a level of support and credibility it
would have otherwise been difficult to win.

Following several more meetings on labour questions Tokonami
and Shibusawa, along with Tokugawa Iesato, president of the
House of Peers; Ōoka Ikuzō, president of the Diet; and Kiyoura
Keigo met in mid-January 1919 to discuss the creation of an
institution designed to solve the labour problem. The organization,
they agreed, should be a national popular organ with neither direct

ties to nor biased toward capital or labour. On that understanding the participants in the January meeting established the following rough framework for the organization's activities:

1 Through lectures and publication activities the organization would seek to educate workers and raise their skill levels.
2 It would act as a research body conducting investigations of foreign and domestic labour and social conditions.
3 It would seek to create a central labour exchange and operate exchanges in appropriate areas throughout the country.
4 It would establish mechanisms for mediating strikes and labour unrest where possible and appropriate.
5 It would endeavour to help workers as much as possible in areas such as working conditions, housing and childhood education.[52]

Tokonami's hopes for the creation of such an organization were given official voice in the final report of the Relief Committee, chaired by his vice-minister Kohashi Ichita.

In late 1918 Tokonami attempted to sound out the Japan Industrial Club (Nihon kōgyō kurabu) on the idea of an organization to reconcile capital and labour. Meeting with Nakajima Kumakichi, Tokonami emphasized that the Industrial Club could not remain bystanders on this important matter. The cabinet, he said, unanimously supported the idea of such an institution and he hoped the Club would support it. Despite this entreaty, Industrial Club leaders Dan Takuma and Fujiwara Ginjirō were opposed.[53] Aware, however, that the labour problem had become a matter of central importance to the business community, in December the Club established a Research Committee on Labour Problems (Rōdō mondai chōsa iinkai) which was intended to conduct studies on various matters pertinent to labour questions.[54]

Despite the initial opposition of some Club members, Tokonami had evidently received private assurances from Nakajima that the Club would consider the matter of a private organ to deal with labour–management problems. So in early 1919 Tokonami solicited officially the opinion of the Club on the issue and asked it to make recommendation for its implementations. The Club responded in May with its recommendation to create what it called the Shinai kyōkai (the True Affection Society). On 28 May Nakajima visited Tokonami and presented him with drafts of the Founding Prospectus of the Shinai kyōkai (Shinai kyōkai setsuritsu shuisho) and the Founding Principles of the Shinai Kyōkai (Shinai kyōkai setsuritsu kōryō). The Prospectus outlined a position much like that taken by earlier opponents of the Factory Law.[55] It asserted that Western countries had been wholly unable to deal with labour–management conflict except through the force of law. Japan, however, was fortunate, the Prospectus claimed, in that the 'beautiful customs of the past continue to exist' making it possible for it to avoid the 'evils' that characterize relations between labour and management elsewhere. The nearly universally shared view among Japanese that workers and capitalists constituted 'a single harmonious whole' (*wachu kyōdō nisha ittai*) allowed the nation to fashion a 'distinctively Japanese solution' to the labour problem. The Prospectus also stated that the Shinai kyōkai would work to build managerial 'social awareness' while promoting education and moral cultivation for workers. In the Founding Principles the organization's task was stated as being 'to bring about harmony and cooperation [*kyōdō yūwa*] between managers and workers by encouraging and aiding in the execution of appropriate social policy activities'.[56] The proposed activities of the organization were similar to those outlined in Tokonami's January draft: research and publication on social policy activities, lectures to facilitate technical and economic education, administration of labour exchanges, and the like.

Despite the broad similarity between the Club's proposal and the January draft outline, the two plans differed in one very important respect: the Shinai kyōkai proposal accepted and used explicitly the language of paternalism; the government draft did not. The difficulties paternalistic language presented were made clear by Tokonami's discussions with another group, the Capital and Labour Problem Study Association (Shihon rōdō mondai kenkyūkai). The Association was a small group of influential journalists and opinion leaders committed to the goal of seeking 'reform of labor–management relations'.[57] In June, after receiving the Industrial Club's proposal, Tokonami met with representatives of the Association to discuss the creation of a private institution for promoting labour–management stability and, specifically, to get its opinion on the Shinai kyōkai proposal.[58] The Association's representatives, Honda Seiichi, Itakura Takuzō, Kamata Eikichi, Kikuchi Takenori and Kubota Fumizō rejected the Club's proposal out of hand. They objected to the name of the proposed organization as an antiquated appeal to paternalist values and rejected the idea of managers and labour as part of a single social group motivated by identical interests.

The Association took the position that industrial reform could best be achieved through private, intermediary agencies because 'the lives of individual governments are brief and they cannot therefore play a durable role in the reform of labour–management relations. Because of this inability, government should act to encourage the development of intermediary groups not subject to political changes' in order to affect the necessary reforms.[59] Paternalistic rhetoric, they believed, was a poor substitute for a living wage and respect for workers. Kikuchi Takenori invoked Fukuzawa Yukichi's famous dictum that 'heaven did not create men above men or men below men' to support the notion that paternalistic, hierarchical relations in industry are insupportable. If this is not recognized, he said, and if legitimate reforms are not implemented, Japan 'cannot be expected to be victorious in the economic war to come'.[60]

Not content simply to reject the Shinai kyōkai proposal, the Association submitted its own proposal for a private labour–management conciliation institution it called the Kyōzonkai (the Mutual Existence Society). In most of its programmatic components the Kyōzonkai was largely indistinguishable from the Industrial Club's proposed Shinai kyōkai. Its underlying assumptions were, however, very different. In place of paternalism, the Kyōzonkai was to be predicated on the belief that workers and capitalists were distinct social entities. A new economic age had dawned in which workers and managers occupied separate but equal places within the economic order. To build a satisfactory relationship between them in this new context required an awareness of each group's respective rights and duties as well as management's respect for individuality and character (*jinkaku*).[61]

Clearly little advance had been made in defining the character of the organization Tokonami hoped to build. Both the Industrial Club and the Study Association proposals added little that was new to the original rough outline drawn up in January. What the proposal process had accomplished, however, was an expansion of participation in the building process. If the organization was to be a private one, dependent upon the support and participation of groups of individuals outside the government, it was necessary to involve potential supporters in the creative process. At the same time the vigorous reaction to the Shinai kyōkai's implicit paternalism alerted Tokonami to the dangers involved in the creation of such an organization. As a keen observer of popular opinion and 'world trends' Tokonami had already been aware that if his organization was to achieve the industrial stability he sought it would have to step very lightly around the paternalism issue. 'World trends' demanded circumspection.

One month after his meeting with the Association, Tokonami along with Shibusawa, Tokugawa Iesato and Kiyoura Keigo met with the press to announce unofficially the intention to establish the Kyōchōkai.[62] The formal announcement of their plan was made on 16 August 1919. The founders' meeting held in the Tokyo Imperial Hotel was attended by nearly two hundred people. Beside the principal sponsors, Hara and several other cabinet ministers were present as well as numerous prefectural governors, mayors and military leaders.[63] Noticeably absent were any prominent representatives of labour. This absence was not for want of effort on the sponsors' part.

Shibusawa had approached the Yūaikai leader Suzuki Bunji to discuss joining the soon-to-be created organization. Shibusawa was ideally placed to court Suzuki's support. They had built up a close relationship over the 1910s while Shibusawa had given decisive support to the young Yūaikai giving credibility to the union's reformist efforts while shielding it in a mantle of respectability. What transpired in their private meeting is difficult to ascertain with any degree of certainty. In statements to the press and later in his autobiography, Suzuki contended that he had spurned Shibusawa's request that he become an advisor to the Kyōchōkai. He claimed that he would only become an advisor if Shibusawa was prepared to meet a number of conditions. The most important of these were:

1. It was essential that a labour union law be advocated and the repeal of Article 17 of the Peace Police Law be demanded by the new organization.
2. The Kyōchōkai had to be independent of the government.
3. The directors of the organization had to include an equal number of workers and capitalists.
4. The organization should not engage in labour-management mediation activities. Its work had to be limited to research and education.
5. The name of the organization had to be the Shakai seisaku kyōkai (Social Policy Institute) since to him Kyōchōkai implied an unwillingness to recognize the absolute equality between capital and labour.

Suzuki concluded his discussion of the meeting by noting that

Shibusawa was unprepared to accept his conditions and, as a result, their relationship came quickly to an end.[64]

Shibusawa's version of the meeting was quite different. He denied that Suzuki had categorically rejected participation in the Kyōchōkai or that he had offered conditions as the price the organization had to pay for his support. In an interview given shortly after their meeting, Shibusawa said that he and Suzuki had discussed broad issues of social policy, the role of the government in social relations, and the general needs of state and society. He acknowledged Suzuki's dismay over government failure to abrogate Article 17. He acknowledged further that Suzuki argued that the Kyōchōkai should not become a stooge of the government. On these issues, he and Suzuki were, he said, 'in general agreement'.[65]

Whatever the content of Shibusawa's and Suzuki's discussion the fact remains that there were no representatives of labour at the founders' meeting nor among the directors of the organization once it was fully established. Even those who sympathized with the goal of labour–management harmony such as Uno Riemon were very disappointed about the absence of labour representatives on the organization and questioned the overall thrust of the organization's proposed activities.[66] How could the Kyōchōkai realistically claim that it could be an unbiased mediator between capital and labour if its members and directors were primarily government bureaucrats and capitalists. It was a problem the organization never overcame. Hara had stressed that the Kyōchōkai 'should be independent not only of capital and labor but unless it is independent of government as well it will lack authority'.[67] Its affiliation with government, however, was never really in doubt. The official-studded founders' meeting and the continuing employment of former bureaucrats as Kyōchōkai directors and employees made the organization's relationship to the government clear. That it had derived support from capitalists was equally clear. Around the time of the founders' meeting the sponsors sought to establish a 10 million yen endowment to cover Kyōchōkai operating expenses.[68] A variety of meetings were held and trips taken to solicit funds for the endowment.[69] Through their efforts sponsors received pledges from ninety-two people for nearly 7 million yen and another 2 million came from the government treasury. Contributions were obtained from many of the most important and largest companies in Japan. Individual contributors included many of the leading names in the industrial world, among them Okura Kihachirō, Nakajima Kumakichi, Asano Soichirō, Inoue Junnosuke, Dan Takuma,

Furukawa Toranosuke, Wada Toyoji and others.[70] The very high level of capitalist participation in funding the Kyōchōkai further eroded the credibility of its statements that it would act as an unbiased mediator between capital and labour.

The announcement of the creation of the Kyōchōkai was regarded with suspicion by workers' groups and a wide variety of intellectuals. Suzuki Bunji acknowledged that its founding prospectus seemed to be based on a recognition of equality between capital and labour but in fact, he said 'it differs in no important way from the ideas of former great capitalists'. Under such an organization, therefore, 'should not workers be concerned about the protection of their legitimate rights?'[71] To Suzuki and other labour activists the Kyōchōkai was nothing more than part of 'a trend to undermine union development'.[72] Surprisingly, many industrialists agreed with these criticisms. By the end of World War I a substantial fraction of businessmen in the Kansai area had come to believe that the legal recognition of labour unions was the most appropriate means of overcoming labour radicalism. The Osaka Industrial Association (Osaka kōgyōkai), the largest organization of industrialists in metropolitan Kansai, as well as the Tokyo Federation of Business Associations (Tokyo jitsugyō kumiai rengokai) passed resolutions in 1919 urging the passage of a labour union law. Such groups, representing small as well as large businesses, were informed by the British labour movement and saw unions as providing a sense of order and discipline to workers and as a result reducing the conflict with management.[73] Typical of this view was a statement by the Kansai businessman Yasukawa Keiichirō, who wrote in 1919 that 'strikes are not necessarily a product of labor unions . . . . The history of other countries shows that the incidence of strikes actually declines with the healthy development of labor unions.'[74] This belief led such men to question the usefulness of the Kyōchōkai. Without labour representatives in the organization and without a statement of forthright support of labour unions and labour issues, the organization, it was widely believed, would be interpreted by workers as little more than a capitalist body cloaking an insidious paternalism in its high-flown rhetoric about cooperation and harmony.[75]

The Industrial Club itself presented a problem. Its views on the character and role of a private industrial cooperation organization had been reflected in its proposal for the Shinai kyōkai. But its position that the organization should be built on a foundation which recognized workers and capitalists as part of a 'single harmonious whole' was rejected by the new Kyōchōkai. Instead the Kyōchōkai's founding documents rejected paternalist rhetoric and posited that workers and capitalists were separate but equal classes with separate but equally important interests.[76] As a result the Industrial Club was more often than not opposed to Kyōchōkai activities and ideas.[77] The question of labour–management equality bothered others as well. The name originally proposed for the organization was the Rōshi kyōchōkai. Yamagata Aritomo argued that such a designation, because it appeared to be based on the idea of treating workers and capitalists as equals could only, he said, 'inflate the ambitions of workers'.[78] He recommended the vaguer, hence safer, Kyōchōkai and claimed that Hara agreed with him.[79] The term '*rōshi*' (labour and capital) was eventually dropped.

Finally on 25 December 1919 the Kyōchōkai was officially launched. The president of the new body was Tokugawa Iesato with the sponsors Kiyoura, Ōoka, Shibusawa and Tokonami as vice-presidents. The important managing director posts were held by Taniguchi Ryugorō, chief of the General Affairs Division; Matsuoka Kimpei, chief of the Activities Division; and Kuwata Kumazō, chief of the Research Division. This organizational scheme was to be short lived but the Kyōchōkai had begun. Even before it was officially open for business it had been rocked by criticism from government critics, workers and capitalists. It was a pattern that would persist throughout the 1920s.

Prior to World War I many Japanese leaders had recognized that modern development was beginning to have a recognizable effect on social and economic organization. The gradual erosion of natural, historical communality and social cooperation was to them a predictable by-product of development. Yet they also believed it was still possible to forestall or to resist the worst social consequences of industrialization – broad social conflict and industrial unrest of a type visible in the West. By linking programmes of institutional reform to time-honoured moral sentiment, they hoped that a new, modern form of moral community could be created to meet the challenges of modernism.

By the end of the war it could no longer be doubted that industrial society was in place; denial or retreat was no longer possible. Workers were no longer an abstract mass; they had become members of an identifiable 'working class'. Labour unrest and social conflict were no longer an alien phenomenon of future concern, they were a domestic reality with domestic causes. No longer could it be said that Japanese industry retained an earlier pre-industrial shape; modern factory organization (and its consequences) had become an inescapable reality.

Despite the new circumstances and the new intensity of social problems, the basic assumptions about how these conditions had to be addressed changed relatively little. Tokonami, like Oka Minoru and other Factory Law supporters, continued to emphasize the need for linking institutional change with moral and ideological inculcation. For Shibusawa a new commercial morality and the ideals of social harmony were no less important in 1918 than they had been in the 1880s. Social problems continued to be regarded as substantially moral problems requiring moral solutions. With the end of World War I these assumptions were invested with new weight by the establishment of the Relief Committee and the creation of the Kyōchōkai. With the support of the new government and its most important minister, Tokonami Takejirō, the quest to recreate and redefine moral community became the central concern of administrative social policy. Although many questioned and attacked the Kyōchōkai's institutional authority, its charge of re-establishing social and industrial harmony through moralist inculcation made the new organization a key player in the long-standing effort to forge a distinctive industrial ideology.

3 Kyōchōkai visions of industrial society

The task of building a 'rich country and strong military' (*fukoku kyōhei*) had been a driving force for a generation of Japanese and in the name of those objectives they had borne heavy sacrifices. Following the Russo-Japanese War at least one of the Meiji goals had been realized: Japan had became a powerful country. It had won an important victory over a Western nation and in so doing gained the respect of the West and the admiration of other non-Western countries. Yet it was still far from being a rich country. Kiyoura Keigo, Minister of Agriculture and Commerce, acknowledged this fact in a speech in April 1905. He was concerned that while industrial growth was taking place in Japan too much of Japan's productive capacity was in small-scale cottage industry and too many structural problems remained within Japan's economy. Nevertheless, he said, 'we are fortunate that because our standard of living is low' and 'since wages too are low' Japan can still compete with the Western industrial economies. But, he warned, 'in the future neither prices nor wages will remain low. Therefore, overcoming European and American productivity will require a new strategy built upon a major revolution in the organization' of Japanese industry.[1] With the achievement of Meiji leaders' primary political goals – consolidation of the new state, a guarantee of political independence and the achievement of military strength – economic goals grew to new prominence. The economy had to be strengthened and consolidated, industrial structure reorganized and invigorated, and the workforce trained and improved.

Nineteenth-century government leaders routinely used potential threats to national independence to win popular acquiescence with its developmental policies. With the new political system secured and its power recognized elites focused on a new threat: the coming 'war of commerce and industry'.[2] Kiyoura's 1905 speech stressed Japan's competitive disadvantages. Yet industrial expansion alone was not sufficient to win the economic war many predicted. Speaking in the Diet in 1920 the Kokumintō representative Uehara Etsujirō expressed a common concern when he said that 'if postwar international rivalries are characterized as a form of economic or industrial competition, those nations that best resolve the problems between labour and capital will be in the most advantageous position'.[3] The labour problem, which had become the most visible symbol of social disharmony during World War I, threatened Japan's ability to mobilize its economic resources. If the economic war with the West were to be won, the labour problem had to be solved and social harmony restored. The Kyōchōkai's principal goals of industrial development and the establishment of social peace were indissolubly linked.

The means by which it hoped to meet these goals were laid out in the official statement of the Kyōchōkai Principles (Kyōchōkai kōryō) and its Act of Endowment (Kyōchōkai kifu koi).[4] These documents enunciated the new organization's broad purpose and specified the activities it intended to pursue. In substance they differed very little from the original proposal of January 1919. As specified in the original proposal, the organization would offer lectures and classes as well as provide libraries and other information resources to help educate workers; establish labour exchanges to ameliorate the problems of the unemployed; help mediate labour disputes wherever possible and practicable; act as a research body on social conditions and social policy questions; and create other necessary agencies and institutions when appropriate and feasible. The founding documents also claimed that the Kyōchōkai would discuss problems of social policy with the government and other public agencies and would make suggestions and write draft legislation on social policy issues. Such activities, of course, were by now familiar as well as general. The Kyōchōkai's role as a semi-official organ, however, gave the proposals a degree of importance they would not otherwise have had. But their real significance was that those activities were linked to a new industrial ideology of which the Kyōchōkai was the most visible and ardent sponsor.

The task of coping with new social norms and challenges to normative ideals faced all Japanese in the second decade of the twentieth century. In the arts, artists and writers began to focus on the modern urban industrial world. To Yokomitsu Riichi, for example, the task for writers had become one of portraying the life of and creating ideals for the 'new age' in which Japan found itself.[5] To create new values and ideals became the goal of much of Japan in the late 1910s. Radical groups of all persuasions hoped that 'education' of the masses would lead to a transvaluation of society and the creation of a new state in which the new ideals would be given expression. Government and social elites were no less active in this effort. Programmes such as the Movement to Foster National Strength (Minryoku kanyō undō), modelled on efforts at moral inculcation begun in the early years of the twentieth century, continued to be important tools for building and sustaining popular support. Like numerous popular groups the Kyōchōkai sought social transvaluation through 'education' of the urban working classes. It developed and sought to inculcate a new corpus of industrial values bundled together under the name of 'harmonism' (*kyōchōshugi*). This notion – which literally meant the doctrine of harmonious cooperation – constituted a new approach to labour–management issues developed under the pressure of late wartime and postwar industrial conditions. The harmonism doctrine, articulated and elaborated by the Kyōchōkai and its members, became a core concept of Japanese labour policy and labour administration in the 1920s. It was not, however, a coherent ideology. It was never rigorously defined, carefully thought out or clearly explained. Nevertheless, it constituted a recognizable doctrine and one to which writers, critics and government policy makers repeatedly referred. Its contours evolved as the Kyōchōkai itself changed and as social conditions changed. This chapter discusses the evolving structure of the Kyōchōkai and its most basic doctrine.

OLD IDEALS FOR A NEW SOCIETY

The parameters of the Kyōchōkai's industrial ideal were first laid down by the chief sponsors of the organization, Tokonami Takejirō and Shibusawa Eiichi. It was these men who defined the basic components of the harmonism doctrine. Their views were repeatedly refined and reconfigured as we shall see, but the harmonism of Tokonami and Shibusawa remained the basic intellectual touchstone for the Kyōchōkai and a generation of policy makers.

As discussed above, Tokonami believed it was necessary for political leaders to be aware of and act in accordance with the 'trends of the times'. 'World trends' could not be flouted without dire consequences. Like most Japanese elites, however, Tokonami accepted the view that social and political action had to be grounded in particularistic cultural and historical conditions. 'World trends' had to be adapted to fit specific domestic conditions. The Western industrial experience served to alert Japan to potential problems and provided models for an official response to those problems. But Japan, Tokonami argued, should not be cowed by the example of Europe. It should instead make a 'fresh start' based on 'new ideas' derived from the realities of Japanese life and culture.[6] Although numerous changes had taken hold in Japan since the Meiji Restoration, Tokonami believed that 'we are unable to transform our mind and our spirit any more than we can change the colour of our skin or the blood that runs through our veins'.[7] Japanese had come to wear shoes instead of *geta* and Western clothes had replaced traditional attire. But it did not follow that they had become Westerners as well. It was essential that the Japanese people 'confront the world as Japanese' not imitation Europeans.[8] The heritage and traditions of each nation forged a 'common character' between the nation's peoples and set them off from other peoples and other nations. The distinctive traits of Japan must therefore be acknowledged and should at the same time guide the quest for solutions to social problems.

Moreover, this awareness of national distinctiveness was the means of winning national greatness. In a directive to Home Ministry officials Tokonami stated that 'The most important task of our time is the quest to achieve genuine national power through the perpetuation of the vital and living customs of the past'.[9] An appreciation of the 'trends of the times' therefore did not contradict maintaining and adhering to a nation's heritage. Rather, both were essential components of a strategy to deal with the upheavals of industrial society while promoting the nation's strength.

Japan differed from Western countries, of course, in a number of respects. Most important of these, at least in so far as it pertained to industrial questions, Tokonami believed, was the differing perceptions of the relationship between managers and workers. In Western countries the emergence of social problems was a 'natural condition' (*shizen no koto*) inherent in the very process of industrial development. In the first place, in Western countries, he argued, labour is seen as a commodity sold, bought and bartered like other goods. Second, conflict between capital and labour is regarded as an unavoidable part of workplace relationships.[10] In Tokonami's view these assumptions were not only contrary to the Japanese character and the history of the Japanese people, they 'ignored the fundamental principles of the universe'.[11] Work could not be regarded as a piece of property subject only to market forces.

> Human work is not an inanimate thing. It is the fruit of life . . . .
> Things pursued for the sake of money alone are of no value.
> When work is properly seen as the fruit of life it must be regarded as sacred.[12]

This humanization of economic life was, to Tokonami, part of the fabric of Japanese culture and, more important, it expressed the eternal truth about the character of economic activity.

Because labour was a human activity springing from human needs, the relationship between the individuals performing their respective tasks in the productive process could not be governed by or understood in terms of some mechanistic model. To say that labour–management conflict is inevitable was to remove it from the totality of human relationships, Tokonami believed. Conflict was necessarily present in industry as it existed elsewhere in human life. But it did not operate according to a predetermined script which called for inevitable conflict between management and labour. The error of Western countries derived from their belief in the value of competition. Competition could of course help propel a society forward. But in the process of doing so it at the same time threatened the progress gained, because competition and conflict were indissolubly linked. Moreover, he emphasized, it ignored the essential oneness of things. All things differed from one another but each was part of a larger whole. Pine, plum and cherry trees are each distinct and unique, but all are trees. Buildings contained both horizontal and vertical beams but rather than working against each other they form differing elements of a single unified whole. Similarly, Tokonami said, 'from the point of view of the state capital and labour are the same thing'.[13] Each had an economic task to perform, each brings differing skills needed in the economy, and each is an equally important and equally necessary part of the economy.

Tokonami believed, therefore, that 'to attempt to solve the labor problem by importing Western ideas of confrontation' was not only contrary to Japanese tradition but, more importantly, was doomed to failure.[14] Human relationships were part of a total organic unity of life. To place particular parts of that unity in a position of arbitrary opposition threatened the total organism. Instead, 'to assure the healthy development of the state', Tokonami said in 1918, 'we must encourage a spirit of cooperation and harmony [*kyōdō chōwa no seishin*] among all segments of the nation'.[15] By 1919 he began to employ the neologism *kyōchōshugi*, or harmonism, to refer to this spirit.[16] Cooperation and harmony between individuals and social units more accurately corresponded to the needs of society, Tokonami asserted, and were at the same time true to the character of the Japanese people. Japan, therefore, could only avoid 'the bitter experience of Europe' by promoting and fostering harmonism in Japanese industry.[17]

Tokonami's advocacy of harmonism was not an effort to reassert the validity of 'master–servant relations' (*shūjū kankei*) or paternalism (*onjōshugi*) in new rhetorical garb. Rejecting early businessmen's arguments, Tokonami believed that while labour and capital were separated by skills and interests, they were functionally united in the working of the social organism. By failing to exercise their responsibilities on behalf of the workers' welfare, and through their unwillingness to recognize the status and the role of labour in the productive process, capitalists had to share in the responsibility for the emergence of the labour problem.

The impressive economic growth of the Meiji era Tokonami regarded as the product of sound policies beneficial to both capital and labour. Japanese could 'be confident about the continued prosperity of our nation's industrial development' only when harmonism is accepted as the basis for ordering labour–management relations in the rapidly changing industrial economy.[18] For Tokonami, harmonism clearly implied a subjugation of particular interests to the needs and demands of society and the nation. Cooperation and harmony were essential for restoring social stability and at the same time fostering a mutually supportive industrial relationship which would increase efficiency and productivity. 'Neither freedom nor equality are absolute', he said, but are dependent upon the needs of the state and must be tempered by an awareness of the welfare of the whole society.[19] As he said in a directive of March 1919, the new postwar conditions demanded that government leaders 'cultivate a sense of community [*kōkyōshin*] and work to bring about a spirit of self sacrifice'[20]. By recognizing their social responsibilities capital and labour would benefit the nation and the state by increasing economic growth. They would also find that a spirit of cooperation between them was mutually beneficial. Production would expand and profits would grow.

Workers' wages would rise and their well-being and security would be enhanced. At the same time, by recognizing their social responsibilities the two groups would benefit the nation and the state by promoting economic strength and helping to forge a unified, stable society.

Because he regarded cooperation and harmony as the essence of Japan's national character and the most effective means of building a powerful economy and state, Tokonami had little use for unions, specifically trade unions (*shokugyō betsu no kumiai*). Trade unions were divisive: they isolated workers from each other and from management. They presupposed the existence of inherently unequal groups in industry and an adversarial relationship between different parts of the economy. As a result, trade unions constituted the institutionalization of conflict in labour–management relations while diminishing the capacity of achieving a cooperative relationship which would lead to increased productivity and efficiency.

Tokonami rejected the idea that by providing a mechanism for representing workers' interests unions could bring discipline to the labour force and thereby reduce labour unrest. 'Labor unions are not a remedy for solving the labor problem', he said; they are instead 'a poison' that in most cases taints the relationship between managers and workers and induces conflict between them.[21] The experience of Western countries made the limitations of labour unions abundantly clear: 'England is the country with the most developed unions. But by themselves labor unions have proven to be incapable of bringing order to today's industrial world . . . . For that reason the Whitley plan [to establish works councils] was devised.'[22] Trade unions, therefore, not only were contrary to Japanese tradition, but also unable to mitigate labour unrest, and indeed were inimical to it.

In March 1919 the Relief Activities Research Committee under the authority of the Home Ministry, publicized its recommendation that unions be permitted to follow their 'natural development'. This position was supported by Tokonami in statements to the Diet and elsewhere.[23] This did not mean, as we have seen, that he favoured trade unions. In a Seiyūkai committee meeting he clarified his position. What was wanted, he believed, was the creation of small-scale vertical (*jūdanteki*) unions which were preferable to nation-wide or industry-wide horizontal (*ōdanteki*) unions.[24] Although he later repudiated this terminology claiming that it misrepresented his actual goals,[25] he continued to support the underlying implications of that earlier position. He saw vertical unions as potential organs of mutual understanding (*ishi sotsu kikan*). They could be established in every factory and would provide avenues of communication between managers and workers. These bodies were referred to by various names including works councils (*kōjō iinkai*), factory councils (*kyōgikai*), or workers' councils (*shokkō iinkai, rōdō iinkai*). The councils, Tokonami argued, were an attempt to implement principles very much like political democracy or local self-government in factories.[26] Each council should include an equal number of delegates representing management and labour. Every worker with at least six months in the company (or preferably one year) would have voting rights and workers on the job two or three years would be eligible for election.[27] Tokonami's discussion of the scope of council authority was vague and the establishment of enforcement mechanisms for the implementation of council decisions non-existent. The main value of the councils in Tokonami's view was that they would provide workers with a medium for an 'exchange of views with managers' thereby helping to reduce tension between the two groups and forestalling a widened conflict between them.

The creation of councils in each factory, Tokonami believed, would be a major step toward solving the labour problem. They would satisfy labour's demand for representation while helping forge between labour and management a relationship based on cooperation and mutual goodwill. Moreover, councils would be based on assumptions very different from trade unions. They presupposed cooperation rather than conflict, mutuality instead of mistrust, and unity rather than separateness. To perform their important work he stressed that the councils had to avoid taking on a corporate or inter-factory character. Rather, it was important 'that they be maintained as purely individual committees'.[28] Tokonami clearly hoped to localize conflict in the individual factory. By providing an alternative source for worker allegiance the self-contained councils would usurp the role of the growing trade union movement and reduce the arena available for worker unrest. By December 1919 the Home Ministry had prepared a draft works council bill. Vigorous opposition to the proposed law, however, forced the bill to be shelved before even reaching the floor of the Diet.

Tokonami's views of the labour problem and potential solutions to it were shared by numerous government and Seiyūkai leaders in the years following World War I. Most feared that despite the prosperity of the wartime boom period industrial efficiency was declining and the tranquility (*heisei*) of the nation was being upset by radical and union agitators. The director of the Police Bureau (Keiho kyoku), Kawamura Takeji, echoed Tokonami when he said:

> Japanese society is different from that of the West. Unlike the cool relations which exist between capital and labor in Western countries, in our country those relations are warm and friendly. This is one of Japan's great virtues and must at all costs be preserved.

To do so it was, he thought, imperative to recognize that labour unions on the Western model were not right for Japan. More appropriate were factory councils and the implementation of social policy programmes such as profit-sharing.[29] The conviction that labour unrest could be thwarted and efficiency improved by factory councils and through educational and social policy programmes directed toward workers led Tokonami and others to spurn demands for legal recognition of labour unions.

These men took the view that the creation of union legislation in England was a product of particular historical conditions, conditions not relevant to Japan. English union laws had been necessary because unions had been earlier proscribed by the Combination Laws of 1799 and 1800. In Japan, by contrast, unions had never been prohibited. No laws, Tokonami argued, prevented the creation of moderate unions and a 'healthy' union movement.[30] Like earlier opponents of the factory law, Tokonami, Kiyoura and a number of other Home Ministry leaders were of the opinion that a union law would not further workers' interests but simply lead to an unnecessary narrowing of Japanese freedom. Moreover, Seiyūkai leaders were unwilling to rescind Article 17 of the Peace Police Law. In a statement to the Diet Tokonami claimed that Article 17 did not 'obstruct the formation of moderate labor organizations'.[31] As the Police Bureau official and later Home Minister Kawarada Kakichi argued, Article 17 prohibited the formation of neither healthy unions nor strikes. The purpose of the law instead was to prevent compulsory union affiliation and the outbreak of strikes incited by agitators and rabble rousers from outside of the factory.[32]

On this issue, however, Tokonami began to shift his position in 1920. His growing interest in the creation of 'vertical' unions and in the inculcation of harmonism led him to reinterpret Article 17. That is, by 1920 Article 17 began to be used selectively to encourage the growth of factory councils. In the event of strikes in industries with councils, Article 17 was not applied but instead every effort would be made to settle the dispute through mediation. The provisions of the bill would only be invoked in the event of strikes precipitated in factories without councils.[33] He thereby was attempting to manipulate the legal system through selective enforcement as a means of altering the institutional relationships which shaped labour–management relations.

Tokonami's views about the solution to labour problems and the nature of the industrial values upon which solutions had to be based included, therefore, a number of elements. First, his ideas and policy initiatives were premised on the conviction that a state could not prosper if divisions existed within it. He accepted the notion of an organic state in which each element of a given society had a role and a place within the whole. If the bonds between any two parts of the social organism were weakened or severed, the whole, not just the particular parts, suffered the consequences.

Second, when seeking to re-establish the nation's social bonds, it was essential that the institutional and legal programmes undertaken correspond to the history and traditions of the nation. It was crucial that Japan understand and, in so far as possible, act in accordance with 'world trends' if it hoped to achieve its rightful place in the international community. Nevertheless, he said, our 'most pressing task is to work to promote our nation's *kokutai*'.[34] Japan's moral values and its distinctive *kokutai* were 'constant and unchanging' and political action in the realm of labour policy, as in all other areas, had to reflect and be in accordance with these fundamental and eternal principles.[35] The labour and social problems were also moral problems and could only be solved by pursuing policies consistent with Japan's time-honoured moral ideals. Simply to import Western ideas and institutions was to ignore the historical character of the Japanese people, threaten the shared values and goals of the nation and, as a result, would ultimately fail to repair the fissures within society brought about by the incursion of Western ideas.

Tokonami therefore rejected Western trade unionism, union legislation and the values upon which they were built. In contrast to the organic principles which defined Japan's *kokutai*, unionization was based on social fragmentation and the conflict of interests. Not only did such ideas clash with Japanese heritage and character, they threatened the strength and stability of the state. This, he believed, was confirmed by efforts in Europe and America to establish works councils for the purpose of fostering more harmonious labour–management relations. Therefore, to oppose legalization of unions was not contrary to world trends but in fact was in accord with them.

Finally, by advocating the creation of works or factory councils, he was convinced that he was acting in support of venerable Japanese labour relations practices. Unlike the Japan Industrial Club and other capitalist groups, Tokonami recognized that old paternalist practices were bankrupt and not capable of bringing about a stable industrial order. By manipulating sentiments of community and notions of industrial democracy, however, he hoped that the councils could bring stabilization to labour relations and promote increased production in industry. By relying on notions of solidarity instead of conflict and democratic ideals instead of class consciousness, he hoped that the councils would win workers away from divisive ideologies and unions so that social stability and national strength could be secured. Just as those concerned with social welfare in the nineteenth century mobilized communal sentiment to solve social problems, Tokonami built new approaches and new industrial values on a refashioned organicist idealization in the hope of overcoming new and more intense social problems.

The other seminal figure in promoting the harmonism ideal was Shibusawa Eiichi. Active in banking, railways and the general promotion of modern industry, Shibusawa was the archetypal Meiji entrepreneur and the most vivid symbol of Meiji industrial dynamism. His legendary stature, however, derives less from his specific entrepreneurial activities than from his personal status as the embodiment of Japanese commercial and business values. His image was defined by his claim that the motivation for all his actions was his concern for state and society. Always active in social welfare issues, following his retirement in 1916 Shibusawa became a tireless, full-time activist in social issues. Among the most important of these was the labour problem.

In an interview in August 1919, Shibusawa observed that although labour unrest and the notions of class conflict had had a long history in the West, in Japan there was no historical basis for the idea of class conflict, and the recent strikes and labour activism were 'the first appearance of such events since the beginning of our history'.[36] While he agreed with Tokonami that the 'intrusion of Western thought' had been critical in plunging Japan into 'a state of confusion and disorder',[37] he believed the principal causes of Japan's labour problems lay elsewhere.

By the 1910s he had come to believe that the problems between labour and management were a product of structural changes within the economy similar to those undergone earlier in the West. Prior to the Meiji Restoration commerce had been on a small scale and manufacturing was generally limited to handicraft production. Because of the simplicity of the country's economic institutions there was, he argued, a 'relative equality' of wealth in the country which minimized the potential for conflict between the various participants in economic institutions.[38] Moreover, relations between employers and workers were those of master and servant (*shūjū kankei*). Between them was a bond of closeness and affection not unlike the relationship between members of a family. As a result, there was little criticism of this relationship. But, Shibusawa argued, the small capitalist or merchant with meagre resources has been replaced by anonymous investors. Workers have come to number in the thousands and the tens of thousands. Therefore, in contrast to his views during the 1890s, he said that in such a situation the relationship between management and workers lacked 'the natural warmth' which had prevailed in simpler times.[39] Technological change and the pursuit of modern economic development, although generally beneficial, had therefore brought fundamental changes in the pattern of interaction between managers and workers. Animosity and mistrust had become common and lamentable byproducts of growth.

Shibusawa believed that to fail to bring about a fundamental, long-term solution to the labour problem jeopardized the country's industrial growth and undermined national strength. When manufacturers and merchants prosper consumers prosper as well by having available the goods and services they wish to buy. Managers and workers, he argued, were part of a similar symbiotic relationship. For management to succeed and industry grow strong, workers must be satisfied and fairly treated. If workers hope to keep their jobs and improve their lot, they must help management succeed by fulfilling their obligation to work as hard and as efficiently as possible. Each side, therefore, prospered only if the other did. The fate of both management and labour was interlocking; strife and mistrust between them affected both adversely. State and society were also affected. Industrial conflict inevitably meant a decline in national output and national wealth. Moreover, even Western nations had begun to recognize the gravity of the problem. The creation of organizations such as the International Labour Organization (ILO) were evidence of the perceived need to address the problems of labour. This collective effort, Shibusawa believed, was part of a world trend to ameliorate the labour problem, a trend of which Japan too must be a part. For if it failed to do so it would be unable to keep pace with the Western nations in economic growth thereby further weakening the nation.

Another world trend identified by Shibusawa was the 'natural development' of union organization.[40] He was not referring to the 'small-scale vertical' unions supported by Tokonami. He believed Tokonami's notion to be an 'unfortunate' relic of the 'era of cottage industry'.[41] While the unions Tokonami hoped to foster might have been feasible in the past, it was nothing more than an impossible dream in the age of large-scale industry that prevailed following World War I. Shibusawa saw labour's urge to organize itself as an inevitable and inescapable concomitant of industrial development. Rather than trying to limit the workers' natural urge to organize as Tokonami was attempting to do, Shibusawa urged that officials and capitalists actively encourage workers to form 'healthy', 'satisfactory' unions thereby 'eliminating the fear that unsatisfactory unions will be formed'.[42] Acting on that belief Shibusawa had earlier supported Suzuki Bunji's Yūaikai and remained a vocal advocate of 'responsible' unionism.

Clearly his support for unions was not open-ended. While he believed that the legal recognition of unions as well as the abrogation of Article 17 of the Peace Police Law were appropriate and useful means of dealing with the labour problem, his view of the character and role of unions was vastly different from the type of organization demanded by workers' groups. In October 1918 Shibusawa observed that

> if unions are formed with no purpose other than to oppose capitalists they are not good. But, if unions are organized to improve the character of workers, elevate their status, or to meet special emergency situations, I am in no way opposed to them.[43]

Shibusawa's view of the role of unions, therefore, was that they should act as self-help cooperatives or mutual-aid societies. That is, they must be like the Yūaikai to which he had given his support earlier. He did not really address himself to the questions of greatest concern to labour leaders and workers in post-World War I Japan; the right of workers to organize freely, the legal recognition of their freely organized unions, nor unions' rights to collective bargaining. Although he accepted that union organization was in accord with world trends and would thus provide a useful antidote to labour unrest he accepted neither workers' nor unions' demands for absolute rights of labour. Before claiming 'rights' workers had 'obligations' that had to be discharged. 'Rights,' he said, 'are not something that we ourselves can insist upon, they must be given.' He despaired that 'among workers who participate in strikes there are many who simply demand rights for themselves while neglecting their responsibilities'. Such a state of affairs was, he said, 'truly regrettable'.[44] 'Rights' had to be earned. The rights of workers, and by extension others as well, were not absolute but conditional upon the fulfilment of their prescribed duties. If they met their obligations, rights would be given to them; how and by whom he did not specify.

By supporting the Kyōchōkai, Shibusawa hoped to create an agent for the creation of 'sound' and 'responsible' unionism. At the same time he was concerned that the organization act as a mediating body between labour and management. Shibusawa shared with other Kyōchōkai leaders the conviction that the fate of managers and workers was completely intertwined and mutually dependent. A successful economic enterprise was the product of 'the combined efforts of both capitalists and workers'.[45] Each side of the relationship was of equal value to society. The tasks of neither could be minimized if Japan's social stability and economic strength were to be assured. In the face of the labour–management conflict that had become apparent by the late 1910s Shibusawa believed that mediation of industrial disputes by someone or some group in a neutral position was essential. He hoped that the Kyōchōkai would do what it could to achieve 'the pacification of labor–management unrest from its position as a third party'. If it were able to do so, he claimed, 'the future of Japan's labor problem is something we need not fear'.[46] Shibusawa was not unconcerned with ideological inculcation, but argued that the fledgling organization could have a more immediate impact in a practical role of dispute conciliation. By so doing it would establish its credibility as a neutral party and would thus be able to effect genuine reconciliation between capital and labour.

It is tempting to see Shibusawa as a 'progressive' or perhaps even as a 'liberal' alternative to Tokonami and other government proponents of the Kyōchōkai. His willingness to recognize horizontal unions and to advocate their legalization, his urging that Article 17 be abrogated and his belief that the Kyōchōkai could most effectively defuse the labour problem through impartial mediation are all ideas which could be used as evidence of liberal goals. As important as the differences between Tokonami and Shibusawa were, however, they should not be allowed to obscure the broad similarities between the two men. It was their areas of agreement which brought them together as co-sponsors of the Kyōchōkai and formed the undergirding of the harmonism ideology that the Kyōchōkai promoted. It was on the basis of their shared assumptions that the Kyōchōkai developed, and it was those assumptions that continued to shape the Kyōchōkai programme and government industrial policy throughout the interwar period.

Both Shibusawa and Tokonami, like most other Japanese elites, placed great emphasis on moral and ethical values as defining the parameters of acceptable political and economic action. Tokonami urged an awareness of world trends but stressed repeatedly that changes must be in accord with Japan's time-honoured cultural and ethical values. Similarly Shibusawa made clear that however much it was necessary to keep abreast of the trends of the times it was even more important that Japan should not 'swallow Western ways whole'.[47] Just as foreign religions like Buddhism and Christianity were successfully absorbed and made into wholly Japanese phenomena, so too should modern systems of human relations in industry reflect an appropriate Japanese character. Such matters as unions, health insurance, labour exchanges and the like should be studied carefully in their Western settings. Nevertheless, he said, those studies should not be regarded as blueprints for the importation of such foreign innovations but as guides which can provide the basis for selecting, rejecting or altering plans and programmes in accordance with 'our nation's *kokutai*'.[48] Shibusawa and Tokonami alike, as they had earlier, hoped to recreate traditionalist moral ideals in a new context.

Also like Tokonami, Shibusawa repeatedly dismissed master–servant relations and paternalism as appropriate means of structuring labour–management relations. He said that of course he was 'not opposed to preserving the good customs which have come down to us from the past,' but he did not believe that 'the problems which beset us today can be solved by relying on those customs'. In view of the changes in the economy and because of the intrusion of Western ideas, he argued that it would be 'extremely difficult' even to attempt to preserve Japan's traditional system of work relationships.[49] There is an air of disingenuousness in these statements. For in the 1920s as in the 1880s Shibusawa hoped to reconfigure traditionalist moral values to fit the new economic setting. His most strongly held belief was that if cooperation between capital and labour were not brought about on the basis of each side's own 'moral decision', 'a satisfactory and durable solution' to the labour problem could not be achieved. What was essential was a complete reciprocity of respect and affection between individuals based on 'moral human feelings' (*dōkuteki ninjō*).[50] Thus, the Kyōchōkai was built upon a belief in what he called *kōonshugi* (literally, warm relationism). That is, its goal was to create 'a warm relationship between capital and labor, a relationship based upon mutual respect, love, faithfulness and tolerance'.[51] Warm relations were merely another way of expressing the goal of harmonism. However much Shibusawa longed for traditionalist social relationships the fact was that the economy and resulting organizational arrangements were profoundly different from what they had once been. Kawazu Sen, a Tokyo University economic professor and Kyōchōkai advisor, expressed the dilemma of Shibusawa and other organicist conservatives in a Home Ministry pamphlet of 1920: 'there are people who think that the [labour] problem can be solved through the old system of master–servant relationships. It would be wonderful were that possible, but too much has changed.'[52] Thus like Tokonami, Shibusawa in the 1920s continued to believe, as he had long done, that Japan's time-honoured customs had to be adapted to the new economic environment. To do so Shibusawa appealed more forcefully than anyone else to what he saw as the source of those customs, Confucian humanistic values.

As discussed earlier, Shibusawa embraced Confucian moral and ethical ideals for their instrumental value, for their capacity to solve real-world problems. Confucianism did not for Shibusawa represent a religious system but a doctrine of practical morality that established guidelines for ordering human society.[53] During the early years of industrial development he mobilized classical Confucian moral constructs to legitimize business activity and to reorder relationships in industry. By the second decade of the twentieth century, however, it was no longer necessary to justify industry. The more pressing task was to overcome its social consequences.

As early as 1907, in a speech to the first general meeting of the Social Policy Association, Shibusawa argued that in industry, 'if workers and capitalist met with each other in accordance with the true spirit of Confucius and Mencius . . . strife and conflict between them would not arise'.[54] A decade later he observed that truly amicable relations between management and workers could be realized only if each side based its attitudes and behaviour on the Confucian ideals of benevolence and humanity.[55] Social and legislative reform were of course necessary, but without a solid grounding in Confucian moral humanism they would not succeed. The Kanegafuchi and Tōyō textile companies demonstrated that with benevolence harmony in industry was possible. Even foreign companies like the Krupp company in Germany made clear that close, considerate relations between management and workers meant a reduction of friction in industrial relations.

Shibusawa's ideal was the classical notion of the 'kingly way' (*ōdō*, in Chinese *wang tao*). This Mencian construct constituted a venerable model of righteous Confucian governance. In it the people were the standard of political action and political virtue. Their welfare was the reason for the state's existence, the principal motivation for its activities, and the source of its strength. Adherence to the ideals of the 'kingly way' was, in Shibusawa's views, the best, most basic guideline for solving the labour problem. For him, the 'kingly way' validated the basic equality of managers and workers. He warned of the 'gravest dangers' if capitalists did not 'alter their attitudes toward workers' and recognize their true equal status.[56] By arguing, however, that workers' 'rights' were dependent upon the successful execution of their 'duties', Shibusawa showed that his belief in the equality of the social classes was conditional. Indeed, Shibusawa shared Mencius's view of social stratification. Distinctions between 'upper' and 'lower' were not distinctions of status or worth but differences in function. Each performed different tasks. Yet the task of each was to provide 'social service'. The 'kingly way' validated this social equality and gave meaning to the benevolent and humane relationships that must, in Shibusawa's view, define the organic moral community.

For Shibusawa, and for many others as well, Confucian moral values embodied the most humane and most just means of ordering and conducting modern society. To be effective in restoring social harmony those values had to be propagated. The Kyōchōkai itself would engage in this effort. So too did a variety of Confucian societies. The Shibunkai, the most prominent of these groups, supported and sought to foster Confucian ethical values as an antidote to the excessive materialism spreading with economic growth. It supported the Confucian moral and social vision as a means of promoting Japan's national polity and its native, as opposed to Western, values.[57] Numerous government leaders and bureaucrats took a similar position. Ōki Tōkichi, the Justice Minister in the Hara government, for example, observed that the social problems being experienced in Japan were a consequence of the 'confusion in people's thinking'. His prescription was that 'the people must be made to understand well the true moral character of Confucianism'.[58] To Kaneko Kentarō, a leading bureaucrat and earlier Factory Law supporter, the diffusion of the ancient Confucian moral ideals of humanity, justice, loyalty and filial piety (*jingi chūkō*) would bring order and harmony to Japanese society. 'If those teachings are preserved,' he said, 'we need not feel anxious about the future.'[59] Those values could serve this function not only because they were right and true, but also, according to Mizuno Rentarō, because they 'constitute the foundation of Japanese morality'.[60] As a result, they were appropriate and consistent with Japanese attitudes and mores. Thus Shibusawa and other important leaders sought to address social problems with and in the name of traditionalist moral goals.

Shibusawa's appeal to Confucian ethical values was double-edged. He was convinced that the humanistic ideas of Confucianism expressed the highest and truest goals for humankind. They facilitated the creation of a morally based society and business mentality. But at the same time, those values had major instrumental value for modern society. Since moral ideals and economic success were mutually supportive and mutually reinforcing, and because Confucianism espoused the most perfect moral and ethical values, not to build society and industry on those values threatened future development of the state and the nation. Moreover, because Confucian values emphasized 'friendliness' and 'harmony' between peoples, a nation that thoroughly embraced those values would be spared the strife and conflict that characterized modern industrial states in the West.

Following the lead of Mencius, Shibusawa stressed the need of the state and society's leaders to secure the people's welfare. Only by so doing could people be content and society well ordered. This conviction led Shibusawa to activism in social welfare programmes and planning. It also was, in large part, a motivation for his espousal of the rights of workers to unionize and the legal recognition of unions. The 'trends of the times' pointed to the necessity of granting workers expanded rights in industry, a trend sanctioned, in Shibusawa's view, by Confucian humanism. To him workers and capitalists were of equal value to society and the state. Despite the differences over the exact legislative course to be pursued, Shibusawa shared with Tokonami, therefore, an organic conception of the organization of society and industry. Each element of society was bound to every other, the whole constituting the common means to common and shared ends. The organicist conservatism implicit in nineteenth-century reforms had become explicit in views of the Kyōchōkai's creators and the harmonism doctrine they advanced.

NEW DIRECTIONS

Despite the optimism of Tokonami and Shibusawa, the Kyōchōkai found itself in the midst of a crisis shortly after its creation. The cause of the crisis was a major strike at the Fuji Gas Spinning Company (Fuji Gasu Bōseki Kabushiki Kaisha). On 14 July 1920 more than 2,000 workers at the company's Oshiage plant went out on strike under the leadership of the Sōdōmei local. The Fujibō strike is an important benchmark in Japan's labour history. It was the first major post-World War I strike that had unionization rights as its sole objective.[61] As a result, it attracted considerable attention. The recently organized Sōdōmei took a particular interest in the strike and the issue that provoked it. As the largest and most influential labour organization in the country it had the greatest stake in the union rights problem and stood to gain the most from its successful resolution.

Sōdōmei leaders gave a great deal of attention to one aspect of the Fujibō strike that was especially troubling to the Kyōchōkai. That is, the president of Fujibō, Wada Toyoji, was at the same time a Kyōchōkai director and major supporter. To Suzuki Bunji this fact merely confirmed his earlier suspicions of the organization. On 16 July the Sōdōmei sent a letter to the Kyōchōkai which criticized the organization for its apparent inconsistency.[62] The Kyōchōkai, according to the letter, claimed that it was formed to seek an equitable solution to the labour problem. Its founding documents asserted that it would act as an impartial intermediary between capital and labour. Yet the attitude of Wada and the failure of the Kyōchōkai to address the issues raised at Fujibō gave rise to doubts about the organization's intentions. The letter concluded with a demand for 'a clarification of the Kyōchōkai's attitude toward this affair'.

The organization responded with equivocation and a pious reiteration of its continued support for 'sound' and 'healthy' unionism. Not surprisingly Sōdōmei leaders were not satisfied with such a formulation. A union statement attacked the 'vague and evasive' statements of the Kyōchōkai. Only one thing had been made clear to union leaders. That is, removing the transparent mask of labour–management harmony behind which the Kyōchōkai hid itself, 'reveals the Kyōchōkai to be in reality a defender of capitalism and capitalists'.[63] It was concerned simply with protecting capitalist interests, not with helping genuine labour organizations. Suzuki Bunji accused the Kyōchōkai of being based on an attitude of what he called bureaucratism (*kanryōshugi*).[64] It had become, as a result, abundantly clear that 'henceforth for us to have any dealings with the Kyōchōkai would be pointless and absurd'.[65]

When the Fujibō strike broke out the Kyōchōkai was little more than seven months old. It had been launched with great rhetorical flourish. Its beginnings had been attended with high hopes that it would play an important role in minimizing the threat from labour and create a social unity and sense of unified national purpose that would have been unique in the industrialized world. By repudiating the repressive tactics of the Terauchi and earlier cabinets and by supporting moderate reformism, Kyōchōkai sponsors hoped to satisfy the minimal demands of labour thereby removing workers' impetus to participate in disruptive strikes and other forms of industrial unrest. But conservative reforms that would have been welcomed in 1900 or 1912 were no longer regarded as adequate by 1919 or 1920. Popular demands had caught up with and surpassed elite willingness to extend concessions. The reformist views of the early Kyōchōkai were no longer adequate to satisfy the calls for change, or 'reconstruction', that were widely invoked. The Kyōchōkai did not meet a grateful constituency. Rather, the Kyōchōkai was proposing a conservative ideology and reformist programme at a moment they were unlikely to be accepted. The Fujibō strike and the fallout from it marked the failure of the first stage of the Kyōchōkai and its industrial ideology. A new approach was needed.

Before a new approach could be pursued, the organization first had to repair the damage the Fujibō strike and its aftermath had caused. The July strike and the attacks on the Kyōchōkai that had ensued destroyed its claim that it was unbiased. Moreover, its failure to help mediate the strike eroded whatever confidence may have existed in its ability to participate in labour–management crises in the active manner the founding prospectus envisioned. To try to patch up its image without jettisoning its underlying principles the Kyōchōkai undertook a major reorganization in October 1920.

The most obvious and visible change was the appointment of a new team of managing directors. As in 1919, three new directors were appointed: Soeda Kiichirō, Nagai Tōru and Tazawa Yoshiharu. Soeda was the most senior of the three.[66] He graduated from the law faculty of Tokyo University (Todai) in 1898 and entered the Home Ministry in the same year. One of his early posts was as a staff member in Hyōgo prefecture. It was there that Soeda met Tokonami Takejirō, at that time a senior official in the Ministry's Hyōgo office. Until his death in 1935 Tokonami acted as Soeda's protector and pulled him up through the Home Ministry hierarchy. When Tokonami became Home Minister in 1918 he named Soeda chief of the important Local Affairs Bureau. As a member of the Relief Research Activities Committee Soeda took a leading role in opposing Takano Iwasaburō's agenda for the body. He argued for the retention of Article 17 of the Peace Police Law and for the provision calling for the creation of a labour–management harmony society. Soeda's effectiveness as a spokesman for Home Ministry labour objectives and principles made him a natural candidate for the position of Kyōchōkai managing director.

Nagai Tōru was proposed as a candidate for a managing directorship by Kiyoura Keigo and assumed his post on 8 October.[67] In 1903 Nagai graduated from the Tokyo University faculty of law. From 1903 to 1911 he held a variety of positions in the Ministry of Agriculture and Commerce. After that time he moved over to the Railway Administration (Tetsudōin). Between 1918 and 1920 Nagai served as a Railway Administration bureau chief under Tokonami, who served as head of the Administration concurrent with his post as Home Minister. Nagai's candidacy as Kyōchōkai managing director, therefore, undoubtedly received the essential support of Tokonami as well.

The third new managing director, Tazawa Yoshiharu, was also a Tōdai law graduate.[68] Tazawa joined the Home Ministry in 1910 and was assigned to its Shizuoka prefecture office. During his four years in Shizuoka, Tazawa developed considerable expertise in organizing and directing educational programmes. He became an important leader of youth education programmes and by 1916 became intimately involved with the national youth group movement. Both Tokonami and Shibusawa were impressed with Tazawa's skills and dedication to education. They saw his wide experience in this area as a useful asset for the new Kyōchōkai organizational scheme. He was persuaded to leave the Home Ministry and assumed the post of Kyōchōkai managing director on 22 October.

Save some minor departmental shuffling and new organizational titles little was changed in the structure of the Kyōchōkai after the reorganization of October 1920. The appointment of the three new managing directors was the only significant change. Other officers, including Wada, remained in place. There seemed to be precious little in the October shakeup that would appease Kyōchōkai critics. Even the appointment of the new managing directors did not seem auspicious. All of the new men were Tōdai law graduates, each had been a career bureaucrat, and none had demonstrated any particular sympathy toward the labour movement prior to 1920. Indeed, each shared with Tokonami and Shibusawa a basic belief in the need to resurrect moral community in the factory environment. Simple institutional reshuffling, therefore, would be inadequate to solve the organization's problems. Rather, what was needed was a refinement and a clarification of its ideals.

Paternalism in the New Society

The new managing directors understood that it was imperative for the Kyōchōkai to make a stronger effort to live up to its rhetoric; it must appear unbiased in deed as well as in word. For this reason, Nagai in particular argued that Kyōchōkai officers must avoid unnecessary contact with the Japan Industrial Club.[69] Symbols of this kind were necessary but more important still was the more immediate need to correct what the new directors saw as a fundamental misunderstanding of the nature of the Kyōchōkai's character and mission. Nagai complained that 'the meaning of labor–management harmony and the principles on which it rests are not clear' to people, often being misperceived as a form of 'anachronistic thinking' out of touch with contemporary reality.[70] To correct this misapprehension, the new managing directors issued in November the organization's new 'manifesto' (Kyōchōkai sengen).[71]

The themes expressed in this new document were familiar; it rejected paternalism, advocated respect for 'personality' (*jinkaku*), opposed the notion of class conflict while embracing a belief that the interests of the various classes differ. Each of these points had been made in the original organizational documents and elaborated in members' writings and speeches. There was a difference however. In both language and tone the manifesto was more conciliatory, more eager to appear neutral and concerned with the interests of workers as much as capitalists. This new tone was to characterize the Kyōchōkai for the next decade.

The issue of paternalism was especially prickly. During much of the early history of the labour union movement, activists embraced much of the language and sentiment of labour–management cooperation and harmony. Both Takano Fusatarō and Katayama Sen hoped to avoid the endemic confrontation that characterized Western industrial relations. Because strikes 'often proved injurious' to both management and workers, Katayama believed that the problem of achieving harmony between the two sides was one of the greatest issues facing Japanese society.[72] Suzuki Bunji had identified his Yūaikai as a reformist union committed to fostering social and industrial harmony. As late as 1917 he wrote that 'harmony based on warm feelings between capital and labor is something for which we all fervently hope'. He noted, however, that 'these feelings must be reciprocal. The demand that workers alone should manifest warm-heartedness and obedience while capitalists . . . disregard workers' well-being and their status is self-serving in the extreme.'[73] Japan's first generation of labour leaders therefore implicitly accepted the paternalist ideal. But, to be meaningful and bring about harmonious relations, paternalism had to be truly honoured by all. It could not simply be an ideology of control, a means of exacting obedience from workers. A letter from an anonymous worker in 1922 expressed clearly the frustration with paternalist rhetoric:

> The hard times we are now experiencing have taught me a few things . . . . Workers are forced to throw away their lives in precarious desperation. This is surely a cause for concern. But there is something that alarms me even more. Although not believers in paternalism . . . if it comes down to eating or not, workers can live with the idea called humaneness [*ninjō*]. The companies, however, when forced to cut back, fire workers mercilessly . . . . The depression has completely unmasked the lukewarm humaneness of employers.[74]

Labour leaders' belief in capitalists' failure to honour their paternalist rhetoric coupled with the radicalization of the labour union movement during World War I led to labour's rejection of the values and language of paternalism. Postwar union leaders voiced three principal objections to the paternalist doctrine. First, they opposed the 'feudal' character of paternalist values. It was an ideology, they claimed that simply fed capitalists' conceit that they were like feudal lords and workers their retainers. Second, paternalism provided capitalists with the rationale for seizing for themselves the benefits and advantages of industrial production. It sanctioned capitalist greed, allowing them to stuff company profits in their own pockets without consulting or considering workers. Finally, capitalists manipulated warm-hearted values as a means of pushing workers harder while demanding their unquestioning allegiance.[75] By the postwar years, therefore, organized labour had repudiated the moderate social reformism that had marked its early years as well as the conciliatory language that had enabled it to tolerate paternalism. By identifying the Kyōchōkai as a defender of capitalists and capitalist values, Suzuki and others were accusing it of supporting paternalism.

From the beginning Kyōchōkai leaders had sought to defuse this issue. The organization's founding prospectus stated that 'labor–management cooperation cannot be achieved by relying on the customs of the past'. Shibusawa had argued persistently that traditional values were inoperative in modern Japan's industrial society. These pronouncements were extremely vague and did little to disguise the early Kyōchōkai leaders' support of 'true' warm relations (*onjō kankei*) in contrast to the distorted paternalism of the Taishō years. During the 1920s the organization tried to appear more unequivocal in its rejection of paternalism. Soeda rightly observed that paternalism was generally perceived as little more than a stratagem (*sakuryaku*) or a policy of appeasement (*kaijūsaku*) adopted, as the manifesto put it, 'by superiors to pacify those beneath them'.[76] Paternalism was not inherently or necessarily evil, Soeda claimed. Yet he acknowledged that it had been abused by capitalists, destroying its credibility and necessitating its rejection. Feelings of warmth between manager and worker cannot be merely adopted for their tactical value, Soeda said. If such feelings are not genuine, industrial harmony and social unity will not be forthcoming.[77] Capitalists cannot expect to be able to hide behind the cloak of paternalism to exploit workers or use it as a means of justifying their superiority over workers. For:

> today the ideas of democracy hold sway throughout the world, and, in these ideas there is no place for distinctions between superior and inferior or high and low when considering relations between people. In such a situation, therefore, the idea referred to as paternalism has lost its capacity to serve as a basis for social harmony.[78]

Thus even if capitalists were not cynical in their use of paternalism, even if they displayed genuine concern and affection for their employees, it would still be inadequate for establishing amicable social relations. Paternalism implies a necessarily hierarchical relationship and is thus contrary to the democratic, egalitarian principles that had become part of twentieth-century industrial society. The establishment of close, friendly relations was of course desirable, but without the recognition of rights and responsibilities they would be of no avail. As a result, Soeda said, 'the acknowledgement of the rights of others and feelings of individual responsibility are ideas embedded in the ideal of harmonism'.[79] Therefore harmonism was not merely a reformulation of paternalism. The two concepts, Soeda claimed, were in no way related. Harmonism was both more comprehensive and more just.

The New Worker and the New Society

The issue of social justice was central to the Kyōchōkai effort. Certainly to solve the labour problem required improving the lives of workers. As Soeda recognized, however, this was not 'simply a question of material progress'. Rather, workers were engaged in a broad 'betterment movement' (*kōjō undō*), seeking improvements 'in both material and spiritual areas'.[80] While not dismissing the importance of issues such as, say, housing or general living conditions, Soeda and the other new managing directors understood that in the postwar period, following European trends, 'workers have other demands'. Those demands included social and political recognition of workers' equality and human worth. If capitalists 'do not wake up to this fact the future of Japan will be very gloomy', Soeda believed.[81]

With the World War I economic boom and a rising level of labour activity during the same period, workers' conceptions of themselves and their social function changed. They came to see heightened value in their labour and gradually became aware of themselves as a corps of producers, not merely nameless and faceless cogs in society's lower order. Increasingly they believed that society perceived and treated them as scum, that industry robbed them of their individuality and human character and that capitalists pushed and manipulated them as if they were little more than animate machines. The basic goal of many workers was that they be treated with dignity and that their fundamental humanity be recognized. This growing sentiment among broad numbers of workers made the call for 'social liberation' (*shakaiteki kaihō*) of the working class one of the principal labour demands of the postwar period.[82] Being partners in the production process, workers came to see themselves as possessing social significance at least equal to capitalists and others. As such they had the right to be treated as human beings, as equal members of the society of which they were a part. A recognizable working class had begun to emerge after the Sino-Japanese War but it was not until the World War I years that a broad cross-section of workers became aware of themselves as members of it. This new view of their role, in part, led the newly organized Sōdōmei to call for social liberation and equality, liberation and participation that reflected the new awareness of Japanese workers.

Workers' 'spiritual' dissatisfaction was partly the result of and was intensified by changes in the nature of the labour force. Numerous changes in the character and use of the workforce manifested themselves during the World War I period. One important change was the educational level of the post-World War I working class. Despite the emphasis placed on education during the Meiji period, a 1905 Education Ministry (Mombushō) survey showed that in that year 57.3 per cent of the nations's factory workers had not attended school.[83] During what would have been the school-age years for those workers, familial poverty, the absence of schools and resistance to school tuition kept about one-third of Japanese children out of school.[84] These figures gradually improved after 1900 when the government began phasing out tuition fees for elementary school attendance. As a result, by 1924 nearly three-quarters of Japanese factory workers had completed at least primary school.[85] By the wartime and postwar years the number of newspapers and periodicals grew sharply with the increasingly literate populace. According to data collected in a 1922 police report, the number of newspapers increased by nearly one-third between 1917 and 1922 while the number of magazines (defined in the report as a periodical distributed less than three times per month) increased from 1,442 in 1918 to 2,236 in 1922.[86] Needless to say, many of the offerings of this publishing bonanza were frivolous; *Motion Picture World* (*Katsudō no sekai*), *Fashion World* (*Ryukō sekai*), or *The Three S's: Screen, Speed, and Sex* (*San-esu*) for example. But many of the publications sought to appeal to important special groups or rising new constituencies. *The Woman's Companion* (*Yūai fujin*) and *The Housewife's Friend* (*Shufu no tomo*) addressed the concerns of middle-class women while *The Examinee's Manual* (*Juken zasshi*) and *Examination World* (*Jukenkai*) tried to provide guidance for those seeking success in the increasingly competitive school entrance examinations.[87] Workers were the intended audience for a growing number of newspapers and magazines. Beginning with the Yūaikai's *Yūai shimpō*, union publications mushroomed. Like the Sōdōmei's *Labour* (*Rōdō*), these publications were written a clear, crisp and very accessible style. These publications helped keep labour union members and other workers abreast of issues not just in industry but in all areas relevant to worker interests. Takano Iwasaburō's famous study of workers' living conditions in Tsukijima revealed that workers' sources of information were not limited to union publications. The survey team's data showed that among those identified as working-class families 79.4 per cent (523 of 657) subscribed to at least one newspaper. Remarkably, 17.8 per cent of the respondents sub-scribed to two or more papers. Among the most popular papers were the respectable *Yorozu chōhō*, *Tokyo nichi nichi shimbun* and the *Mainichi shimbun*.[88] Workers were better informed than ever and better educated. These were important conditions that had a significant impact on workers' sense of their place in society.

Twenty years earlier Yokoyama Gennosuke had identified an emerging urban working class that was distinct from the vague category of the poor. By the World War I period, this new working class had grown in size and definition. Structural changes in industry and labour force utilization abetted workers' recognition of their position in society. With the growing sophistication and educational achievement of workers themselves, they took a greater interest than ever in the ideas and events of their world. Of course, none had greater power or currency than the ideas of democracy and social equality. To try to win the support of labour and the general acceptance of its programmes, the Kyōchōkai, more than ever, had to appeal to those new ideas and build a programme on them.

Soeda Keiichirō's denunciation of paternalism stressed the prevalence of democratic ideas and the resultant inappropriateness of hierarchical, antidemocratic paternalist practices. The new Kyōchōkai leadership suggested its commitment to democracy with its repeated use of the phrase 'respect for personality (*jinkaku sonchōshugi*, literally, respect for personality-ism). Shiozawa Masatada, an important Kyōchōkai leader and later Waseda University professor, wrote that 'warm relations [*onjō kankei*] will develop naturally' if both managers and workers act in accordance with the spirit of respect for personality.[89] It was respect for personality, not the inherently unequal paternalism that would enable workers and managers to come together to build a harmonious industrial society.[90] Industry had grown rapidly and the use of labour increasingly rationalized, but 'as labour is treated as a type of commodity the relationship between managers and workers . . . becomes purely an economic relationship, a relationship between buyer and seller, completely separate from humane and moral ties'.[91] In such a situation dissatisfaction and conflict are inevitable. But, 'before being capitalists or workers,' Tazawa said, 'all of us are first people. The terms capitalist and worker are simply economic terms, and, as such, they are not reasons for assigning differences in each group's human value.'[92] Each person, whether worker or capitalist, must be judged not by their relative economic position but must be respected and treated as individual human beings. The personality of each person within society is equal and of equal social value.

It is important to note that during the 1910s the term 'personality' had come to have profound philosophical implications. Beyond the conventional understanding of personality the term had come to denote human dignity. When applied to human nature or character, therefore, it referred to what might be called dignity status or human worth.[93] This understanding of personality underlay one of the most important philosophical trends of the Taishō period.[94] Nishida Kitarō, Tomonaga Sanjurō, Kuwaki Gen'yaku and others grappled with the significance of personality. But it was the philosopher Abe Jirō who devoted the greatest energy to this issue. Abe believed that personality constitutes the supreme value. The significance and classification of all other values are determined by reference to this principal value.[95] This view was a direct challenge to the traditional bureaucratic understanding of state and society in which the state had a life of its own apart from the people and groups that constituted it. Abe's views necessarily diminished the state's role as the arbiter of truth and value. Abe's 'personality-ism' (*jinkakushugi*) saw the source of truth and value as emanating from within the individual. Each individual therefore possessed a unique and powerful dignity or worth and it was from within the individual that all truth and value flowed.

Matsumoto Sannosuke has criticized the emphasis on personality and personality-ism as an intellectually elitist position. Abe argued that personality-ism was completely contrary to materialism. It was ethical and moral concerns that were central. Matsumoto concludes that this anti-materialist bias divorced a potentially liberating philosophy from the realities and operation of actual society.[96] Nevertheless, it was precisely this emphasis on morality and character that lay beneath what has come to be called Taishō Democracy. Yoshino Sakuzō, the leading voice of liberal democracy in the Taishō period, believed that the ideal government was 'government by the wise and good' (*tetsujin seiji*). Government, therefore, was to be led by a morally enlightened minority or *jinkakusha*, men of character and judgement.[97] This emphasis on the moral underpinnings of political leadership linked Yoshino's political ideas with the philosophical thrust of personality-ism as developed by Abe and discussed by others. It had become, indeed, a major component of Taishō liberal thought. Therefore, the term 'personality' was an important part of the conceptual vocabulary of Taishō liberalism.

By embracing and promoting the notion of respect for personality, the new Kyōchōkai leadership actively sought to appeal to the democratic yearnings of Japan's liberals and labour leaders. Their understanding and application of the personality concept, however, differed from the idea as articulated by Abe, Yoshino and others. First, it was a concept put forth for its instrumental value. That is, in contrast to Abe's belief that personality or the individual human character was the ultimate definer of value and the source of truth, Kyōchōkai leaders promoted the doctrine of respect for personality as a means of achieving social harmony. This instrumentality was implicit in the statements of Shiozawa. Nagai Tōru made the point explicit. He argued that the organization of industry was based on a triangular relationship between labour, management and capital each of which was essential for the successful production of society's goods. If each of these groups together, he said, 'push vigorously toward the development of social industry [*shakai sangyō*] with an awareness of their duties and a respect for the personality of each other then true harmony will easily develop'.[98] Harmony, 'true harmony', was the objective; respect for personality the means to achieve it. Within this kind of formulation, personality was stripped of the significance that gave power to the liberal invocation of the term. It was reduced to little more than an amuletic slogan expressing the hope that workers and managers would be respectful to one another. It thus differed little from the earlier didacticism of Tokonami and Shibusawa who had admonished capitalists to uphold their paternalist duty toward their workers.

Moreover, in the above statement Nagai discusses the importance of duties but says nothing of rights, individual or otherwise. Implicit in the notion of personality-ism articulated by Abe was the freedom or right of the individual to act upon or in accord with his internally generated values or truth. The new Kyōchōkai leadership emphasized instead the individual's 'sense of responsibility' as Soeda put it, or his duty to society.[99] Shiozawa dismissed rights as an inappropriate Western legalism not necessarily applicable to the individual. Duty (*honmu*) was the basis of rights. Without duty there are no rights.[100] By emphasizing duty and responsibilities the Kyōchōkai rendered the conceptual power of personality impotent and from the point of view of its critics, undermined the organization's credibility as a proponent of liberal democracy.

Finally, Abe, Yoshino and others who relied on the concept of personality-ism were concerned with eliminating the state's role as the source and definer of value. They sought to break the cycle where the value and spiritual needs of the individual were perpetually subordinated to the needs of the state. But as used by the Kyōchōkai leaders, personality was an instrumental ideology intended to further state goals of social and industrial harmony. Not only were state goals not made subordinate to individual aspirations, those goals were the very reasons for the organization's existence, the rationale of industry and society, and the motivation behind the invocation of the term personality itself. The Kyōchōkai, therefore, by adopting the respect for personality phrase made a significant nod toward the increasingly vociferous demands for democracy. It acknowledged the importance of those demands and the need to address them. It was clear that it was no longer possible casually to dismiss the liberal democratic groundswell taking place in postwar Japan. At the same time, however, the new leadership was unwilling to go beyond the hortatory nostrums of Shibusawa. They hoped that by promoting respect for personality, workers and managers would be awakened to each other's worth and importance in the industrial process, and as a result, a new-found mutual respect would naturally ensue. Social and industrial peace would be the inevitable result of this happy situation.

The Question of Class

The final theme that the new leadership sought to clarify was the question of class and class conflict. The rhetoric of the Kyōchōkai founders stressed the importance of keeping abreast of world trends. Unfortunately, the precise nature of any trends, world, national or otherwise is seldom clear. By their very nature trends are very much in the eye of the beholder. This was no less true in the post-World War I years. For many in Japan, the victory of the allied powers and the compelling idealistic vision of Wilson signalled that liberal democracy was an inexorable world trend. But a sizeable portion of Japanese saw a different world trend. For this group the Bolshevik Revolution and the German social revolution signalled that the world was moving toward socialism. Class consciousness and a breakdown of the capitalist order were inevitable outcomes of the new postwar world. The leading social policy thinker Kuwata Kumazō argued, however, that world labour trends were 'greatly misunderstood' in Japan.[101] The belief that revolution was a world trend reflected, he said, a fundamental misapprehension of the Russian and German revolutions and the nature of socialism in those countries. Socialist development in those founts of revolution was a result of economic and social conditions unique to them. An important factor that set those countries apart was the breakdown of economic production as a result of the war and a variety of other causes.[102] As a result, Kuwata concluded, the Russian and German revolutions 'were a product of unique national conditions' and were not indicative of world revolutionary or socialist trends.[103] Given the predisposition to see social harmony and cooperation as characteristics embedded within Japanese tradition, it is hardly surprising that the Kyōchōkai regarded socialism and the idea of class conflict with hostility.

In their approach to class conflict and the question of class, the new leaders took largely the same approach as that taken by Tokonami and Shibusawa. They regarded the ideology of class conflict as 'illogical' and 'contradictory'.[104] It was a doctrine that advocated conflict for its own sake when struggle should be 'the final step taken only out of sheer necessity'. But even then it should be a course pursued only in matters of justifiable defence.[105] In practice the notion of class conflict devolved into little more than name calling. Workers see themselves as just and virtuous and must everywhere smite the wicked, scheming capitalist; while to capitalists, workers are ignorant troublemakers who deserve no respect. It was therefore an empty ideology based on an attitude of 'wiping out wickedness and restoring virtue' (*haja genshō*).[106] Moreover, those who accept class conflict fail to take into account the essential cooperative nature of economic production. Workers and managers were like husband and wife or 'like the wheels of a cart or the wings of a bird, if either . . . is missing growth in production is not possible'.[107] Workers and managers thus must meet their 'common objective' of productive output through cooperation and attention to their respective responsibilities.

While the new leadership denied the validity of class conflict as a workable social doctrine, like the Kyōchōkai founders they supported the notion that capitalists and workers had differing interests. Because these groups had different interests conflict between them and between other groups in society was inevitable. Although the Kyōchōkai sought to build an industrial system and social structure characterized by cooperation and harmony, that did not mean, Soeda said, that their position required 'a complete absence of controversy in human society. We must recognize that dispute is a fact not only of contemporary life but is also unlikely to be eliminated from any future society'. Indeed, he continued, 'controversy between people is one of the means by which human society steadily advances'.[108] Therefore, to 'attempt to eradicate conflict from within the existing social order' is completely contrary to the thinking and intentions of the Kyōchōkai.[109] While it repudiated the validity of class conflict, it accepted the ideas that differing classes did indeed exist and that the interests of those classes were often at odds with one another. Cooperation thus would only be achieved by a frank avowal of those differences and by establishing institutions and programmes undertaken to try to seek accommodation and compromise between the welter of competing interests that characterized modern society.

The Kyōchōkai was created to provide an institutional mechanism to facilitate the re-establishment of moral community in Japan's economy and society. This aspiration was shared by both of its principal founders. Although Tokonami and Shibusawa differed sharply in their specific proposals, each supported a programme of conservative reform designed to shape a harmonious, integrated society that conformed to their organicist ideals. Moreover, each recognized that a judicious blending of time-honoured moral values and reforms corresponding to the 'trends of the times' was best suited to the achievement of their goal.

Despite their use of the vocabulary of equality, Tokonami and Shibusawa shared a bias toward a hierarchical, top-to-bottom vision of social organization. In turn their respective strategies for solutions to the labour problem flowed from this bias. Tokonami's position was very much like the social monarchism of the Meiji oligarchs. Social reform and the gradual accommodation of popular demands was to derive from an independent state that stood above particularist interests. Similarly, Shibusawa regarded change as flowing downward from a morally conscious elite. His emphasis on the 'kingly way' reveals his vision of society as a pyramid in which a concern for the welfare of the people and specific reforms for its achievement radiated down from the apex. Therefore, workers alone were not the object of their concern. It was also essential that managers and capitalists as well be made aware of their duties. As we have seen, neither Tokonami nor Shibusawa laid the blame for industrial problems solely on workers. Managers had failed to create a satisfactory environment for workers and displayed an inadequate regard for safeguarding either workers' interests or safety. Each level of society, managers no less than workers, had its proper duties which had to be fulfilled. By pointing to the good example of the German Krupp industry or to Kanebō, Shibusawa made clear the importance of sound management principles and managerial concern for workers. This emphasis on managerial principles and on the creation of a managerial mystique is one which characterized Kyōchōkai attitudes and activities. To foster managerial expertise and to sensitize management to its responsibilities became a major Kyōchōkai theme.

The Krupp and Kanebō examples offered by Shibusawa also point to the early Kyōchōkai approach to labour unionism. Shibusawa gave his approval to horizontal unionism and Tokonami too came to support expanded organizational rights of labour after 1920. Yet this support was highly conditional and was offered for its instrumental value in moderating labour and fostering 'responsible unionism'. The goal was to bring about reforms and to create an ethical environment in which there would be no further need for unions. To restore the organic unity of the state and to preserve the essence of Japan's *kokutai* were shared objectives of Tokonami and Shibusawa; permanent, separate labour unions as well as managerial scorn of workers were inimical to those objectives. World trends and the conscientious response to them was an important means of accommodating the altered structure of industrial Japan. Yet the response to world trends could not be allowed to overwhelm their primary goal nor force Japan to lose sight of its heritage and ethical foundations.

The 1920 strike at Fujibō represented a sharp challenge to the Kyōchōkai. The reorganization of that year was intended to bring credibility to Kyōchōkai claims of impartiality and fairness. Despite the dramatic changes, however, the basic values and policies of the organization remained largely unchanged. As before, the leadership rejected the notion of paternalism but failed to offer convincing evidence that this was any more than a tactical ploy to achieve a paternalist system under some other name. The new leaders endorsed sound unionism but gave little indication that they had gone beyond Shibusawa's formulation of unions as mutual aid societies. Also, they sought to give clearer and more unequivocal support to democratic ideals. But this effort was couched in terms of respect for personality or respect for the dignity and worth of each individual. Thus Kyōchōkai support for democratic principles was limited to a vague ethical doctrine while the organization was seemingly unwilling to endorse the institutional and legal apparatus of democratic constitutionalism.

The Kyōchōkai after 1920, therefore, was little different from what it had been before. It remained committed to a programme of conservative reform. The language of the new leadership was considerably more 'progressive' but their basic attitudes were unchanged. The emphasis on communality remained central as did the organicist conservatism that had shaped the views of both Shibusawa and Tokonami. To understand the impact of these ideals it is now necessary to consider the actual policies and programmes pursued by the Kyōchōkai.

4   To create society anew

The Kyōchōkai was the first agency established under the auspices of the Japanese government that had labour and social problems as its principal, or more accurately, its sole concern. In this capacity the Kyōchōkai and its individual leaders and members expended a great deal of effort attempting to define the problems, discussing their origins and character, and positing broad theoretical approaches to solutions to them. These were crucial tasks for the recently industrialized Japan. The formulation and advocacy of the doctrine of harmonism, a central component of this Kyōchōkai effort, for example, had a profound impact on the government response to social and labour problems over the whole interwar period.

The institutional role of the Kyōchōkai was not limited, however, to abstract debates over doctrine. Rather, it played an active part in the effort to realize its organicist vision of modern Japanese society and institute its conservative reform policy. In doing so it took two basic approaches. First, it emphasized thought guidance. The Kyōchōkai hoped to build popular acceptance of national goals by inculcating the proper Confucian ethical values and social norms. It regarded as essential that workers 'awaken' to their duty to the state and society, that is, that they come to understand that their task was to work, not in the name of individual class interests but in the interests of the state. Second, it pursued those institutional and legal reforms it regarded as minimally necessary to overcome opposition to the goal of achieving industrial harmony. Such reforms were pursued in the name of moral objectives: the re-establishment of moral community and a renewed acceptance of social communality. Studies of the state's approach to social problems during the 1920s commonly emphasize the use of government power to suppress opposition. This chapter seeks to show, however, that the use of power was complemented by a range of positive programmes aimed at inducing social unity.

SOCIAL WORK: LABOUR EXCHANGES AND SETTLEMENT HOUSES

A key concept in the formation of the Kyōchōkai was social policy (*shakai seisaku*). Social policy thinking dominated government policy making from about the 1890s up to World War I. It sought governmental intercession on behalf of workers and others in order to mitigate the social amorality of *laissez-faire* capitalism. Social policy was not, however, simply a programme of welfare distribution or support for those disenfranchized by industrial and social change. Rather, it constituted a comprehensive system of organizing social relationships and defining the role of various elements of society in the industrial world. Social policy thinkers urged government intercession as a means of bringing about social justice and equality, goals they believed were conspicuously absent in Anglo-American doctrines of capitalism. It was this understanding of social policy that prompted Soeda Keiichirō to call 'the complete realization of social policy' the 'slogan' of the Kyōchōkai. This achievement he claimed, would bring about social solidarity and provide economic well-being for all.[1] The major journal published by the Kyōchōkai was entitled *The Social Policy Review* (*Shakai seisaku jihō*) in keeping with the thinking suggested by Soeda. Yet, by the 1920s, social policy did not generally refer to this type of broad theoretical understanding. Social policy instead was reduced to the distributive function inherent in the theories of Kanai, Kuwata and others. Social policy had come to be understood by government and bureaucratic leaders as initiatives undertaken by the state to ameliorate specific problems of primarily the lower classes. But it was not, as it had earlier been, a policy position intent on fundamentally altering the balance of the capitalist system. Therefore the Kyōchōkai's social policy activities can be understood as relief or welfare activities and as such they represented a relatively small but important portion of the organization's substantive work.

One social policy programme undertaken by the Kyōchōkai was the creation of a national labour exchange. Employment bureaux had existed in Japan for some time, but the Kyōchōkai's Central Labour Exchange (Chūō shokugyō shōkaisho) was the first non-profit, public employment bureau intended to embrace the labour pool of the entire country. Employment bureaux had their beginnings in the Tokugawa period. The pre-Restoration agencies were private, profit-making ventures. These early agencies worked at finding places for domestic servants, waitresses and prostitutes. During the first twenty-five years of the Meiji period this remained the pattern. The private agencies were the source of numerous abuses and beginning in 1872 local governments took repeated steps to control their activities. The laws had little effect. The city of Tokyo, for instance, was forced to revise and strengthen controlling legislation repeatedly over the Meiji period.[2] Theft of deposits and fees was common as was blatant deception of young female applicants. As late as the Taishō period reports of young women seeking domestic employment who had been virtually sold into prostitution scandalized the country.[3]

Beginning in 1892 new services for the unemployed began to emerge. In that year the first free employment placement service was initiated by the newly created YMCA in Tokyo's Kanda district. This service established the prototype for numerous other employment services created in the following decades. First, it was created by a religiously sponsored social service organization. The YMCA, the Salvation Army and Christian settlement houses all sought to find employment for those workers who needed it. The free employment system in Japan, therefore, had its roots in the welfare programmes of Christian social activism. Second, the new employment bureaux no longer catered exclusively to hiring out female domestics and entertainers. Rather, their services were in the main rendered to the newly emerging urban working class. Day labourers, rickshaw pullers and other unskilled male workers constituted the bulk of those served by the new exchange. Finally, the services of the bureaux were rendered free of charge. Instead of being a front for extorting money from helpless young girls, these new organizations functioned as welfare agencies providing services without charge. As early as 1901 various local governments too began to establish free public labour exchanges.[4] During the first decade of the twentieth century most of Japan's major cities established employment bureaux to deal with unemployment problems in their own cities.

With the World War I economic boom the growth of local labour exchanges all but ceased. Unskilled as well as skilled labour could and did move into the workforce in great numbers. Finding employment for workers thus became a low priority. This situation quickly reversed itself during the postwar recession. Sharply reduced demand drove a number of firms out of business and forced most others into a period of sharp retrenchment. Moreover, the dilemmas involved in forcing wages down induced companies toward Japan's first major wave of 'rationalization' and the substitution of capital for labour expenditures.[5] The unemployment issue was yet another manifestation of the general 'social problem' and as such posed, in the eyes of government leaders, a threat to the Japanese state and society.

Abe Isoo argued that a complete solution (*konponteki kaiketsu*) to the unemployment problem, a solution 'in which unemployment is completely eliminated, requires nothing less that a fundamental alteration of the capitalist system'. That is, the establishment of a socialist system alone would eradicate unemployment because 'the phenomenon of unemployment is a disease peculiar to a capitalist society'.[6] As a practical matter, however, labour unions and supporters sought the immediate creation of programmes to cope with the severe problems brought on by the postwar recession. Typical of union efforts was a list of policy recommendations made by the Alliance of Labour Unions (Rōdō kumiai dōmeikai) in July 1920. The Alliance, an umbrella organization of mainline and anarchist unions, sought long-range changes such as the establishment of a system of labour insurance and factory law revision. But it also hoped to have a number of measures put in place that would deal with the immediate issue of unemployment. The most important was the recommendation that a national system of labour exchanges be created and that a more comprehensive system of controls on activities of private labour exchanges be put in place.[7] However much the leaders of the respective unions within the Alliance may have agreed with Abe's evaluation of the situation, they recognized that immediate ameliorative steps had to be taken to protect workers. An important step in that direction was the creation of labour exchanges.

Government leaders and members of the Kyōchōkai were quite naturally unimpressed with Abe's prescription. But they recognized that the problem was real and one to which a solution had to be found. Some hoped wistfully that if simply enough employed workers could be induced to return to the countryside from which they had come, the problem would in large measure be solved. Kawamura Takeji, the Home Ministry Police chief, for instance, argued that since many of the present unemployed had come to the city earlier to improve their lives during the wartime boom it could be a good thing if in the current circumstances they returned to their villages. By doing so they would not only relieve the burden of urban unemployment they would provide the needed manpower for work on important state tasks (*kokka jigyō*) such as maintenance and repair of dikes and canals, road repair and the surveying of agricultural croplands.[8] There were a variety of roadblocks to urban–rural migration as a policy agenda, not least of which was local opposition to returnees.[9] Nevertheless, simply hoping for urban out-migration did not seem to be an adequate response to what was perceived as a serious and immediate concern. Like union leaders many government officials saw employment exchanges as a key strategy for coping with the growing numbers of unemployed.

As in so many other areas, interest in exchanges at the state policy level was signalled in a report of the Relief Activities Research Committee. In a position paper submitted to Home Minister Tokonami in March 1919, the committee recommended that the government 'encourage the creation and/or expansion of labour exchanges administered by public agencies or organizations operating in the public interest (*kōeki dantai*), and, take steps to support cooperative ties (*sōgo renraku*) between the exchanges' in various urban areas.[10] Like the proposals of the first ILO conference made later in the year, the authors of the committee report saw exchanges as part of a broad policy initiative toward unemployment protection. More important, the committee report perceived labour exchanges for the first time as part of a national as opposed to a local agenda. The operation of the labour market had become a matter of direct concern to national policy makers, and by extension state intrusion into that market was valid.

During 1920 the number of free, public interest labour exchanges in Japan grew dramatically, At the end of 1919 there were forty-eight exchanges of this type. By June 1920 there were fifty-two; by early September, ninety; and by the end of the year there were 145 separate exchanges.[11] The problem with the labour exchanges before 1920 was that there existed no mechanism for dealing with unemployment on a nation-wide basis. Indeed, since most had been set up by urban governments they were incapable of even acting as regional agencies. Recognizing the inherent weaknesses of such an approach eight prefectures proposed in early 1920 that they establish an exchange system that would link individual exchanges in their respective prefectures.[12] Nevertheless, the first exchange system that sought to service a national as opposed to a local or regional constituency was the system established by the Kyōchōkai.[13] At the behest of the Home Ministry, the Kyōchōkai set up the Central Labour Exchange (Chūō shokugyō shōkaisho) on 1 June 1920.[14] The new national exchange was the first concrete manifestation of government interest in the work of labour exchanges and the first institutional response to the recommendation made by the Relief Activities Research Committee.

The organization's exchange was set up at its Yurakuchō headquarters under the authority of Kuwata Kumazō. Although its objective was to build a nation-wide network of exchanges, the Kyōchōkai did not build such a system from the ground up. Rather, it sought to act as a clearing-house for statistics and information submitted by locally established exchanges. It was to act as a 'centralized body' for building 'cooperative ties' between hitherto separate local exchanges. The activities of the exchanges were to include publishing regular reports synthesizing data submitted by participating local exchanges, conducting research on labour exchange activities and potential programmes, leading lecture and educational programmes on establishing new exchanges, doing general research on specific problems of unemployment and labour dynamics, and creating an advisory office for various public interest exchanges in the Tokyo area.[15] Following the passage of the Labour Exchange Law in July 1921, the Central Labour Exchange was renamed the Central Labour Exchange Bureau (Chūō shokugyō shōkai kyoku) and was designated the official, authorized central exchange by the Home Ministry. In March 1923 the Kyōchōkai's labour exchange was taken over by the Home Ministry's newly created Social Bureau (Shakai kyoku).

While it can scarcely be said that the Kyōchōkai followed an activist policy in the area of labour exchanges, the Central Labour Exchange constituted an important component of the Kyōchōkai mission. It acted as yet another medium for research on social issues; through its work as a clearing-house, the Central Labour Exchange was able to gather some of the most complete statistical data on the problem of unemployment and steps being taken to alleviate it. Exchanges also represented institutions through which the Kyōchōkai would be seen as acting in the interest of workers. That is, by providing a centralized agency that could more effectively and efficiently find suitable employment for those without jobs, the Kyōchōkai hoped that its labour exchange would play a critical role in helping solve a pressing problem of the working class. The Kyōchōkai adviser and Osaka exchange official Yatsuhama Tokusaburō stressed that the primary purpose of the exchanges was to alleviate the personal suffering that was a natural consequence of unemployment while at the same time satisfying industry's need for labour. A welcome by-product of this work was that exchanges help promote social harmony while contributing to the nation's prosperity. Thus, Yatsuhama argued, exchanges were not so much welfare organs as they were 'industrial institutions'.[16]

Also by establishing a central labour exchange at the behest of the Home Ministry, the Kyōchōkai was taking the first tentative steps toward active state involvement in the general economic arena, an involvement that in later years would be a defining characteristic of the Japanese economy. The state had been an active participant in the economy earlier, but its role had been confined to certain well defined areas – the national railways, naval shipyards, arsenals and the like. It had acted to shape the economic process through its control of these key sectors as well as through legislation and macro-economic policy. But in the postwar era government leaders, particularly in Tokonami's Home Ministry, perceived the social problem as a major systemic crisis and sought to respond to that crisis by intruding the state into the working of the economy. In the years following the Russo-Japanese War, Tokonami played an important part in thrusting the state into the fabric of rural life. Following World War I he took the lead in pursuing a very similar policy for the urban industrial areas. The Kyōchōkai was a central player in this programme and the creation of a national labour exchange, one of the first substantive policies aimed at its fulfilment.

The Kyōchōkai was active in a variety of other social policy programmes as well. One of the most notable was its work in the settlement house movement. As in the case of labour exchanges, settlement houses were not a product of the post-World War I period. Japan's first real settlement house was established in March 1897 by the Congregational Mission in Japan.[17] Named Kingsley Hall after the well-known Christian socialist Charles Kingsley, Japan's first settlement house was modelled on the Southend Settlement House in Boston and the famous English settlement houses Toynbee Hall and Oxford House. According to Kingsley Hall's charter, its purpose was to improve the welfare of the people and educate them about the true nature of social conditions. Katayama Sen, the Hall's first director said that he hoped the house would 'become a connecting link between higher and lower classes' while at the same time providing residents with educational opportunities they could not otherwise obtain.[18] The new organization hoped to reach out to as broad a constituency as possible by minimizing the religious character of the Hall. Article 3 of its charter said that while Kingsley Hall believed in and was committed to the principles and ideals of Christianity, it would 'adopt methods appropriate for the circumstances and in accordance with the conditions' in which it found itself in order to realize its higher goals.[19]

Like the YMCA and the Salvation Army, the Settlement House Movement had its roots in the working class and poor sections of the major cities of England and the United States. By 1900 there were over one hundred settlement houses in the United States. The goal of the houses was to provide an orderly, wholesome environment for recent arrivals to the city from the countryside and earlier arrivals who were experiencing problems in the city. Most American settlement houses had resident volunteers who sought to recreate a model middle-class household and instil middle-class values. Settlement house leaders were alarmed by what they saw as the moral degeneracy rampant in the burgeoning cities. Stripped of traditional communal restraints, new urbanites drifted away from piety and positive social values. The leaders of the houses hoped to establish the social ties and instil the moral righteousness that characterized, they believed, traditional values. Settlement houses, therefore, were to act as sanctuaries from urban depravity and secular havens for instilling moral values of sufficient strength to withstand the temptations of the city.[20] Japanese settlement houses were not so uniform in the values they promoted. Nevertheless, they shared with their American counterparts the notion that the new urban industrial world had in some very important ways altered the character and composition of society and that the settlement houses were useful institutional mechanisms for shaping and cultivating the new urban citizen.

Between 1917 and 1926 forty-three new settlement houses were built in Japan by various groups. Twenty-three of these were established by religious groups (thirteen Buddhist and ten Christian) and of the remaining twenty houses, local governments set up ten, semi-governmental groups eight, and the remaining two were university established.[21] Typical of the semi-governmental settlement houses was the Zenrinkan opened by the Kyōchōkai in mid-1921. Kyōchōkai leaders acknowledged that the Zenrinkan was not Japan's first settlement house, but they claimed it was the most well organized and most effective.[22] Established in Tokyo's Fukagawa ward, the Zenrinkan provided, Kyōchōkai leaders believed, a stable and salutary environment for the labouring poor and unemployed. Beside a healthy living environment, space was allocated for recreational facilities, workshops and meeting rooms. As in Katayama's Kingsley Hall, the Zenrinkan also sponsored a kindergarten, adult night school classes and general education programmes for house residents and others.[23] The Zenrinkan, therefore, like the first Christian settlement house and those that followed, had an important social mission as well as a welfare function. It provided not only a clean wholesome environment for those who needed shelter but served as an educational institution for residents and non-residents alike. Social education was the principal task of the Zenrinkan and other settlement houses. What distinguished the various houses was not their function but their differing visions of the ideal nature of the new urban man.

The Zenrinkan typified what one scholar has called the social solidarity and labour–management harmony type (*shakai rentaiteki rōshi kyōchō*) of settlement house.[24] The person in charge of the house and of promoting the values of social solidarity and industrial harmony was one Tatsuno Sadaichi. Tatsuno had taught at middle schools in Kyoto, Hiroshima and Kagoshima before taking charge of the Zenrinkan in 1921. He had been greatly influenced by Ninomiya Sontoku and the Hōtokusha and, as a result, saw the task of education as a central means of performing social service. He modelled the actual activities and operation of the house on Jane Addams' famous Hull House in Chicago.[25] However, the education programme that was a key element of the house's operation rested not on Christian piety but on Confucian social ethics and moral values. Like the Kyōchōkai as a whole, Tatsuno sought to solidify and expand the ideal of moral community and social organicism. Tatsuno hoped that by centring on these ideals, the educational programmes offered by the house would contribute to stabilizing society and breaking the cycle of poverty and despair that characterized Tokyo's urban ghettos.

Tatsuno returned to Kagoshima in 1923. The Kyōchōkai continued to operate the Zenrinkan for another four years, at which time it was turned over to a private social work group. Despite its brief link to the Kyōchōkai, the Zenrinkan was representative of the organization's interest in social education through relief work. Other groups operating settlement houses took a similar approach but with differing ideological objectives. Instead of social solidarity and labour–management harmony, other settlement houses attempted to inculcate democratic values while still others promoted proletarian liberation. The differing ideological bases of the Japanese settlement house movement were part of the broader competition for allegiance of the new urban proletariat in the postwar period. The most consistent and durable arena in which this competition was waged was in the area that the Kyōchōkai broadly referred to as education – an area identified in the organization's founding documents as central to its mission of promoting social and industrial harmony.

THE PUSH FOR SOCIAL EDUCATION

No metaphor was more ubiquitous in the years following World War I than the idea of awakening or becoming conscious (*mezame*, *jikaku* or *kakusei*). Women's groups sought to 'awaken' women to their second-class status through lectures, study groups and publications. The National Levelers Society (Zenkoku suiheisha) hoped to open society's eyes to the oppression of Japan's special communities (*tokushu burakumin*) so that steps could be taken to end discrimination. Opening the eyes of the nation's workers was of especially great importance. Labour leaders hoped to raise the consciousness of the working class by building a greater awareness of their shared fate. In 1914 Ōsugi Sakae, for example, argued that it was crucial that workers be mentally, spiritually and psychologically prepared for revolution and ready to take their place in the new society. To achieve this state of proletarian readiness, Ōsugi believed that 'workers' spiritual education is the essential thing'[26]. The more moderate Yūaikai, later reorganized as the Nihon rōdō sōdōmei (Japan General Association of Labour) too emphasized the need for educating workers. The Yūaikai promoted popular lectures on issues relevant to workers and beginning in 1916 sponsored lecture tours for its branches throughout the country. It also published a newspaper and magazine devoted to labour issues.[27] The Sōdōmei went to even greater lengths to cultivate a politically educated labour class. It set up a variety of labour schools (*rōdō gakkō*) to promote democratic values and develop workplace skills. The curriculum of the schools included classes in trade union principles, economics, law and history as well as programmes of vocational education. While Sōdōmei education programmes did not concentrate on building labour class consciousness,[28] they did attempt to address one of the principal demands of postwar workers: the demand for recognition of their status as important and equal members of society. This goal would be achieved with an expansion of knowledge and the inculcation of a social ethic built on individual moral virtue. There was, therefore, a generalized concern among private, special interest groups that an 'awakening' of the masses was critical for the success of their goals, whether those goals were the implementation of true democracy or the launching of revolution. Government and bureaucratic elites were no less convinced of the need for people to have their eyes opened. In the Meiji period social policy thinkers emphasized the need to shape the consciousness of society as a key means of preventing the outbreak of social problems. 'Thought guidance' (*shisō zendō*) became the central element in building an ideology that would lead to social cooperation and stability rather than social conflict.[29] Social unity, according to this line of reasoning, could be built most effectively through positive programmes of education.

The belief in the utility of positive social education led to the creation of a variety of programmes such as the Local Improvement Movement, the Patriotic Women's Association and the national coordination of youth groups and reservists. With World War I and the recognition of the emergence of the social problem, the urgency of establishing broad educational programmes was seen more clearly than ever. To pursue this goal was, in large measure, the rationale behind the creation of the Kyōchōkai. As shown earlier, Kyōchōkai founding documents pointed to education and research as one of the main tasks of the organization. Nagai Tōru wrote in 1921 that among the various activities of the Kyōchōkai none had greater importance than 'publicizing and propagating' the values of harmonism and more generally 'guiding social thought' through schools, lectures and publications.[30] The 'education and enlightenment [*kyōiku kyōka*] of workers', he said, 'is the primary issue' the Kyōchōkai must address.[31] He doubted that the Kyōchōkai could act as an effective agent in strike mediation or that it could establish an adequate system of labour exchanges. Not being a government body, it lacked the legal authority and institutional strength to perform those functions. Moreover, it did not possess the ties to local areas that would permit it to act as an agent of social welfare. Given those limitations the Kyōchōkai's greatest efforts should be devoted to education. Education, enlightenment and thought guidance were legitimate and realistic activities, he believed, activities the Kyōchōkai could effectively perform.[32] To Nagai and the other new leaders of the Kyōchōkai, the organization's objective, therefore, was not to be a mediator of strikes; it was to prevent strikes by building understanding between labour and capital by guiding and shaping the consciousness and values of both.

In its advocacy of 'thought guidance' and 'education and enlightenment', the Kyōchōkai constituted a logical extension of the values and methods of Meiji period social reform thinkers. In the context of the 1920s, however, it had become only one agent competing to win the allegiance of the new industrial class. Like Shibusawa in the 1880s, it hoped to shape the values not only of workers but management as well. For the labour and social problems, as Nagai pointed out, were ultimately part of an 'industrial problem' (*sangyō mondai*).[33] Solutions to this larger problem required not only moral exhortation but also an expansion of productive output. Workers had to come to understand that a growth in output meant that they had to work more efficiently. Hard work and skill enhancement would benefit the individual worker and society as a whole. Thus solutions to the 'industrial problem ultimately depend upon the awakening of workers' to the significance and importance of expanding productivity.[34] Productivity expansion could not, however, be achieved by workers alone. Rather, it was the responsibility of management to create the industrial infrastructure and environment in which labour skills and dedication could be maximized. Thus it was necessary to awaken managers to their duties and to the techniques that could most effectively mobilize and utilize the workforce.[35] Maximization of labour output could not be won with oppression. Only a positive programme of incentives and education coupled with sound managerial practices could achieve this end. Oppression of workers leads not only to labour unrest but also to a long-term weakening of the very fabric of industry and society. The labour problem is significant, Nagai concluded, not simply because of the tragedy of social unrest but precisely 'because a stable and satisfied labour force is an essential component of a healthy economy' and a keystone in the foundation of state and society.[36]

Kyōchōkai leaders saw their educational function as a form of didactic conciliation. Workers and managers alike required training and instruction. Each side in the prevailing social struggle had to be awakened to their responsibilities and duties. The restoration of moral community was the essential objective of all Kyōchōkai educational activities. Social education in this broadly defined sense would then be crucial in solving the central crisis of postwar Japan; it would solve the labour and ultimately the social problem, it would lead to domestic economic expansion and prosperity through rising productivity, which would in the long run lead to Japan's success in the economic war with the West. If indeed awakening people could accomplish all its advocates claimed, it is hardly surprising that social education was given such high priority by the Kyōchōkai and the nation's bureaucratic leadership.

In 1928 the British observer A. Morgan Young wrote that the Kyōchōkai squandered the 'manifest opportunities' presented to it to deal with social discontent. 'It might have made militant trade unionism both unnecessary and impossible', he argued, but instead it simply 'frittered away time and money on the publication of a magazine, which nobody read, and the collection of futile statistics.'[37] Young misunderstood profoundly the mandate and function of the Kyōchōkai. For the things about which he complained were the very tasks the organization deemed central to its purpose. The gathering of statistics, detailed studies of domestic and international social conditions and the propagation of that data were seen to be key elements in the overall Kyōchōkai educational mission. If policy makers, managers and workers were well informed about the exact nature of social and economic conditions and if they were aware of sound and effective methods for coping with problems both at home and abroad then correct policies could be implemented and a healthy social order built.

The principal publishing vehicle for Kyōchōkai research was a monthly magazine entitled *Shakai seisaku jihō* (*Social Policy Review*), subtitled in English *The Social Reform*. The first number of this journal was published in September 1920 and continued monthly until 1946. By 1923 5,000 copies of each number were being produced.[38] The journal aimed at intellectuals and scholars interested in social issues. Each month articles on some aspect of labour or social conditions, labour law, social policy or international labour appeared. A typical issue included five or six articles on topics such as these. It also included a section on Kyōchōkai activities, and irregularly, Kyōchōkai or government policy positions, draft legislation or recently enacted social/labour legislation. The breadth of problems discussed and the generally high quality of the research made the *Review* one of the most respected journals of its time and it remains today one of the best available resources for studying interwar Japan's labour and social conditions.

The Kyōchōkai also published book length manuscripts on labour and social issues. Between 1920 and 1945 it published hundreds of books and pamphlets from enormous compendia and sourcebooks such as *Saikin no shakai undō* (*Social Movements in Recent Years*) (1929), or *Kakkoku rōdō chingin tōkei* (*Statistics on Wages in Various Countries*) (1926) to narrow monographic studies such as

Bōseki jokō no eisei jōtai (*The Health Conditions of Female Textile Workers*) (1921) or *Totei seido to gijutsu kyōiku* (*The Apprentice System and Technical Education*) (1936).[39] These works as well as numerous translations of Western scholars' works form an important bedrock of data for understanding interwar Japan and the social issues it confronted. But, for Kyōchōkai members and its bureaucratic supporters research like that in the *Shakai seisaku jihō* and numerous Kyōchōkai published books had a more immediate and important purpose. As we have seen, more than a generation of Japanese leaders saw that there was a real need for research and study of the social problem. Men as different as Kanai En and Yamagata Aritomo had emphasized the need for research as a crucial first step in solving social problems. The Kyōchōkai leadership took this as its task with the belief that with a clear understanding of the issues and a thorough grasp of the details solutions would be found.

Not all Kyōchōkai publications and publicity programmes were so high minded. Scholars, intellectuals and policy makers required hard data and substantive research. Not so the less well schooled. If *Shakai seisaku jihō* took the high road of social research, a second magazine, *Hito to hito* (*People Together*), was more directly concerned with guiding social thought. The Kyōchōkai's goal of shaping popular consciousness and leading workers toward healthy ideas was most visible in this publication. *Hito to hito*, which began publication in April 1921, was conceived as a popular journal, a 'workers' magazine'. Written in simple and direct language *Hito to hito* was intended to expand the knowledge and enrich the spirit of workers through the presentation of 'healthy reading materials' (*kenzennaru yomimono*).[40] Each issue contained brief articles on work-related subjects such as industrial hygiene and safety, legal issues or information on recent technical advances. In the hope of 'cultivating refined taste' (*kōshōnaru shumi o kanyō*) *Hito to hito* also regularly published serialized novels, short stories and poetry. These offerings tended to be less refined than didactic; counselling hard work, frugality, honesty and fidelity. A regular feature was a section called the 'Labour News' ('Rōdō shimbun') in which a variety of activities pertinent to workers appeared. Often included in this section was news of the establishment of a works council, the successful mediation of a strike, or the implementation of a plant-based health insurance plan. There was also an irregular feature entitled the 'Female Workers News' ('Jokō shimbun') that included similar material directly pertinent to women.

As its title suggested, *Hito to hito* hoped to build the values and ideals from which cooperation between people could emerge. Tazawa Yoshiharu wrote that 'the solution to the social problem comes down ultimately to the issues of "people"'. For that reason, he said, 'the Kyōchōkai invariably emphasizes "people" problems while working toward the realization of social policy'.[41] In *Hito to hito* this emphasis on 'people' meant demonstrating to workers that their interests were linked inexorably with capitalists, with their firms, with the economy as a whole, and with the totality of society. Japanese society and the national economy were made up of and could only function if 'people together' worked and lived with the full understanding of their linkage to one another. The organicist conservatism of a generation of social reformers, therefore, was given voice in *Hito to hito*.

The Kyōchōkai also used one of the newest technological developments to promote the values of cooperation and moral community: moving pictures (*katsudō shashin*). In early 1921 the Kyōchōkai solicited synopses and scripts that would elucidate 'sound and healthy ethical precepts' (*kenjitsu onkennaru kyōkun*) in themes on factory life.[42] Later solicitations were made for stories specifically on female workers and agricultural problems. In three separate solicitations eleven synopses were selected out of 248 submissions. At least two of the eleven were actually made into moving pictures.[43] A review of one of these should make clear what constituted 'sound and healthy ethical precepts'. This epic entitled *The Human Heart* (*Hito no kokoro*) told the story of a strike at an unnamed electric power generating station. As luck would have it a child of one of the strikers was ill, she required an operation or she would die. Just as the operation began the electricity went off, a tragic consequence of the growing confrontation at the power station. Despite heroic efforts to save her, the child died. The striking father was overcome with remorse when he realized the consequences of his intemperate action. The damaging results of a lack of cooperation were only too clear.[44] *The Human Heart* and a second film, *A Young Girl's Determination* (*Shōjo no kesshin*), were shown in public auditoriums, movie houses and numerous factories, as well as being screened for employer groups and social welfare organizations. Through popular magazines, films, as well as public lectures by organization members, the Kyōchōkai sought to reach out to the broad society to propagate and instil the values of social cooperation and harmony. How effective maudlin stories were, either in the form of 'healthy reading material' or in 'moving pictures', in inculcating these values is impossible to say. What is clear, however, is the Kyōchōkai's interest in fostering the ideals of the moral community through all available media.

In the task of educating workers and managers to their responsibilities to each other and in bringing about a stable economic relationship between them on which productivity expansion could be built, the broadcast method of inculcation was, as we have seen, important. Yet the Kyōchōkai and government leaders pursued a more directed approach as well. The establishment of schools and organized study programmes was a critical component of the organization's overall educative mission. The Kyōchōkai's work in directed training was part of a broad government effort to regularize and upgrade the factory workforce. Major changes in the scope and character of the emerging industrial economy made suitable training a critical component of economic development. The state therefore encouraged the establishment of appropriate schools set up by local governments, Chambers of Commerce and other public and private groups.[45] The Kyōchōkai, as part of this general effort, set up a variety of schools aimed at both workers and managers.

An important example of schools established by the Kyōchōkai was the Workers' Training Programme (Rōmusha kōshūkai). Tazawa Yoshiharu, a Kyōchōkai managing director, was the director and principal instructor of the Programme. The goal of the Training Programme was to attempt 'to bring about an awareness of the true meaning of social cooperation (*shakai kyōchō*) and to foster a healthy understanding of social problems'.[46] Tazawa's most basic message was encapsulated in the motto of the Programme: 'Before being workers or capitalists we are first people.'[47] The curriculum included discussion of thought problems, economic organization, social policy, and health and safety issues. What distinguished the Workers' Training Programme from other workers' schools, Tazawa claimed, was its spirit of absolute equality. Together students and teachers shared meals and lodgings 'seeking mutual understanding through friendly conversation'.[48]

The Workers' Training Programme offered courses consisting of six-day blocks. The first programme included seventy-two students, all workers from government enterprises: the Tokyo Naval Shipyard, military arsenals and the national railways. The students in this first course were ordered to attend by their employers.[49] According to his biographer, Tazawa recognized that many workers regarded the

Kyōchōkai as an institution intended to pacify the labour movement, and as a result, he believed that it was necessary to order
government workers to attend the programme until such time as
workers in private plants became convinced of its usefulness.[50]
Tazawa himself, however, claimed that workers in private industry
were not averse to attending but their employers were unwilling to
compensate attendees. The Kyōchōkai was in the midst of
negotiating this issue with private companies and until negotiations
were completed the programme would have to content itself with
government workers alone.[51] By the programme's fifth session, held
in October 1921, students from private companies were in
attendance. During this session eighty students from several
Sumitomo plants and from the Mitsubishi Shipyards enrolled in the
Programme. During 1921 and 1922 sixteen separate course blocks
were held, twelve in Tokyo, two in Hiroshima, and one each in
Nagasaki and Kyoto with a total of 1,911 students. Most students
were workers in government plants but with a steadily increasing
number coming from private industry.[52] By 1929, 105 meetings of
the Training Programme had been held in Tokyo and throughout
the country with nearly 11,000 students enrolled.[53]

The Workers' Training Programme typified the Kyōchōkai
approach toward workers and its efforts to guide and shape
industrial ideology. By establishing close personal relations with
workers, Kyōchōkai leaders believed the Training Programme
provided a compelling course of spiritual and political education
(*seishin kyōiku, seiji kyōiku*). By demonstrating the Kyōchōkai's
commitment to equality and human concerns Tazawa was convinced
that the Programme acted as a responsible and ethical agent of
labour–management cooperation and social harmony. Because,
Tazawa remarked, a sound system of education 'must be education
for both intellectual and moral advancement, imparting information
alone is not adequate'. Instead, he said, 'cultivating morality . . . is
of the greatest importance'.[54] Fostering a 'healthy' moral and ethical
sense was the principal objective of Kyōchōkai education efforts. If
workers had a 'sound' and 'healthy' understanding of ethical
behaviour they would inevitably resist confrontation and conflict-
based ideologies and organizations and would seek to establish a
more cooperative relationship with capitalists and society as a
whole. Thus 'healthy' moral and ethical values led inexorably to an
acceptance of the value of organic community and educational
programmes were supposed to lead to the re-establishment of moral
community. The inculcation of those healthy moral values, Tazawa

and other Kyōchōkai leaders believed, could best be accomplished through close relationships and the force of example. Therefore resident programmes like those of the Workers' Training Programme as well as social work activities such as settlement houses represented a key educational strategy. Thus the Kyōchōkai pursued a Confucian approach to education: first, education was regarded primarily as a moral enterprise, and second, the most effective method for producing the morally superior man was through the moral example of superiors conveyed through close personal ties.

The Kyōchōkai also set up and conducted a variety of other educational programmes as well. There was, for example, a short resident programme established specifically for female workers. The Female Workers Training Programme (Fujin rōmusha kōshūkai) offered, like its counterpart for men, a short-term course block on general economic and social issues conducted in an intensive live-in atmosphere.[55] The organization also established a Social Policy Institute (Shakai seisaku gakuin), led programmes in vocational and technical training, and helped fund numerous private worker training programmes.[56] The Kyōchōkai's Osaka branch, established in November 1921, also created a Labour Institute (Rōdō gakuin) aimed at providing area workers with basic social education.[57] The Kyōchōkai's zeal in these educative functions rested on the belief that 'a modern state requires an educated citizenry and advances in efficiency'.[58] Thus, a sustained, broad-based programme of supplementary education (*hoshū kyōiku*) was a key component of any strategy intended to strengthen the state and the national economy. But an educated citizenry was not simply one that was capable and skilled. Rather, it was one wherein people possessed a 'healthy' ethical value system that recognized the mutual and reciprocal duties of each person. For Tazawa and other Kyōchōkai leaders sound education stressed 'moral cultivation' as the bedrock of an educated society. The moral man was the necessary prerequisite for the establishment of the moral community and the development of industrial and social harmony.

Despite the emphasis given to worker education it was clear from the beginning that Kyōchōkai objectives would not be realized concentrating on workers alone. According to Nagai Tōru, the labour problem was in fact an 'industrial problem' that could, in the final analysis, only be solved by changes within industry itself. He quoted with approval the American economist John R. Commons who denied the Marxist notion that capitalism grows as a blind natural force, saying instead that it moves and grows 'by the will of management'.[59] At its inception, Kyōchōkai founder Shibusawa had noted the importance of sound management pointing to the Krupp industries in Germany and Japan's Kanebō as examples of plants that engaged in managerial practices that created a salutary work environment in which workers felt no need to adopt confrontational tactics. By the 1920s the Kyōchōkai also emphasized other managerial skills as well. With the postwar depression and the perception of economic competition between Japan and the West, Kyōchōkai leaders regarded enhanced managerial skills as essential for raising productivity and strengthening Japan's industrial competitiveness.

In 1922 Nagai argued that productive expansion was a central component of any solution to the labour problem. Expansion of output could only be achieved through increased productivity and the removal of impediments to increased output. Capitalists' monopolistic practices, lack of managerial expertise and labour unrest all undermined productive expansion. Such conditions merely increased costs and raised consumer prices. Thus both profits and real wages declined. Therefore, since the goal of workers is to make gains in real wages, to impede production through labour unrest and work stoppages only frustrates the achievement of those goals. The issues considered by labour unions, such as wages, hours of work and working conditions were inseparable from the basic issue of production. That is, 'wage increases and the reduction of work hours are unachievable without corresponding increases in output and reduction in prices'. These conditions, however, 'are impossible to realize without increased efficiency and reduced production expenses'.[60] Thus productivity growth through rising efficiency was at the root of the solution to the labour problem. And rising efficiency began with management.

The Kyōchōkai concern with output growth was part of the broad interest in industrial 'rationalization' that emerged in the post-World War I years. Rationalization was pursued to escape the postwar depression and to regain and ultimately expand international markets. There was another concern as well. 'Even the most radical European socialists,' Soeda Keiichirō claimed, 'acknowledge that the recent Russian and German revolutions were a result of shortages in production'. It is impossible to deny, he said, that declining production or 'even maintenance of current production levels will lead to grave human misery', the wellspring of social unrest. To avert this calamity, 'it is essential that there be ceaseless capital growth and an adequate number of resourceful, skilled managers'.[61] Therefore rationalization sought to solve both short-term economic problems and long-term social problems. The interest in the development of 'resourceful, skilled managers' and the enhancement of industrial efficiency were major elements in the larger drive toward rationalization.

Japanese leaders' concern with managerial expertise and interest in efficiency coincided with the growing interest in 'scientific management' in most of the industrialized world during the 1910s and 1920s. 'Scientific management', or 'Taylorism', after its American originator, Frederick W. Taylor, was promoted as a movement of factory organization to enhance industrial efficiency. 'Scientific management', its adherents claimed, would also eliminate conflict between capital and labour over just returns on their respective inputs because it would provide a scientific determination of what would constitute a fair day's work. These goals would be accomplished through the creation of elaborate apparatuses for measuring work and waste, calculating machine speeds and organizing factory lines and storage areas. Scientific management, despite its name, was not an exact science. Instead it existed as a broad movement, a way of thinking about industrial production. Protégés of Taylor and the movement's various evangelists differed over the precise components of the system. All agreed, however, that the enhancement of production could only be achieved through a rational application of scientific and technical skills to shop-floor organization. The transfer of Taylorism's industrial rationalism to industrialized and industrializing countries around the world began around the turn of the century. Around the time of World War I Taylorism or scientific management had become a world-wide movement in which its various components were shaped to meet local needs.[62]

Taylor's *Principles of Scientific Management* (1911) was introduced into Japan by Ikeda Tōshirō soon after publication.[63] By the end of the war a variety of research institutes had been created to study and further scientific management principles. Ikeda for instance, established and led the Efficiency Study Association (Efuishonshii kenkyūkai) and the Lion Toothpowder Company created a Workshop Efficiency Research Centre (Sagyō nōritsu kenkyūjo). The Osaka Chamber of Commerce also set up a Factory Management Institute (Kōjō kanrihō kōshūkai) and several higher commercial schools instituted programmes in industrial efficiency.[64] Given the Kyōchōkai's interest in management efficiency, it is hardly surprising that it sponsored an efficiency programme of its own.

Ueno Yoichi headed the Kyōchōkai's Industrial Efficiency Institute (Sangyō nōritsu kenkyūjo). Ueno had ambitious goals for the Institute. He hoped it would:

1 sponsor public lectures and other courses on the principles of efficiency;
2 publish reports and research findings on issues related to efficiency;
3 dispatch experts to provide advice and consultations on improving efficiency;
4 devise and administer aptitude and skill tests and formulate appropriate testing procedures;
5 study physiological and psychological relationships to improvements in efficiency, and
6 introduce machinery and apparatus that would be more conducive to increases in efficiency.[65]

The Institute occupied a wing of the Kyōchōkai's new headquarters building in the Shiba ward of Tokyo. Given the contacts and high visibility of the Kyōchōkai, the Institute acted as a mecca for managers and scholars interested in scientific management and efficiency.[66] The Kyōchōkai's Industrial Efficiency Institute also demonstrated the nature of Japan's adaptation of scientific management. With the exception of Lillian Gilbreth, a psychologist, the leaders of the American scientific management movement were all engineers and technical experts. Despite being promoted as a way of thinking, scientific management in the United States emphasized precise knowledge of the production process in an effort to reorganize and systematize every aspect of the process. To reduce each worker's task to precisely defined and distinct activities underlay scientific management and was the rationale for such well known innovations as time-and-motion analysis. In contrast to the American efficiency engineers, the head of the Kyōchōkai's Institute was a psychologist.[67] After a stint in a Nagasaki mission school, Ueno studied psychology at Tokyo University. He was an early translator of John Dewey's educational writings and the editor and publisher of the leading professional psychological journal of the Taishō period, *Psychological Studies* (*Shinri kenkyū*). Ueno came to the attention of Kyōchōkai leaders with a number of public speeches given on the 'psychology of efficiency' (*nōritsu no shinri*). As can be seen from his goals for the Institute, Ueno saw it as primarily an educational and consultative mechanism. Rather than concentrating on the complex paraphernalia of American scientific management, Ueno and the Institute placed greatest importance on group discussion and personnel testing procedures. Rather than furthering new bookkeeping and accounting methods, the calculation of machine speeds, motion studies or any of the array of technical methods for efficiency expansion, the Institute promoted aptitude tests, special skill training and shop-floor problem solving.

It is hardly surprising that the essentially technical character of scientific management would become so quickly distorted in the hands of Ueno and other Japanese promoters of management efficiency. Taylorism was promoted in the United States in the context of an effort to substitute machinery for labour. Labour itself under such a regime would become more skilled, presumably more machine-like. Moreover, strong American trade unions saw in scientific management a mechanism for strictly delimiting job determination and providing a 'neutral' method of calculating wage determination. In Japan, however, an abundant labour force coupled with the absence of a tradition of union intrusion into management's prerogatives of determining job content and internal worker mobility rendered American-style scientific management an unattractive option from the point of view of both management and workers.[68] But by concentrating on the aspect of Taylorism that emphasized that efficiency represented a change in the way of thinking, Ueno and the Kyōchōkai were able to dovetail scientific management with the organization's overall educational effort. By motivating workers to seek cost reductions, by encouraging shop-floor consultation, and by promoting both individual and workforce discipline, the Kyōchōkai hoped to build a managerial system that would lead to a more efficient and productive industrial structure. Of course, such an emphasis was also completely consistent with its organicist, communitarian view of factory and social organization. By helping to build a managerial system of this kind the Kyōchōkai hoped to contribute to forging a solution to both the economic and social problems it regarded as so pressing.

The educational programme devised and pursued by the Kyōchōkai was a central component of its overall effort to strengthen society and the state. Through broadly conceived programmes of hortatory admonition, general education and vocational training the Kyōchōkai sought to build a more skilled labour force and at the same time one attuned to the interests of their companies and to society as a whole. Promoting cooperation based on an understanding of the mutual and shared responsibilities of various groups was a key component of the educational programmes. It was also necessary to recognize, Tazawa argued, that 'labor is itself a timeless virtue'. People do not work simply to satisfy animal desires. 'Labourism' (*kinrōshugi*) is the moral grounding of social interaction and the ultimate point of unity and equality between rich and poor, labourer and capitalist. Each must work for each has duties to fulfil. Each must work 'for the sake of the progress of state and society'.[69] This was the strong and persistent message of all the Kyōchōkai's educational programmes. The recognition of people's harmony of interests and goals was essential if the social and industrial peace upon which Japan's progress depended was to be secured. But it was also necessary that effective means of directing and mobilizing industrial development be found. Therefore the Kyōchōkai gave great importance to trying to improve productive output through the promotion of efficiency and managerial expertise. For to fail to expand production jeopardized Japan's social foundations by giving rise to poverty and despair. The Kyōchōkai activities in worker education and training and in the promotion of efficiency and managerial skills, therefore, were mutually reinforcing and complementary activities.

THE MECHANICS OF NEW INDUSTRIAL RELATIONS

In its social policy and educational activities the Kyōchōkai sought to institute programmes that would help eliminate human deprivation and misery while promoting 'healthy' social values. If successful in accomplishing these tasks, the leaders of the Kyōchōkai were convinced that workers would eschew confrontational tactics, labour unrest would be minimized, the economy would prosper, and social peace and stability would be secured. Yet, even if they were completely successful in inculcating cooperative ideals, Kyōchōkai leaders recognized that disputes and conflict could not be wholly eradicated. For if, as they argued, workers and capitalists had differing interests, disputes would continue to arise. The task was to convince both sides that cooperation and compromise could and should be sought in solving problems between the two sides. Therefore the Kyōchōkai Manifesto of November 1920 included the statement that 'while our main concern is to take steps so that disputes will not develop, in cases where labour unrest has broken out, this organization will not shrink from involvement in mediation efforts'.[70] Despite Nagai Tōru's conviction that the Kyōchōkai could not act as an effective mediator, it acted as a mediator or was involved in some way in over 300 strikes between 1921 and 1940.[71]

Why did the organization involve itself in so many strikes? There are two reasons. First, the Kyōchōkai was conceived with the belief that strikes tore the very fabric of the state and economy. Workers and capitalists alike lose money during strikes, profits decline and consumers' ability to purchase the goods they want or need diminishes. Therefore strikes impose 'a hardship on the entire nation'. The losses incurred during strikes are not just minor inconveniences. Rather:

> the damage brought about by strikes . . . is analogous to the loss of military materiel in wartime; reports of losses of equipment are just numbers expressing only a superficial reality. What are important are the losses not reflected on the surface.[72]

The less visible losses brought about by strikes included a fracturing of social unity and a weakening of the general economy. Strikes, therefore, impeded Japan's ability to compete with the West in the 'economic war' that marked the years following World War I. The Kyōchōkai, whatever Nagai's reservations, sought to minimize those invisible losses through strike mediation.

Second, in its social policy and education programmes the Kyōchōkai was throwing over bridges to workers. By establishing and encouraging settlement houses and through the medium of close personal relations in the Workers' Training Programme, the Kyōchōkai leadership attempted to build a constituency of supporters for harmonism, its most fundamental cooperativist ethic. Likewise, strike mediation was perceived as yet another mechanism allowing the Kyōchōkai to establish relationships in factories and workplaces. Therefore strike mediation provided another vehicle whereby the Kyōchōkai, and ultimately the government, were able to penetrate the economic infrastructure while overcoming important industrial problems.

Among the important strikes in which the Kyōchōkai participated were the Fujinagata Dockyard strike (1921), the Sumitomo Besshi copper mine strike (1925–6), the Noda Soy Sauce Company strike (1927–8), the Japan General Motors strike (1931) and the Tokyo Electric strike (1934). In none of these cases was Kyōchōkai involvement truly decisive. Rather, the Kyōchōkai mediators, primarily Soeda Keiichirō, provided an outside forum for face-to-face negotiations between the parties. In the long Noda strike, for example, the conflict between labour and management had become so laden with emotion that it had become impossible for any kind of talk even to take place.[73] Ultimately, the Kyōchōkai was brought in to act as an outside observer (*tachiainin*) in discussions between the union negotiator Matsuoka Komakichi and plant manager Namiki Shigetarō.[74] It also helped bring about a final settlement of the strike by shuttling between the various players. Key Kyōchōkai members, notably Soeda and Machida Tatsujirō, moved back and forth in a form of shuttle diplomacy in an effort to reach an agreement. Even Shibusawa, still a Kyōchōkai vice-president, held discussions with the head of the Sōdōmei, Suzuki Bunji, as well as with Matsuoka and Namiki.[75] In strikes conducted by unions more radical than Sōdōmei affiliates the Kyōchōkai also played a similar role. The 1926 strike at the Japan Musical Instrument Company in Hamamatsu, Shizuoka prefecture, for instance, was led by an affiliate of the communist influenced Japan Labour Union Council (Nihon rōdō kumiai hyōgikai). Nevertheless, Soeda acted as a go-between in the dispute and ultimately drew up a conciliation plan that provided the basis for a settlement.[76]

The Kyōchōkai's involvement in strike mediation reflected a common role in Japanese discussions on many types of issue. That is, whether in marriage or labour negotiations the presence of a go-between or middleman is welcome. A go-between occupies a place between the parties, ostensibly concerned with the interests of both, and charged with the responsibility of building rapport between them. The fact that the Kyōchōkai played this part so frequently suggests that it was more widely seen as uncommitted, if not absolutely unbiased, than the early vitriolic rhetoric of its labour critics indicated. This is reinforced by the fact that it was not just management that sought Kyōchōkai mediators but negotiators for labour did as well. Kyōchōkai mediation efforts must also be seen in a larger context of elite interest in mediation in the interwar period.

During the 1920s and 1930s a series of conciliation laws (*chōtei hō*) were enacted. Among them were the Land and House Lease Conciliation Law (Shakuchi shakuya chōteihō) (1922), the Farm Tenancy Conciliation Law (Kosaku chōteihō) (1924), the Commercial Affairs Conciliation Law (Shōji chōteihō) (1926), the Monetary Claims Temporary Conciliation Law (Kinsen saimu rinji chōteihō) (1932) and the Personal Status Conciliation Law (Jinji chōteihō) (1939). The passage of these conciliation laws was intended to reduce the rising tides of lawsuits that characterized the 1920s.[77] For the purpose of this book, however, the more significant characteristic of interwar conciliation was that it sought to impose solutions to problems on the basis of the parties' moral responsibility rather than through adjudication based on legally defined rights.[78] Conciliation was pursued to ensure that dispute outcomes were consistent with moral rather than legal guidelines. The settlement of a dispute was by itself not significant. The conciliation process could be and usually was used by the mediator to educate the parties to their respective duties and responsibilities. This process of 'didactic conciliation' was a central element in the conciliation laws of the interwar years and a main element of the overall Kyōchōkai programme.

Despite the misgivings of some Kyōchōkai members about the wisdom of the organization's involvement in strike mediation, the fact is that this task meshed perfectly with its overall mission. Mediation gave the Kyōchōkai opportunities to insert itself into the industrial structure. By offering settlement plans, as in the case of the Japan Musical Instrument strike, or by being a key party to negotiations the Kyōchōkai could help shape industrial relationships to achieve its goal of labour–management harmony. In so doing, Kyōchōkai mediators could and did act in an educational capacity, instructing each side in their duties and responsibilities. Soeda and other Kyōchōkai mediators acted in accordance with the Kyōchōkai ideology enunciated by Shibusawa, Nagai, Shiozawa and others. That is, the key to building industrial and social harmony lay in the realization of what they regarded as time-honoured Japanese moral principles and in the inculcation of people's duties. Strike mediation constituted the perfect means to solve problems while at the same time furthering the ideological values on which the organization had been built.

The interest in mediation points to a basic dilemma within the Kyōchōkai programme of conservative reform. The validity of one's actions was determined by the extent to which they conformed to the moral responsibilities of the actors. The determination of legal rights gave way to judgments of moral justification. Shibusawa, Tokonami, Soeda and Tazawa all emphasized the superiority of moral and ethical determinants of action. There were no 'natural rights'. Rights were won by those who understood and acted in accordance with their responsibilities to their families, the community and society as a whole. The 'living customs of the past' embedded in Japan's *kokutai* demanded the subjugation of the individual to the well-being of the whole, the rejection of individual rights in favour of communal goals of social stability and national strength. Yet the Kyōchōkai had been created specifically to cope with challenges to this idealized order. The growth of an urban working class and the belief that increasingly radical labour unions threatened the organic unity of the Japanese state prompted the creation of the Kyōchōkai as a body designed to cope with these challenges. If indeed labour posed the threat that government leaders believed, pointed rejection of its demands would have been impossible. But labour's strongest demands were for the very things ostensibly denied by the Kyōchōkai and much of the government, that is recognition of union rights of organization and collective bargaining. The Kyōchōkai directed the bulk of its efforts to social work and education in an effort to 'awaken' workers and capitalists to their responsibilities to each other and to society. But if it was to succeed in the task of fostering social and industrial harmony, the Kyōchōkai could not, as the Fuji Gas Spinning strike demonstrated, avoid the questions of labour law and worker organization. Therefore the Kyōchōkai took an active part in the debates over works councils and labour union legislation that animated the 1920s.

Works councils had achieved importance during World War I in Britain, the United States and in Germany. In October 1916 the British government set up a committee chaired by J.H. Whitley charged with suggesting means of improving relations between management and labour and considering methods of securing better conditions in the future. In a report of May 1917 the committee recommended the creation of representative bodies made up of employers and workers that would work toward improved conditions for all. The 'Whitley spirit' was conceived with the 'idea that the comradeship of the trenches would be brought into industry'.[79] The resultant Joint Industrial Councils were generally regarded as supplementary organs to labour unions and management groups. In the United States works councils began with the US entry into the war. Councils were promoted by the National War Labor Board as a means of fostering amicable industrial relations and aiding the wartime production effort.[80] Shop committees became common in war industries and several were mandated as part of strike mediation settlements. Because the committees brought some form of organization into industry, a defender of the committees wrote that they encouraged unionism. 'The Shop committee . . . is not a device of capital to prevent unionism; its seeds lie deep in the soil of unionism.'[81] This belief notwithstanding, the committees allowed war industries to maintain production while avoiding difficult problems of union recognition. In contrast to the promotion and creation of councils by the British and American governments, in

Germany works councils were the spontaneous creation of workers themselves. Influenced by the Russian Revolution, German workers established councils on the model of soldiers' and workers' soviets.[82] The councils were to be the agents for achieving workers' control of industry through true industrial democracy. In the new Weimar Constitution, workers were given the right 'to cooperate [with employers] in the regulation of wage and labour conditions as well as in the whole economic development of production' through workers' councils. But workers proved unable to agree on the precise role the councils would play and they quickly lapsed into innocuous grievance committees.[83]

These Western developments help explain the very wide interest in works councils in Japan as well in the postwar years. Workers, managers and government leaders alike saw the councils as a means of achieving their objectives. Workers and labour groups favoured the councils because they implied a democratic relationship in the factory. Influenced by the labour movements in Britain and Germany, 'industrial democracy' and 'workers control' were at the centre of many of the strikes of the early 1920s.[84] Suzuki Bunji asserted that as equal partners in the productive process, workers deserved and demanded a voice in the actual management of industry. Suzuki believed that Sidney Webb was correct when he said that 'industrial democracy' was the just and inevitable wave of the future.[85] The Christian labour leader Kagawa Toyohiko wrote in 1920 that contemporary capitalists had become more powerful than the former daimyō. The daimyō, he said:

> were not capable of employing thousands of workers daily. Nor did they maintain factories or organizations that operated around the clock day after day, year after year. But today, wielding chains of gold, capitalists shackle women and children to a factory for fourteen hours a day.

The only means of breaking those chains and achieving workers' rights, he believed, was through factory constitutionalism (*kōjō rikkenshugi*).[86] Works councils provided the method of achieving 'industrial democracy'. As a result, in 1921 alone demands for the creation of works councils were a factor in twenty-five strikes.[87]

Employers and government leaders as well became interested in works councils around the same time. Their interest in the councils sprang from sources that differed from those of workers, however. Shortly after the turn of the century public companies began to turn to relief programmes and mutual-aid unions in an effort to stabilize labour–management relations. The newly nationalized railway system under Gotō Shimpei established a mutual-aid union (*kyūsai kumiai*) and emphasized a family system model of labour–management relations.[88] Numerous military arsenals followed a similar course. The Kure Naval Arsenal in Hiroshima prefecture, for example, established in 1903 the Kure Workers' Mutual Relief Association (Kure shokkō kyōsaikai).[89] In Kure, Yokosuka and elsewhere it was hoped that this type of cooperative society would strengthen paternalist bonds within the factory and mitigate labour tension that was becoming increasingly prevalent.

For the same reason works councils became popular in larger firms following World War I. According to Kyōchōkai figures, industry established fourteen councils in 1919 and twenty-one in 1920 alone.[90] It is difficult to obtain a precise reckoning of the number of councils established during the 1920s but what is clear is that by 1926 more than a hundred councils had been established by government and private industries. As with the mutual-aid unions, many councils were established in government and strategic industries. In October 1921 the Army Clothing Depot, for example, formed the Workers' Discussion Association (Shokkō kondankai) to provide a regular forum for the exchange of views. Yawata Steel created a council in April 1920 to foster 'mutual understanding and cooperation' following a major strike at the plant earlier in the year. The most prominent example of a public industry council was the works council system established by the National Railways under Tokonami in May 1920.[91] Whether in public or private firms, the goals of the councils were generally similar. First, as the Yawata case makes clear the factory owners and managers who established works councils hoped that by establishing councils and discussion associations they would be able to promote more amicable relations within the company. Workers goals for the councils included the achievement of 'industrial democracy' and a level of 'workers' control' in plant decision making. With but one exception, however, council discussion focused primarily on welfare and working conditions issues.[92] Councils therefore, as in Britain and Germany, had become little more than grievance committees. But by giving workers a feeling of involvement, managers believed the councils provided an ideal forum for reducing worker militancy. Managers also saw in the councils the means of deflecting growing union demands for collective bargaining rights.[93] By offering discussion groups within the factory intended to deal with genuine workers' concerns (but with no enforcement mechanisms) managers believed councils could act as substitutes for outside, 'horizontal' union interference into the individual factory.

Given this role of the works councils, unions quickly recognized that they were not destined to be agents of 'industrial democracy' and came to oppose their creation. From its inception, however, the Kyōchōkai embraced works councils and continued to promote them throughout the 1920s. In the positions taken by Kyōchōkai spokesmen, works councils were capable of realizing the goals pursued by both managers and workers. As discussed earlier, Tokonami had been among the first to advocate works councils. Councils, he believed, were the ideal antidote to the 'poison' of class conflict promoted by nation-wide or industry-wide 'horizontal' unions. As a medium for the exchange of views between managers and workers councils represented institutions capable of minimizing industrial conflict but at the same time conformed with Japanese traditions. In the letter accompanying its 1921 draft works council bill, the Kyōchōkai stated that 'the labor unrest that has broken out in recent years in this country is a result of the absence of understanding and compassion, resulting in a rift between management and labor'. Western countries, the letter said, tried to deal with such conflict through the creation of a system of works councils. Yet the conflict between the two sides is of such long standing and is so bitter that councils have not been very effective. But 'in Japan, the evils of European and American labor–management relations are not so deep-seated or pervasive. Therefore we believe that if a works council system is established properly and universally it will be successful'.[94] Kyōchōkai leaders were convinced that councils could solve labour problems by building bridges between labour and management. Establishing personal ties between the two sides would inevitably restore the 'compassion' and 'understanding' that would lead to a diminution of labour unrest and the rebuilding of a healthy country and society.

The Kyōchōkai and a variety of government leaders emphasized that a spirit of democracy was implicit in works councils. In a letter to Prince Saionji in 1919, the vice-minister of the Home Ministry wrote that the solution to the labour problem rested on two ideas: (1) the cultivation of a spirit of 'cooperation and self-restraint' in workers and (2) the demonstration of a spirit of 'cooperative management' by capitalists.[95] Soeda Keiichirō equated works councils to city or local government. As those governments were elected to serve local interests under Japan's constitutional structure, likewise works councils were elected bodies designed to promote the exchange of views between different interest groups and to evaluate and solve problems that arise within the factory. In this sense 'a works council is an institution for putting a factory constitution system into effect'.[96] The Kyōchōkai promotion campaign for works councils, therefore, extolled, as Tokonami said, their capacity to 'preserve the reliability [*kenzen*] of workers while encouraging understanding between top and bottom', thereby minimizing conflict.[97] But at the same time it emphasized that the councils constituted a giant step in realizing the world trend of egalitarian democratic relations in industry. Therefore, Soeda wrote, 'in both logic and fact, works councils are the key to harmonizing labor and capital'.[98]

In the hope of furthering works council creation the Kyōchōkai leadership employed a number of tactics. One was to include works councils as part of a strike settlement package during mediation efforts.[99] The subject of works councils was also an important part of the curriculum in the various Kyōchōkai schools. More important, perhaps, the Kyōchōkai and its leaders were key players in promoting works council legislation. Three separate drafts of a works council law were drawn up. At Tokonami's instigation, the Home Ministry drew up the first works council law in late 1919. The draft, which provided the model for the works council adopted by the National Railways in the following year, proposed the mandatory establishment of works councils in factories and enterprises employing more than fifty workers (article 1). It mandated council election procedures (articles 2–9) and prescribed matters to be considered by the duly elected councils (article 15). Issues for council consideration were limited to health and safety issues, working conditions, labour welfare matters and education needs.[100] The law did not provide for enforcement mechanisms for council decisions nor did it sanction council deliberation of wage issues or labour involvement in actual plant management. Moreover, it provided that the chairman of the council would not be an elective position but was to be filled by managerial appointment (article 17). Opposition to the draft from party politicians in both the Kenseikai and Seiyūkai forced the government to withdraw the draft before it was submitted to the Diet.

Nevertheless, the Kyōchōkai itself proposed a works council law in October 1921. Submitted to the cabinet, the Home Minister and the Minister of Agriculture and Commerce, the Kyōchōkai draft differed from the Home Ministry bill of two years earlier only slightly.[101] In its eleven articles the draft was far less detailed than the Home Ministry proposal. It required the creation of councils in all firms with more than a hundred workers (article 1) and discussed voting procedures and outlined council organization guidelines. Unlike the Home Ministry version, it did not prescribe acceptable issues for council deliberation or the method for selecting council chairmen. Like its predecessor, the Kyōchōkai draft never made it to the Diet floor. But in 1929 a slightly modified version was finally submitted to the Diet.[102]

In each case the proposed law was rejected for the same reasons. First, critics argued that it was inappropriate and wrong to make works councils a mandatory form of organization. In its rejection of the Kyōchōkai draft, a government statement argued that while the council objective of bringing about labour–management understanding was itself 'not improper' it would be best, it said, 'to limit ourselves to stimulating [works council development] . . . rather than compelling their growth through legislation'.[103] Second, opponents of the legislation objected to the fact that none of the drafts provided means of enforcing council decisions. Without giving binding power to council deliberations they would be reduced to vapid debating clubs.[104] The most difficult question was the relationship of councils and labour unions. Labour groups opposed the bills arguing that 'council objectives cannot be realized with the existence of labour unions'.[105] Therefore, before considering works council legislation the first step should be legal recognition of union rights of organization and collective bargaining. Soeda, in defence of works council legislation, argued that the Kyōchōkai agreed with the view that the creation of a labour union law was necessary and for that reason labour union legislation is under serious consideration in the Kyōchōkai and elsewhere. But he said, 'there is no harm in establishing a works council law separately, prior to the completion of these discussions. Councils should operate together with unions but are not necessarily dependent upon them'.[106] By 1929, when the bill was finally presented to the Diet, management too had come to oppose councils. Initially, management supported their creation as a means of stemming union organization. However, with the growing 'realism' of the Sōdōmei and the deepening depression in the late 1920s which tempered labour radicalism and unrest, management lost interest and indeed objected to the coupling of councils and labour unions made by the Kyōchōkai and government supporters of the bill.[107] With opposition from both management and labour the bill failed.

The Kyōchōkai defence of works councils reveals much about

its approach to the labour problem and solutions to it. As we have seen, cabinet rejection of the Kyōchōkai bill saw informal encouragement as the best means of achieving council development. Management groups' opposition to the 1929 bill was couched in similar terms. This had been the tack taken by management groups to all forms of social legislation beginning with the debates over the Factory Law. The Kyōchōkai was convinced that 'the creation of a council system would too often not be achieved if left to the discretion of managers'.[108] Since it saw managers, like workers, as deficient in their understanding of the true nature of social problems, it feared that management would either ignore councils or set up weak window-dressing bodies as simple grievance committees with no real decision-making capability. Its fears were well founded for that was precisely the type of works council that was created and that dominated the movement.

Works councils were deemed important for the values they fostered in the workplace. Kawazu Sen observed that 'in the Kyōchōkai our advocacy of works council creation is nothing more than an attempt to bring about labor–management harmony in each factory through the spirit of social policy'. It is a programme, he said, that embraced the principles of respect for personality (*jinkaku sonchōshugi*) and responsibility (*sekininshugi*).[109] Kyōchōkai leaders believed that by creating a medium in which personal contact was made between managers and workers, 'friendly', 'warm' relations between the two sides could be attained. This belief was built on the classical emphasis on personal relationships of individuals within a society. Confucian ideals stressed the personal, moral ties that bound individuals within social groups. This approach seeks not simply understanding but 'friendship'. Just as Tazawa hoped to build close personal ties between the instructors and the students in the various Kyōchōkai schools, it was hoped that the works councils would act as a forum in which 'friendly', 'warm', 'healthy' and 'understanding' relations between managers and workers could be forged. With an institutionalized works council system in place, it was argued, 'between managers and workers friendly negotiations and discussions conducted in a spirit of harmony and cooperation will be possible'.[110] In this way a harmonious industrial system would emerge naturally and inevitably.

At the same time works councils would, it was believed, solve real problems. The Kyōchōkai recognized 'that there are a number of deficiencies in contemporary factory organization'.[111] Capitalists could not be relied upon to implement genuine labour reforms in the firm, but mandatory works councils would help to rectify this. As discussed earlier, Kyōchōkai members recognized that workers' dissatisfaction arose out of legitimate grievances about working conditions and the absence of respect for their labour. The latter problem would be addressed through the personal relationship built through councils. The councils would also provide the means of satisfying more tangible workplace grievances. Sample works council constitutions written by the Kyōchōkai indicate that it expected councils to concern themselves with a number of issues:

1   health and safety problems;
2   health and injury benefits;
3   matters of work hours and general conditions;
4   education and recreation issues;
5   welfare and relief concerns;
6   issues related to improved efficiency, and
7   'other issues of common interest to workers'.[112]

The Kyōchōkai believed that reforms undertaken through the council discussions and initatives would help satisfy many worker complaints. In so doing, worker unrest would be mitigated by accommodating many of the workers' demands. Yet, like all other council proposals, the Kyōchōkai draft law contained no means of enforcing council decisions. Soeda argued that while ideally enforcement mechanisms should exist, 'in the present state of Japanese industry it is impossible to bring such things into being'.[113] The vigour of capitalist opposition to the 1929 draft suggests the correctness of Soeda's position. Nevertheless, Soeda and other Kyōchōkai leaders believed that by establishing close relations in the firm, councils would lead to genuine reform.

Finally, for councils to be truly effective, ultimately, as Soeda pointed out, there would have to be legal recognition of labour unions. By the early 1910s a number of men who would become important leaders of the Kyōchōkai recognized that a sound union movement would provide the means of solving the labour problem. In 1912 Shiozawa Masatada, for example, argued that strikes and labour unrest were not due to workers alone: 'in a dispute both parties must share the blame'.[114] Capitalists frequently ignored the fact that labour dissatisfaction sprang from workers' just grievances. Therefore communication between the two groups was essential. Cooperative unions (*kyōdō kumiai*) and even regular trade unions, he believed, could provide the channels of communication between the parties that would lead to a lessening of tension. This same belief led Shibusawa and Kuwata to give their support to Suzuki Bunji's Yūaikai. After World War I a sound union movement was seen as more necessary than ever. Shiozawa wrote that with the growth of industry, the expansion of education, and workers' growing awareness of class interests, unions were becoming increasingly prominent. He continued:

> It is impossible to arrest this development, this is a historically verifiable fact. Therefore, with respect to workers' organization, what are most essential are measures to guide a sound union development . . . . The recognition of labor unions, however, must not involve ignoring mutual relations between employers and workers. Rather, it would be appropriate, I believe, to see unions as one step toward the establishment of just, healthy relations between the two groups.[115]

Shiozawa's statement typifies the Kyōchōkai view of labour unions and its approach to labour union legislation. First, he stressed that labour unions were part of an unavoidable world trend. Rather than denying that trend, it was best to take steps to direct the character of union development. Second, like Shibusawa, Shiozawa relied upon 'sound' unionism. He believed that 'healthy' mutual-aid type unions should be encouraged as a prophylactic against a spontaneous emergence of radical unions committed to class conflict. The promotion of healthy unionism, therefore, was important for its instrumental value. Third, the encouragement of 'sound' unions was but one part of an overall strategy of accommodating worker demands. Unions were 'one step' toward 'healthy relations' between managers and workers. Works councils, effective strike mediation, improved conditions through Factory Law revision, and political and social education were all necessary if unions were to perform the function of furthering social harmony.[116]

Given the potential value of labour unions in solving labour and social problems, the Kyōchōkai supported the creation and passage of a labour union law throughout the 1920s. Soeda Keiichirō, representing the Kyōchōkai, was a member of the Hamaguchi Cabinet's Social Policy Review Council (Shakai seisaku shingikai) that was charged with the responsibility of deliberating labour union legislation.[117] As a council member, Soeda supported the passage of a union law and submitted a draft bill for council consideration early in its deliberations.[118] Soeda contended that labour union legislation does nothing more than provide uniform criteria guiding legal union development. There is no reason whatsoever to suppose there is an ulterior motive that encourages conflict. The improvement of labour conditions, even if by legally imposed means, will solidify the moral basis of labour–management relations and enhance the stature (*jinkaku*) of workers. In so doing a great contribution to industrial peace will be made. Therefore, the passage of a labour union law will lead not to labour unrest but to labour–management harmony.[119]

In 1929 Yoshida Shigeru, head of the Home Ministry's Social Bureau, and beginning in 1931 a Kyōchōkai managing director, gave the government view of union legislation in language strikingly similar to that of Soeda:

The purpose of a Labor Union Law is to eliminate social obstacles facing the labor movement and make it more moderate and orderly. Labor unions are the natural product of the present economic system and because they have no status in law, there have been unnecessary disputes between labor and management . . . . The government always intends to promote the sound development of industries through cooperation between labor and management and a genuine cooperation can be achieved with giving the labor unions a legal position and working with them.[120]

The Hamaguchi cabinet submitted to the Diet in 1931 a labour union bill drafted by the Social Bureau. Although supported by the government and by organized labour, the bill never made it out of the House of Peers. As in previous attempts to legalize unions, the 1931 attempt met furious opposition from business interests. Given the large representation of businessmen in the House of Peers this opposition made its importance felt in the upper house's shelving of the bill.[121] After more than a decade of interest in labour union legislation, the failure of the 1931 attempt marked the end of government efforts to legalize labour unions.

A significant aspect of the Hamaguchi cabinet's support of union legislation is that the reasons given for that support mirror the views promoted by the Kyōchōkai since 1919. The essential congruity of the statements by Shiozawa, Soeda and Yoshida make this point clearly. Earlier union drafts by the Home Ministry (1920), the Kokumintō (1922), and the Social Bureau (1925) among others lacked a supporting constituency within the government or outside it.[122] By 1931, however, a broad coalition in the government had come to accept the idea of labour union legislation as one aspect of an integrated policy designed to cope with labour and social problems. Labour union legislation had become a key component of what Kawazu Sen called 'the spirit of social policy'. Coupled with social welfare work, educational programmes and works councils, 'healthy' labour unions sanctioned by labour union legislation could build the social and industrial harmony that had been the goal of the Kyōchōkai from the beginning. By 1931 Kyōchōkai conservative reformism had become government orthodoxy and the quest for moral community a national imperative.

5 The moral community in crisis

Despite broad official agreement on labour policy during the Hamaguchi cabinet, a growing sense of crisis forced a sweeping re-evaluation of that policy. Although leaders remained committed to the ideal of harmonism, they had become uncertain about how it might be pursued. The failure of the labour union bill coupled with economic depression and international tension brought on by the Manchurian Incident seemed to demand a new strategy. By 1937 the effort to formulate this strategy led to a Patriotic Industrial Movement, or Sampō (*Sangyō hōkoku undō*), that absorbed, by 1940, the last remnants of an independent labour movement. Harmonism provided the ideological basis of the new movement, but in wartime Japan the ideology was advanced in a new way. Rather than rationalizing legal and institutional reform in the name of national goals, harmonism justified direct government representation of what the government itself defined as workers' interests. Bureaucratic leaders of the Patriotic Industrial Movement replaced labour organizations as the defenders of workers against capitalists. But there was no one left to defend workers from their new representatives, representatives concerned above all else with industrial harmony.

SOCIAL BUREAUCRATS AND SOCIAL POLICY IN AN ERA OF CRISIS

One aspect of the debate at the Paris Peace Conference in 1919 was discussion of the role of labour in the postwar world. The Commission on International Legislation on Labour, one of several commissions operating under the auspices of the Conference, was charged with responsibility for devising a programme and establishing guidelines for dealing with labour questions. The result of

Commission deliberations was the creation of the International Labour Organization (ILO). Proponents of the Convention on International Labour sought universal compliance by its signatories. In a private meeting held on 1 April Japan's delegate to the conference, Makino Nobuaki, expressed Japan's position on the issue. He said:

> Labour conditions in Japan are very different from those prevailing in Europe and America . . . . The object of the Labour Conference was to establish throughout the world uniform standards. These standards in some respects are very remote from those at present prevailing in Japan. Should they be enforced in Japan the result might be a destruction of Japanese industries.[1]

As a result, Makino demanded 'some elasticity in the application of the principles set out in the draft Convention'. He suggested that Japan's 'final attitude' toward the Convention depended upon a recognition of Japanese realities and that if some leeway was not granted, 'Japan would not be able to accept the Convention'.[2] As a result of Makino's blatant threat, Article 405, Paragraph 3, of the peace treaty provided that:

> In framing any recommendation or draft convention of general application the conference [ILO] shall give due regard to those countries in which climate conditions, the imperfect development of industrial organization, or other special circumstances make industrial conditions substantially different and shall suggest the modification, if any, which it considers may be required to meet the case of such countries.[3]

Makino agreed to this amendment to the original convention and Japan became a permanent member of the Governing Body of the ILO.

Despite the strong language Makino used at the Conference, back home he took a different tack in urging government acceptance of the pact. In a report to the cabinet in August, Makino stated that 'Japan's political organization has kept pace with world thought'. Similarly, he said, 'I believe the future of labour must in the same way be dealt with in international terms'. Japan should be a participant in the International Labour Pact because 'a safe policy in accord with present trends is preferable to [yielding] to inevitable outside pressure or [facing] an irrevocable disaster inspired by outside radical movements'.[4] At the same time as Makino's report was being considered, Kyōchōkai sponsors were calling for a new labour policy that was in accord with world developments. As has been suggested earlier, major industrial changes taking place during World War I made the question of the role of labour critical and gave great importance to the quest for a new labour policy. The quest for a new labour policy and the appropriate administrative apparatus to conduct that policy was a major theme of the postwar years.

Prior to 1922, administrative responsibility for labour issues was scattered among several government agencies. From the mid-Meiji period the Ministry of Agriculture and Commerce had taken responsibility for labour protection activities and had led the fight for passage of the 1911 Factory Law. The Home Ministry, charged with maintaining internal security, concerned itself with monitoring labour activities and ferreting out radical agitators among workers. In 1920 each ministry sought to widen its authority in the labour policy arena. In August of that year the Ministry of Agriculture and Commerce established a new Labour Department (Rōmuka) that was intended to take a more activist role in the area of labour protection. Around the same time the Home Ministry elevated its Social Department (Shakaika) to the level of a full bureau (Shakai kyoku) and enlarged its responsibilities. Each ministry presented drafts of labour union laws in the same year and each took a more active role on general labour policy issues. The important Social Bureau official Kitaoka Juitsu has argued that these activities are evidence of bureaucratic 'sectionalism' that prevented efficient and effective labour policy formulation and administration.[5] It is a mistake, however, to see the postwar competition between the Home Ministry and the Ministry of Agriculture and Commerce primarily in terms of simple bureaucratic squabbling over turf. While turf was certainly at stake, the competition between the two ministries can be best understood as the first tentative struggles to forge a new labour policy for post-World War I Japan. It is in this context that the efforts of the Kyōchōkai must be seen.

The Kyōchōkai represented the first institutional effort linking the traditional concerns of the Home Ministry and the Ministry of Agriculture and Commerce. The new organization took an active part in providing and promoting labour protection programmes, formulating educational programmes, devising social and labour union legislation proposals and encouraging their passage. It also was critical in developing an overall approach and set of values for labour and social issues, that is, the ideal of harmonism. Yet, from the beginning, Kyōchōkai leaders argued that its position as a private, non-governmental agency prevented it from acting in a decisive manner to implement its views on labour issues. For that reason the Kyōchōkai took the lead in supporting the creation of a single government agency responsible for labour policy and administration. In the spring of 1922 Nagai Tōru wrote a proposal calling for the creation of a Ministry of Labour (Rōdōshō). The idea was initially opposed by the Japan Industrial Club. The Kyōchōkai director and Industrial Club leader, Wada Toyoji, therefore suggested that the proposal be revised; it should not be a labour ministry but one of general social administration. Through Wada's negotiations with Dan Takuma, the Industrial Club withdrew its objection.[6] Finally, in July 1922 the Kyōchōkai submitted a formal proposal for the creation of a single government agency that would coordinate and administer labour and social policy programmes.[7] In November 1922 the cabinet created the new Social Bureau (Shakai kyoku). The new body was not simply an expanded version of the 1920 Home Ministry Social Bureau. Rather it was created under cabinet authority as an independent 'external bureau' (*gaikyoku*) outside the usual chain of command, responsible directly to the Home Minister. It was to be responsible for administering all government labour and social programmes.[8] Therefore, within its jurisdiction were all the matters that had been divided between various departments within the Home Ministry and the Ministry of Agriculture and Commerce. The Social Bureau, then, constituted the first major government reorganization emerging out of the new industrial world of post-World War I Japan.

The ties between the Kyōchōkai and the Shakai kyoku were very close. Among the drafters of the final Kyōchōkai plan for a single government labour policy agency were the head of the 'old' Social Bureau, Tago Ichimin, and the head of the 'new' Social Bureau from September 1923 to December 1924, Ikeda Hiroshi.[9] The head of the Bureau's First Department (Dai-ichibu), Kawarada Kakichi, had been among the original planners and advocates of the Kyōchōkai in 1919 and its managing director from 1935 to 1937. Yoshida Shigeru, head of the Bureau from 1929 to 1931, left to become managing director of the Kyōchōkai. There were also the more general ties between the Kyōchōkai and the Home Ministry. Of course, the Kyōchōkai had been created at the instigation of the Home Minister, Tokonami. Mizuno Rentarō, another of Hara's protégés, was Home Minister in the Katō Tomosaburō cabinet when the Social Bureau was created and was later president of the

Kyōchōkai (1940–6). Moreover, between 1920 and 1937 all of the managing directors of the Kyōchōkai had been Home Ministry bureaucrats.

There was, more importantly, a congruity of interests between the two bodies. In March 1923 the Social Bureau took over the Central Labour Exchange set up by the Kyōchōkai three years earlier. It exercised vigorous leadership of government efforts to promote programmes of labour protection. In March 1923, encouraged in large measure by ILO conventions concerning working conditions, the Diet passed a bill proposed by the Social Bureau revising the 1911 Factory Law. The revised law mandated shorter working hours for women and children and forbade nightwork altogether by either women or children under the age of 16.[10] The bureau also took the lead in the fight to abrogate Article 17 of the Peace Police Law, in proposing the passage of the Labour Disputes Conciliation Law and in lobbying for the passage of a labour union law. The Kyōchōkai supported all these ventures and prior to the creation of the Social Bureau had been the principal bureaucratic activist in these areas. The congruity of the Kyōchōkai and Social Bureau positions on social questions during the 1920s suggests one of the Kyōchōkai's most significant roles.

Although conceived by Tokonami as a means of undermining a burgeoning labour movement and promoting values of industrial harmony, in its institutional form the Kyōchōkai performed another function as well. Influenced by Shibusawa, Kuwata and the social policy experts that dominated day-to-day operations, the Kyōchōkai foreshadowed the creation of the Social Bureau. Tokonami's fear of labour and the potential impact he believed it had on the fabric of society led him to create unwittingly Japan's first agency of labour and social specialists. It was in this forum that the beginnings of a unified labour policy took shape. And on the foundations built by the Kyōchōkai the Social Bureau took shape. This does not mean that the Social Bureau was simply a carbon copy of the Kyōchōkai. It was not. But the vision of conservative reform that had characterized Kyōchōkai members' writings and the programmes undertaken by the organization were given voice in the new bureau, the government body responsible for labour and social policy. And the programmatic agendas of the new agency, no less than the Kyōchōkai, were built on assumptions rooted in the belief in moral community and ethically based social relationships.

Supported in their reform efforts by increasingly powerful mainline Home Ministry officials such as Gotō Fumio, Yoshida

Shigeru and Nagaoka Ryūichirō, bureaucrats in the Social Bureau and in the Kyōchōkai constituted the leading edge of labour reform leadership during the 1920s. The question of what to do about labour had been the critical domestic concern following World War I and remained central throughout most of the 1920s. The ILO, labour union legislation, universal suffrage and the continuing concern with 'dangerous thoughts' were all problems that revolved around the urban working classes. The perception of 'world trends' coupled with the threat posed by the growth of the 'labour problem' made labour policy and related issues paramount during the 1920s. The morally driven conservative reform programme embraced and promoted first by the Kyōchōkai and later by the Social Bureau represented the dominant means of dealing with this critical issue.

Yet by 1932 the Kyōchōkai leadership was calling for a 're-examination of social policy'. A special number of the Kyōchōkai's *Social Policy Review* published in November 1932 featured articles by numerous scholars and government officials each seeking to widen the scope of social policy concerns. Upon assuming his post as Kyōchōkai managing director in 1931, Yoshida Shigeru declared that it was necessary to give 'new meaning' to social policy and the long-standing Kyōchōkai goal of labour–management harmony (*rōshi kyōchō*).[11] The Kyōchōkai and its social policy agenda had been formed during a period when great changes in the economy and in the realm of ideas had made the focus upon labour and labour problems natural and justified. But both domestic and international conditions had changed. Strikes and labour unrest were but one part of broad new patterns of social unrest. In the new situation prevailing in Japan 'the task of social policy should be to bring about healthy social conditions characterized by harmony and unity and to temper the strife and discord prevalent in all strata of society'. Yoshida pointed out that:

> at present social disharmony and strife are not confined to problems between labour and management. Rather, between large firms and small, between financial markets and industrial concerns, between cities and villages, between department stores and small shops, and throughout every other area of society, conflict is becoming an increasingly obvious trend.[12]

During Yoshida's tenure as managing director, therefore, the Kyōchōkai turned from its traditional emphasis on labour–management harmony (*rōshi kyōchō*) to a more broadly conceived concern with achieving social harmony (*shakai kyōchō*).[13]

An immediate cause for the change of direction was the deepening Great Depression. The growing evidence of rural poverty, small business failures and general economic distress compelled the Kyōchōkai and government policy leaders to try to forge new policies and programmes to cope with growing economic problems. But as serious as the economic problems were, they seemed to be overshadowed by a variety of domestic and international crises. In late 1931 the Manchurian Incident destroyed the foundations of the cautious, internationalist foreign policy that had characterized Japanese foreign relations since at least World War I. The incident began Japan's 'fifteen years war', the period many refer to as Japan's dark valley (*kurai tanima*). Japanese Army activities in Manchuria brought increasing militarization of the state and an increasing sense of isolation to Japan's leaders and people. In February 1932 the Minister of Finance, Inoue Junnosuke, and Dan Takuma, president of the Japan Industrial Club, were assassinated by members of the right-wing Blood Brotherhood Group (Ketsumeidan) and three months later the Prime Minister, Inukai Tsuyoshi, was killed by a group of young naval officers. Thus was begun what one foreign observer called a period of 'government by assassination'.[14] All of these problems – deepening economic catastrophe, growing international conflict and spreading political terror – gave rise to a pervasive sense that the nation was in a time of crisis (*hijōji*, *jikyoku*, or *konnichi no nankyoku*).

In such a situation a social policy that concerned itself almost exclusively with devising and implementing a reformist programme aimed at labour was deemed inadequate. As early as June 1931 Yoshida called for a broadening of Kyōchōkai interests to reflect the problems that were becoming evident under the weight of the Great Depression. In March 1932 he created the Crisis Period Counter-measures Committee (Jikyoku taisaku iinkai), as an adjunct body as a first step in this direction. The committee was chaired by Okabe Nagakake, a peer and former Foreign Ministry official. Twenty-eight men made up the committee, twenty of whom were Kyōchōkai members including Yoshida himself, Tokonami, Soeda Keiichirō, Tazawa Yoshiharu, Kawazu Sen, Nakajima Kumakichi as well as the former head of the Social Bureau, Tsukamoto Seiji, and a key member of the Ministry of Commerce and Industry (Shōkōshō), Shijō Takafusa. Committee members from outside the Kyōchōkai included Gotō Fumio, Oka Minoru, Yoshino Shinji and the labour leader Suzuki Bunji. The purpose of the committee was to 'research and discuss important issues related to the period of crisis' Japan was experiencing.[15] The committee met irregularly from May 1932 to October 1934 when Yoshida left the Kyōchōkai to join the new Okada cabinet. Among the issues discussed by the committee were 'policies to overturn industrial poverty', 'policies to overturn rural distress', 'policies to overcome unemployment', 'policies toward Manchuria' and the like.

Typical of the committee's approach was its proposal on 'policies to overturn rural distress' issued in August 1932. In its report to the cabinet, the committee stated that in the face of Japan's economic crisis, 'it is imperative that we formulate and implement comprehensive plans for the regeneration (*kōsei*) of the nation's economy'.[16] Nowhere was this more necessary and more urgent than in the countryside. It was important that rural communities seek to deal with their problems through their own collective efforts. But this was not enough. New government policies must also be initiated. The proposal made by the committee was in seven parts. Part one concerned reforms in farm management including advocacy of farm self-sufficiency and the reduction of family cash disbursement, promotion of cooperative local manufacturing and increased rural rationalization, and advice on local agricultural cooperatives. The committee also discussed debt rescheduling, reforms in credit cooperatives and widening the availability of credit. It also advocated changes in commodity control regulations that would satisfy demand without destroying farm livelihood. The committee took particular interest in 'rural peace' (*nōson heiwa*) and the spiritual character of rural people. It advocated assistance be given to agricultural committees (*nōgyō iinkai*) and 'healthy, harmonious organizations' (*kenzennaru kyōchōteki dantai*) be developed as a means of furthering peaceful rural development. At the same time the committee proposed promoting Japan's time-honoured spirit of cooperation (*kyōdō no seishin*) and the cultivation of the 'beautiful customs of frugality and hard work'.[17] This proposal reflects clearly the Kyōchōkai's new interest in rural problems. Economic distress in the countryside was not only a disaster in its own terms but right-wing terrorist groups claimed to represent and act in the interest of local agricultural society. Rural problems, therefore, came to be seen as an important source of social problems and social unrest throughout the country.[18] This conviction gave a sense of urgency to Kyōchōkai activities aimed at social harmony and was also the motivation behind the general Regeneration Movement (Kōsei undō) led by the Home Ministry that was so prominent in these years.

While the Kyōchōkai altered its focus, the agenda it pursued was in many ways unchanged. While it abandoned advocacy of the major structural reforms that it had sponsored up to 1931, reform remained an important element in its approach. It deemed legal and institutional changes that brought economic relief essential if any progress was to be made in coping with the intense problems of the 'period of crisis'. But at the same time the Kyōchōkai emphasized 'harmony' and 'cooperation' and encouraged organizations and groups that would bring these virtues into being. Local self-reliance, frugality, hard work and a 'spirit of cooperation' would be instrumental in solving rural economic problems. Education and proper thought would improve people's lives and restore social harmony. Thus, despite the change in the focus of social policy, the basic approach to social problems was of a piece with more than a generation of thinking on the issue.

The Kyōchōkai change of direction beginning with Yoshida Shigeru's assumption of the position of managing director cannot be understood apart from the sense of crisis that developed after 1931. But this crisis period alone does not explain developments in the organization or in bureaucratic social policy thinking in general. The new direction only makes sense when considered in light of labour policy issues themselves.

Tokonami Takejirō had conceived of the Kyōchōkai nearly thirteen years earlier as an organization that would help end labour unrest and undermine the growing labour movement. But even Tokonami recognized that it was imperative that labour policy be considered in light of the 'trends of the times'. This meant that by the early 1920s Tokonami's goal of restoring Japan's organic institutional and social character became coupled with a push for a pragmatic programme of legal reforms, the most important of which was to be the legal recognition of workers' right to organize. With the Social Bureau, a cluster of other Home Ministry officials, and a number of Minseitō dietmen, the Kyōchōkai became a key actor in the fight for European-style labour reforms. Factory Law revision, the Health Insurance Law and the Labour Disputes Conciliation Law were some of the fruits of this effort. But progressive-style reformism had been adopted as a pragmatic response to social conditions, valuable as a tactical weapon to bring about industrial and social harmony. Even when most vigorous in advocating legal reform, the Kyōchōkai continued to conduct its various schools and educational programmes coaching social unity and stressing national goals. As late as 1926 Soeda continued to advocate works councils that would awaken workers to the dilemmas of industry while rebuilding the unity of labour and management. The Kyōchōkai promoted the labour reform programmes of Western liberalism for their tactical value, shorn of their intellectual underpinnings. Reforms were grafted on to Tokonami's original goals of increasing national power and strength, preserving Japan's national polity and reforging the national and social unity that had been sabotaged by heretical ideas. Nagai Tōru had been forced to resign as managing director in 1926 largely because he had come to see reform not simply as an instrumental value for the achievement of nationalist objectives.

It was with little difficulty, therefore, that the Kyōchōkai leadership began to turn away from the reformist strategy. By the late 1920s the mainline of the labour movement as embodied in the Sōdōmei had abandoned its earlier radical posture, the radical Hyōgikai was disbanded, and the Communist Party was in tatters. Nationalist and Japanist labour unions were growing in number and importance. As the depression grew in intensity, political and social concerns shifted to providing relief and aid to unemployed workers and impoverished agriculturalists. The reform programme that had characterized Kyōchōkai activities for the previous decade was seen as anachronistic, out of step with the times. The failure to pass the labour union bill only served to confirm this. With Soeda's resignation from the Kyōchōkai in May 1931 the linkage of nationalist objectives and Western-style reformism had come to an end.

THE QUEST FOR INDUSTRIAL PEACE

During the 1920s the Kyōchōkai had been a key player in the debate over labour and social policy issues. It had paved the way for the Home Ministry's Social Bureau. It had defined the essential contours of post-World War I labour policy and formulated the ideological character that underlay official labour policy initiatives. It was instrumental in educating workers, managers and political and social elites about the nature of social problems and the range of acceptable solutions to them. Finally, the Kyōchōkai leadership was active in offering and defending social legislation in the cabinet and Diet. But the changes in the labour and social movements and the growing sense of crisis beginning in 1931 eroded the Kyōchōkai's sense of purpose and its institutional effectiveness. From 1931 to 1935 the organization floundered and government labour policy was without direction. The effort to 're-examine social policy' was symptomatic of the dilemma the Kyōchōkai faced.

With the failure of the labour union bill, the Kyōchōkai like the government as a whole, was left without a labour policy. It was in this vacuum that the new managing director, Yoshida Shigeru, sought to broaden the agenda of the Kyōchōkai from simply building labour–management harmony to fostering general social harmony. The new concern with rural distress manifested itself in the creation of the Crisis Period Countermeasures Committee and the establishment of what amounted to Kyōchōkai research substations in several areas. In 1934 the new managing director, Ōshima Tatsujirō created the Tōhoku Problem Emergency Research Association (Tōhoku mondai rinji chōsakai) with the same objective in mind.[19] These various groups were a mirror image of the more broadly conceived Regeneration Movement that absorbed the energies of many of the 'new bureaucrats' in the government. But despite Yoshida's assertion of a 'new direction' for the Kyōchōkai after 1931, these bodies, which were the physical manifestation of that direction, were of no real significance. The Countermeasures Committee did little more than offer platitudes about the pitiful conditions in agriculture and small business and suggest minimal solutions to the problems. The Tōhoku group was disbanded in 1935 having accomplished no more.

Despite the 'new direction' labour was not ignored. But there was no real programme, no general labour policy enunciated by the Kyōchōkai in the early 1930s. Instead Kyōchōkai leaders limited themselves to the pious hope that 'industrial peace' (*sangyō heiwa*) could somehow be brought into existence. Machida Tatsujirō, for instance, fell back on the old Tazawa prescription that an appreciation of each individual's fundamental humanity was critical. 'The secret of industrial peace,' he said, 'lies in understanding that it is truly a "human" problem, a problem of the "heart" [*kokoro*].'[20] This basic fact, he believed, had been overlooked in the headlong rush to bring about structural and legal changes in industrial relationships. Stripped of the elements of its earlier labour policy, Kyōchōkai spokesmen were limited to the prescriptive language that had characterized its first decade without the accompanying substantive policy programmes necessary to bring their goals to fruition.

Forces were at work, however, that made 'industrial peace' an increasingly generalized principle in the Japan of the 1930s. One of these forces was the emergence of industrial 'control' (*tōsei*) as a concept for overcoming the economic problems made clear during the depression. Industrial rationalization had been important since the post-World War I depression. It had been concerned with raising efficiency through technical innovation, reforms in workshop organization and, most important, by training workers and improving personnel procedures. By 1931, however, rationalization became linked with industrial control.[21] The goal was to replace industrial competition with the sanction of legal cartels in order to achieve economic stability. Cooperation in industry, not competition, would put the Japanese economy aright. Yoshino Shinji, a key Ministry of Commerce and Industry official and leading proponent of industrial control wrote that:

> Modern industries attained their present development primarily through free competition. However, various evils [in the capitalist order] are gradually becoming apparent. Holding to absolute freedom will not rescue the industrial world from its present disturbances. Industry needs a plan of comprehensive development and a measure of control.[22]

Yoshino's objection to 'free competition' was by no means new. Objections to *laissez-faire* economic principles had been the basis for social and labour policies since the late 1880s. This effort to rein in excessive sectarian impulses formed the bedrock of the Kyōchōkai's ideology of labour–management harmony. But in the hope of reversing the economic crises that beset Japan in the new decade, Yoshino harnessed the goal of harmony to the structural coordination of industry. The Important Industries Control Law (Jūyō sangyō tōseihō) passed by the Diet on 1 April 1931, just days after the failure of the labour union law, sanctioned the creation of cartels in 'important' industries in an effort to restore the economy and improve the country's competitive position.

From 1931, successive cabinets were preoccupied with the problems of national economic recovery, and after the Manchurian Incident, militarization. These concerns, to be achieved through industrial control, put increasing pressure on the already fragile labour movement. With the failure of the labour union law and the effective repudiation of the reformist programmes that had characterized labour policy before 1931, the police became, by default, the principal definers and enforcers of labour policy. The police had long been active in monitoring labour activities and enforcing the Factory Law as well as the various public safety laws. After 1931, however, the police increasingly became the most prominent agency in strike mediation. The 1926 Labour Disputes Conciliation Law had provided the apparatus for official mediation, but it was such a cumbersome process to put the official machinery into operation that informal mediation was overwhelmingly used.[23] With the growing emphasis on industrial peace and the tradition of police involvement in labour issues, the police role in strike mediation grew steadily. By 1932 the police acted as mediators in 204 of the total 626 strikes settled by informal mediation. By 1936 these figures had risen to 505 out of 817 settlements.[24] This is not to suggest that the police entered strikes on behalf of management to suppress workers. Communists and radical agitators were arrested as were those who resorted to violence. But in other cases the police played a generally unbiased role, and in some cases favoured workers. In 1935, for example, the second strike that year against the private Toyokawa Railway in Aiichi prefecture, police mediation resulted in a complete victory for the union.[25] This victory was perhaps due to the fact that the Toyokawa union was a patriotic Japanist union. Nevertheless, even in strikes conducted by mainline social democratic unions the police took a generally even-handed approach to settlement negotiations.

What needs to be pointed out is that police officials were part of the same bureaucratic network as officials in the Social Bureau. Indeed, most of the 'progressive' bureaucrats of the 1920s had in the course of normal ministerial rotations been involved in police activities. Kawarada Kakichi, for example, who became managing director of the Kyōchōkai in 1935 and Home Minister in the Hayashi government in 1937, had extensive experience in both the police and social bureaus. From 1922 to 1927 he had been the chief of labour affairs in the Social Bureau. But from 1913 to 1920 he had held various middle-level police posts. Yasui Eiji had been one of the most visible and important supporters of labour union legislation while a member of the Social Bureau in 1922 and again in 1931. But in 1919 he had become chief of the infamous Special Higher Police, charged with controlling 'thought criminals', and beginning in 1930 was concurrently chief of the Police Bureau's Security Division. There was no contradiction between those two areas: a major goal of each was labour–management harmony and 'healthy' union development. Until at least 1935 police mediation efforts and the general involvement of police in labour activities continued to be premised on harmonism in which negotiation between competing groups was central.[26] Therefore police involvement in labour issues was not necessarily contrary to union development.

Nevertheless, growing police activism in labour matters symbolized a political agenda obsessed with bringing about industrial peace. Beginning in the early 1930s mainline social democratic unions did everything they could to avoid strikes. The Sōdōmei hoped to make clear its commitment to industrial peace and 'industrial cooperation' (*sangyō kyōryoku*) when it abandoned strikes as a tactic in 1932. It hoped that by making clear its support for national goals, 'sound unionism' would continue to be supported and sanctioned by the police and others.[27] But these unions were not simply being pressured from above; they were also threatened by the growing prominence of right-wing nationalist unions from below. The growth of the nationalist and Japanist labour movement in the early 1930s not only called into question the patriotism and loyalty of the various socialist unions but also brought into high relief the sectarian, class-based character of those unions.

Unions were tolerated, just as reformism was supported in the 1920s, for pragmatic reasons; they were supposed to act to moderate labour unrest and guide the 'healthy' development of the workforce. But despite labour's vow to support industrial peace, labour unrest did not dissipate. In every year from 1931 to 1937, with the exception of 1936, there were more that 500 strikes (in 1936 there were 498). In each of those years nearly 2,000 incidents of all kinds including strikes, lockouts and go-slows took place.[28] By 1937, when there were 2,126 disputes involving more than 213,000 participants, it had become clear that the mainline unions were not capable of providing a moderating influence on labour unrest. The 26 February Incident in 1936 and the outbreak of war with China in the following year made it abundantly clear that vague hopes for 'industrial peace' were inadequate. A well-defined labour policy had to be formulated and institutional mechanisms put into place. The Kyōchōkai played a part in the effort to create this new system.

THE INDUSTRIAL PATRIOTISM MOVEMENT

By 1935 efforts were underway to devise institutional mechanisms for ordering and regulating labour relations. Police mediation efforts and monitoring of labour activities served an essentially negative function; police officials simply watched developments and settled disputes once they had broken out. But police involvement provided no framework in which industrial relations could be institutionalized and disputes prevented. The failure to pass a labour union law and the discrediting of Western-style reformism stymied policy makers from 1931 to 1935. The task was to conceive of a system that would not be attacked by the business community, as earlier reform policies had been, while at the same time, serving to regularize industrial relations and meet the pressing needs of productive output to meet emergency defence needs. Beginning in 1935, therefore, the Social Bureau began a vigorous campaign promoting the expansion of works councils. In a bureau directive of July 1935 local Home Ministry officials were informed that:

> Because they foster mutual understanding and deepen mutual trust between labor and management, works councils [*rōshi kondankai*] constitute an excellent means of bringing about a spirit of cooperation in industry and preventing industrial conflict thereby providing a solution to a variety of labor–management problems.[29]

In November 1936 the bureau wrote a Draft Legislation to Regulate Industrial Labour Based on Cooperative Councils (Kyōryoku iinkai o chūshin to suru sangyō rōdō – chōsei ni kansuru shohōritsuan) modelled on Germany's National Labour Control Law. The draft proposed expanding official strike mediation efforts and providing legal sanction for the creation of works councils.[30] This legislative effort went nowhere, but growing Social Bureau interest in works councils led to zealous promotion and sponsorship of councils by local police officials and capitalists.[31] Even before the Social Bureau became interested in their development, works councils became increasingly prevalent after 1931. Between 1932 and 1935, eighty-four separate works councils had been set up, mainly in large industries.[32] Capitalists had been the principal initiators of council creation. In the period of crisis beginning in 1931 and with the failure of the labour union law, managers saw works councils as an ideal means of moderating workers' demands and further weakening the already severely crippled labour movement.

The value of council development seemed to be confirmed in 1937. The near record number of labour disputes in that year involved an all-time high number of participants. What was noteworthy, however, was that most of these disputes broke out in small or medium industries, industries in which workers were represented by unions or where there was no worker organization of any kind. Large plants and government factories in the main escaped labour unrest in that year. Government leaders attributed this fact to the diffusion of company unions and works councils in those plants. The correlation between in-house unions or works councils and the absence of labour unrest demonstrated to government leaders the effectiveness of councils as a prophylactic against labour unrest.[33] Interest in some form of council development or plant-specific organization grew as a result.

A council arrangement of some kind was seen as a desirable model of general workshop organization within the Social Bureau and within the Home Ministry at large. Around the same time, however, several plans of varying degrees of complexity were put forward by both individuals and official agencies to regularize the entire system of labour relations.[34] The plans ranged from highly systematic legislative programmes to vague programmes of spiritual mobilization and management self-control. Each of the plans called for the dissolution of unions and the unification of labour and management for the purpose of rationalizing the industrial system and mobilizing the nation's economic resources. Many of the plans recognized, however, that workers had legitimate grievances and it was in the best interest of workers as well as the nation as a whole that those grievances be addressed. The Emergency Countermeasures Labour–Management Regulation Plan (Jikyoku taisaku rōshi seichōan), otherwise known as the Arakawa Plan after its drafter, which was made public in December 1937, was one such plan. It called for the creation of works councils in each factory and provided for the submission of workers' grievances to a dispute settlement committee made up of workers, management personnel and government officials. If the grievance could not be settled through negotiation it would be sent to a settlement committee made up of government officials where it would be resolved through binding arbitration.[35] The plan also gave local officials the right to curb management prerogatives in wage determination and settling hours of labour. The Arakawa Plan, therefore, sanctioned direct government intrusion into the managerial process and as such was strongly opposed by business leaders. What is significant about the Arakawa Plan and others offered for consideration is that they served to draw the line between the participants in the debate over the form a new labour relations system would take. On one side, the Arakawa Plan and a predecessor, the Minami Plan of 1936, signalled official hopes of a more prominent role for the government in protecting and mobilizing the workforce through direct intervention in the economy. On the other side, plans that advanced spiritual mobilization and managerial autonomy were proposed in order to win business support for the construction of a new national economic order. By 1937, therefore, the hope of bringing about industrial peace by creating a coherent system of labour relations led to a contest over who would control these relations, government officials or businessmen, a contest that persisted for the next eight years.

The Kyōchōkai acted as one of the players in efforts begun in mid decade to construct a uniform and regularized system of labour relations. As we have seen, during Yoshida Shigeru's tenure as managing director, the organization's activities shifted to a quest for a general programme of social harmony and vague hopes for industrial peace. This was generally marked by uncertainty about the course the organization should follow. By 1935 the Kyōchōkai, like the Social Bureau, began to take a new interest in the structural character of industrial relations. This new interest was made clear by the organization's new managing director Kawarada Kakichi. Kawarada emphasized in late 1935 that a diffusion of a spirit of harmony was essential if Japan were to meet the social, economic and military requirements of the day. Yet, 'along with stimulating a form of self-regulating labor–management harmony, in view of the unremitting demands of the day', there must also be developed, he said, 'healthy, organized methods' for structuring industrial relations.[36] Four months later he made his point more explicitly:

> The most basic goal of this organization has been to contribute to the furthering of a satisfactory regulation of labor–management relations. That goal is unchanged. The relations between the two, however, have come to be disentangled from the confrontational values that had been so pronounced in the past, and each side today displays unmistakable cooperative tendencies. This is perhaps a result of the times. But, it is also evidence that the spirit of labor–management harmony and industrial cooperation emphasized over many years by the Kyōchōkai has permeated and been understood and accepted throughout society. We must continue to work to perfect this fundamental spirit. In light of the crises now facing the state and society, however, it is, at the same time, essential that we thoroughly reconsider labor–management relations and formulate an appropriate national industrial labor policy to meet the demands made upon our country by these dangerous times.[37]

Kawarada was convinced that the Kyōchōkai's basic ideal of harmonism had permeated society and had had a very salutary effect on social relationships. Nevertheless, it was clear to Kawarada and other members of the organization that labour policy could not continue to be ignored. The continuing inability of labour unions to control strikes made some kind of response apparently necessary. The 26 February Incident spurred Kawarada to consider a 'national industrial policy' necessary as social turmoil seemed to threaten the very foundations of society.

Although Kyōchōkai leaders shared a renewed concern with labour policy, not all were convinced of the need or desirability of nationally directed programmes of labour coordination. Machida Tatsujirō was one such person. Machida, who had risen through the Kyōchōkai ranks as a labour specialist, succeeded to the position of managing director in February 1937 when Kawarada joined the new Hayashi government. Machida was the first managing director since 1920 who had not at one time been a Home Ministry bureaucrat. Two other non-bureaucrats, Nagaoka Yasutarō and Gamō Toshifumi, joined him as managing directors two months later. These men, rather than pushing for a labour policy synthesis, supported the need for a 'spiritual movement' to mobilize society to meet the current crisis. Machida said when he assumed his post that:

> We must work together toward the realization of industrial peace and labour–management oneness [*rōshi ittai*], correcting ideas of individualism and guiding people toward a concept of service to the state and society . . . . Labourers, managers, and the government should join hands in a true spirit of harmony; three separate entities becoming one.[38]

A 'national spiritual movement' (*kokumin seishin undō*), he argued, had to be the basis for building industrial order.[39] Machida expressed distrust of institutional responses to labour issues as early as 1932, preferring to emphasize human relations and human personality.[40] At the same time one Ōsawa Tsutomu of the Nagoya branch of the Kyōchōkai published his 'Personal Opinion for the Implementation of the Emergency Countermeasures Labour–Capital Regulation Plan [Jikyoku taisaku rōshi chōseian jitsugen ni kansuru shian]'. Ōsawa's plan was intended to win acceptance of Nagoya area businessmen for the Arakawa Plan. What it did instead, however, was to gut Arakawa's basic prescriptions. It made works council development an issue to be determined 'in accordance with conditions in individual factories'. It also rejected the creation of standing factory grievance committees and made grievance settlement an issue for individual factory resolution.[41] What Ōsawa's plan and the attitude toward achieving industrial peace taken by Machida and the other new managing directors made clear is that the Kyōchōkai was sharply divided over the approach to take on labour relations. On the one side Kawarada and other old-line social bureaucrats favoured government intervention and the organization of industrial relations in order to protect workers and to mobilize industrial output. Machida and his allies, however, supported spiritual mobilization and a belief in the basic unity of labour and management. These positions were mirror images of the larger debate taking place outside the Kyōchōkai between bureaucrats and businessmen.

The outbreak of the war in China in July 1937 gave new impetus to the search for a coherent labour policy. By September it had become clear that the 'China Incident' was not going to be quickly resolved. Based on this realization, the Kyōchōkai launched a flurry of discussion groups to attempt to reach some consensus on the course the mobilization of labour and industry should take. Between September and November the Kyōchōkai led a roundtable group at its Tokyo headquarters in the hope of reaching some agreement on wartime labour policy issues.[42] The group, known as the Wartime Labour Countermeasures Discussion Group (Senji rōdō taisaku kondankai), was made up of twenty-two men including the Kyōchōkai's managing directors, five Social Bureau officials, two military representatives, three representing capitalist interests and the remainder from various government agencies and private research organizations. The group's specific agenda items included: issues of labour control including labour supply and mobilization; adjustment of labour–management relations, including labour union policy and thought control; national programmes of social policy, including concerns of general social conditions, housing, and the like; and working conditions, including wages, hours of work and health and safety issues.[43]

The Kyōchōkai organized several other groups to discuss wartime policy. On 16 September it convened the Social Education Organizations Discussion Group (Shakai kyōka dantai kondankai) to exchange ideas on effectively promoting 'spiritual mobilization (seishin sōdōin)'.[44] It also organized a Labour Organizations Discussion Group (Rōdō dantai kondankai), a Managers Discussion Group (Jigyōshū kondankai) and a variety of other groups in major cities and industrial areas throughout the country.[45] None of the groups organized by the Kyōchōkai in late 1937 made any effort to formulate specific policy proposals. Rather, the task of these groups was to build a consensus on the need for such proposals.

By October, labour unions had given their enthusiastic support to industrial mobilization and national unity.[46] Discussion between government bureaucrats and a variety of business leaders made clear their united support for some kind of programme to promote industrial peace and labour–management unity. Based on this broad understanding, the Kyōchōkai formed a second Crisis Period Countermeasures Committee (Jikyoku taisaku iinkai) in January 1938 which, in the months that followed, established the guidelines for the Industrial Patriotism Movement. The committee was organized in three parts. The first part was the main committee made up of thirty-one members many of whom were Kyōchōkai members as well as government officials, scholars, and also included four members of the business community.[47] The second part was what was called the First Specialist Committee (Dai-ichi semmon iinkai) composed of eighteen members most of whom were bureaucrats.[48] Finally, there was the Second Specialist Committee (Dai-ni semmon iinkai) which included fourteen members representing business and labour.[49] There were six items on the general committee's agenda: (1) policies on behalf of military casualties, (2) domestic social policy issues, (3) labour-supply regulation policies, (4) labour protection policies, (5) policies dealing with labour–management relations, particularly in major industries, and (6) thought policies. Responsibility for these items was divided between different parts of the committee: items 1 and 2 were to be discussed by the First Specialist Committee; items 3, 4 and 5 were the responsibility of the Second Specialist Committee; and the main committee was responsible for the final item.[50]

The work of the First Specialist Committee presented few difficulties. Chaired by Yoshida Shigeru, the committee met eight times between 2 February and 30 March. The committee was most concerned with the issue of disabled veterans. A satisfactory policy in this area was necessary not simply to make a humanitarian gesture of thanks for the sacrifices of soldiers. Rather, the committee agreed that the failure of the European belligerents during World War I to set up a satisfactory disabled veterans relief policy was an important reason for the postwar social unrest that rocked Europe.[51] Therefore the committee urged that a variety of programmes in this area be established. Among the recommendations were programmes of re-education and training, the creation of a broadened medical rehabilitation support system, aid to families of the wounded, and a publicity campaign to educate the public about the sacrifices made by veterans and their readjustment needs.

The Second Specialist Committee's meetings were marked by controversy from beginning to end. Chaired by Kawarada Kakichi, this committee met six times during February and March. It was in this committee that the conflict between bureaucratic objectives for labour mobilization and the efforts of businessmen to preserve managerial autonomy came to a head. The bureaucratic position was presented by Narita Ichirō, the head of the Labour Bureau in the newly created Welfare Ministry (Kōseishō). Narita said that to build cooperation between labour and capital to meet the difficult challenges facing Japan it would be best 'to create a mechanism for regular labour–management consultation'. While the government had no 'definite plan' to achieve this end he said it would be advisable to 'devise a concrete policy suitable to all factories and conditions', and recommended that the committee do so.[52] Narita, therefore, was re-emphasizing the position taken by social bureaucrats since at least 1935. Morita Yoshio, a representative of the employer's group Zensanren, countered saying that 'creating the guiding spirit of our country's industrial relations' must be the first priority. For 'if the fundamental guiding spirit is put in place will not the establishment of the methods inevitably, and easily follow?'[53] Morita's position echoed earlier objections raised by business groups to the Minami and Arakawa plans designed to organize industrial relations.

Business leaders, of course, had no objection to works councils or consultative committees *per se*. They had, after all, been instrumental in forming many of them during the 1920s and 1930s. What Morita was objecting to was the institutionalization of a council system through a 'concrete policy suitable to all factories and conditions'. For, as the Arakawa Plan had made clear, bureaucratic interest in systematizing works council organization was linked to official intrusion on managerial prerogatives. Businessmen favoured works councils if their creation and operation was at the discretion of management. Just as the business position was intended to realize the time-honoured goal of management autonomy, the bureaucratic position was taken to meet long-standing objectives. Legally sanctioned works councils created with labour representation and charged with addressing issues related to work conditions would serve to protect workers. Councils, by protecting labour interests and promoting workers' welfare, would therefore alleviate the central causes of labour unrest. This conception of councils is virtually identical to Tokonami Takejirō's earlier advocacy of works councils as 'vertical unions' to replace rising trade unionism. Works councils in the new bureaucratic view would perform union-like functions in every factory and it was precisely this to which Morita was opposed.

The debate continued along these lines until 26 March.[54] The result was a report entitled the Labour–Capital Relations Regulation Plan (Rōshi kankei chōsei hōsaku).[55] The plan, submitted to all the relevant ministries in May, represented a synthesis not a consensus. In its two parts the plan seemed to provide something for both the bureaucrats and businessmen. The first part discussed the 'guiding spirit' of industrial relations. It expressed the view that industry was an 'organic entity' that is sustained by the duties of managers and workers. Managers provide for workers' welfare while workers serve the nation by recognizing the spirit of the 'firm as a family' (*jigyō ikka*) and 'familial allegiance' (*kazoku shinwa*) within the factory. 'Industrial patriotism' and service to the imperial state was the fundamental duty and obligation of managers and workers alike. The second part of the plan concerned the means of implementing and diffusing the guiding spirit. This section called for the creation of organs in factories to disseminate the principles. This task would be carried out in educational and training programmes and it called for a central organization to coordinate implementation and propagation of the principles. Despite lip-service given to implementation, the plan concentrated primarily on spiritual mobilization. This suggests that it was easier to reach an agreement on principles than institutions. By advocating the creation of 'industrial patriotism societies' (*sangyō hōkokukai*) in each factory and by endorsing the role of works councils, the plan did provide something to satisfy the bureaucrats. Nevertheless, the plan must be seen as a victory for business interests. First, the plan endorsed the idea of the firm as a family. Since the 1880s businessmen had supported this notion. In 1919 the Japan Industrial Club, the parent organization of Zensanren, had pushed for labour–management oneness as the underlying principle of the yet-to-be-formed Kyōchōkai. In 1938 business leaders finally succeeded in making this principle the 'guiding spirit' of official labour policy. Second, the plan imposed no uniform formula for national organization of industrial relations. Rather, the plan's vagueness implicitly sanctioned continued management autonomy.

Between April and July Kyōchōkai leaders and Zensanren representatives promoted the plan around the country.[56] On 30 July the government established the Industrial Patriotism Federation

(Sangyō hōkoku renmei) on the basis of the Labour–Capital Relations Regulation Plan. Kawarada was appointed director and most federation posts were occupied by Kyōchōkai and Zensanren members. The Federation's founding documents endorsed its commitment to labour–capital oneness (*rōshi ittai*) and the organic unity of capital, management and labour. Its objective was 'to thoroughly diffuse the spirit of industrial patriotism throughout the industrial world'. In industries around the country industrial unions and works councils were renamed industrial patriotism societies. These local units were nominally under Federation authority. In fact, however, Federation ties to local organizations were very loose; it was essentially a relationship of non-intervention. Indeed, only a very small number of local societies were formally affiliated with the Federation. Thus its leaders confined their activities to publicity and education.[57] Through 1938 and into 1939, therefore, the Industrial Patriotism movement pursued the spiritual mobilization programme advocated by business interests.

The role of the Kyōchōkai in the debates over the creation of a national labour relations policy was subsumed in the larger clash between bureaucrats and businessmen. As discussed earlier, the Kyōchōkai leadership tended to be divided between the two sides. Kawarada and the other old-line social bureaucrats favoured systematic organization and government intervention in labour relations. Machida Tatsujirō led a group favourable to spiritual mobilization and business interests in general. The Industrial Patriotism Federation came to reflect the Zensanren position in large measure because Kawarada and the bureaucrats recognized that business support was crucial in any labour relations plan. By 1939 Machida sought a merger of the Kyōchōkai and the Federation. He hoped in so doing to accomplish two things. First, by bringing the largely business-oriented Federation into the Kyōchōkai he hoped to overthrow the idea of labour–management harmony (*rōshi kyōchō*) that continued to be subscribed to by the Kyōchōkai as a group,[58] an ideology that sanctioned works councils and their legalization. Second, he hoped to strengthen the Federation which was coming under increasing attack because of its failure to bring about any substantive changes in industrial relations. His merger plan was rejected by the Kyōchōkai membership, however, and the Federation sank into insignificance shortly after being eclipsed by more vigorous organizations.

The role of the Kyōchōkai in the industrial patriotism movement should not be overstated. Its principal functional position was that it supplied the forum in which the competing business and bureaucratic interests came together to hammer out an agreement, however weak and vague it may have been, about the nature of industrial relations in wartime Japan. Like the three labour representatives on the Second Specialist Committee, the Kyōchōkai members did, and could do, little more than provide support to one side or the other. The clash between businessmen and bureaucrats was endemic in every arena of the wartime economy, including labour relations, and the Kyōchōkai could do little else but choose sides.[59] Yet, as one contemporary writer said, the Kyōchōkai was 'the spiritual womb of the industrial patriotism movement'.[60] In its various guises the movement drew on all the elements of the conservative reform programme promoted by the Kyōchōkai for two decades. Bureaucrats emphasized the need for reform of industrial relations and labour protection. A works council system was the favoured form for achieving these goals. Underlying these bureaucratic reform goals was an implicit reliance on the labour–management harmony ideal created by the Kyōchōkai and promoted since its inception. Business leaders and supporters favoured spiritual education, publicity and an emphasis on human relations aimed at building a correct understanding of industrial relationships that would inevitably lead to sound labour practices. Individuals, not institutions or legislation, were most crucial to the creation of a system of industrial relations that would benefit state and society. Thus, while the Kyōchōkai in its institutional form did not play a decisive role in the development of the industrial patriotism movement, the ideology it had created did. The ideals of harmonism and moral community formed the parameters within which the movement developed and wartime labour policy was formed.

Afterword

Historically, national development and modern nation building have involved both efforts of creation and recreation. Even as developing states pursued new institutional and organizational arrangements they have selectively drawn on the past, repackaging and reconfiguring national values and ideals to meet new needs and solve new problems. The comfortable language and attitudes of an idealized past were mobilized to provide continuity and meaning for a turbulent present. But with a changed context, altered institutional linkages and differing priorities new traditions emerged in the guise of the old, traditions that resonated with the moral authority of history but which were at the same time distant from it. Japan's invention of a culture of harmony as a normative economic value is an example of this pattern.

In the years following the Meiji Restoration the leaders of the new imperial state invoked the ideal of the self-contained rural community to solve the problem of relief distribution. Also, as we have seen, many Meiji entrepreneurs stressed the importance of communality in the new industrial work places. Factories were, in effect, defined as functional analogues of pre-industrial social and economic arrangements. By the 1890s reformist bureaucrats sought to regulate the operation of free-enterprise capitalism. Their concern was that unregulated market economies created social problems that threatened future growth and social stability. At the same time theirs was a moral concern; they aimed at the recreation of a structure of economic relationships that would restore the attitudes of harmony and cooperation that they believed had once existed in a now idealized past. Meiji elites therefore invoked traditionalist ideals and values to address problems brought into being by the transformation of Japan's political, social and economic institutions. Theirs were acts of myth-making, efforts aimed at the creation of a civil culture built on and supportive of the values and norms of a living history.

These efforts represented the beginnings of a new social orthodoxy. The organicist conservatism that formed the basis of Meiji myth-making remained a constant in the continuing elite attempt to address social problems. By the second decade of the twentieth century the most pressing of those problems seemed to be the issue of industrial labour. In 1919 Home Minister Tokonami Takejirō spoke for many when he described Japan's industrial system as having reached a crossroads. The state could choose, and seek to build, harmonious and cooperative industrial relations, or it could allow social conflict and industrial tension to grow unchecked. Tokonami's concern reflected a broad post-World War I belief that the creation of a coherent labour policy had become an absolute necessity. Prior to 1918 Japan's government leaders felt no compelling need for an elaborate labour policy. Up to that time labour had remained as but one part of a substantially undifferentiated lower class. It was only with the explosive industrial growth that accompanied World War I that the question of labour came to be regarded as a distinctive problem requiring a distinct, coherent response.

Labour unions and labour unrest were repeatedly suppressed following World War I. Police consistently monitored union activities. Article 17 of the Peace Police Law continued to be an impediment to union growth and development and the Peace Preservation Law of 1925 provided the legal justification for harassment and, when desired, arrest of union leaders and activists. Nevertheless, it would be a mistake to see the forcible repression of labour as the overriding element of interwar labour policy. Rather, the objective of Japanese leaders was not simply to control labour but to mobilize workers in the service of strategic national goals. For a substantial fraction of Japan's political and bureaucratic leaders the best way of bringing this about was through the inculcation of a new industrial culture, a new civil religion centred on communitarian values and cooperativist ideals. For this purpose Tokonami along with Shibusawa Eiichi led in the creation of the Kyōchōkai in 1919. From its inception until at least 1938 the Kyōchōkai employed a subtle mix of propaganda programmes and the advocacy of institutional and legal reform in the hope of absorbing workers into a smoothly operating industrial system. Supported by repression and systemic crisis forcing an erosion of commitment to independent trade unionism, the Kyōchōkai's model of industrial harmony came to dominate the intellectual and ideological character of interwar labour relations.

Japan's leaders, both within the Kyōchōkai and outside of it, were consciously or unconsciously committed to a preindustrial model of social homogeneity and organic unity as the goal of their efforts. Much the same as Meiji era reformers, these leaders sought the recreation of an idealized moral tradition drawn from the nation's living history. They did not deny that significant changes had taken place within Japanese society. Rather, they believed that the key to the nation's social stability and its ability to foster economic strength lay in recreating an organic community tied together by shared moral and social values. To this end Kyōchōkai members developed and promoted a new economic and social ideology centred on the notion of harmonism (*kyōchōshugi*). Like earlier formulations extolling the place of moral community in modern society, harmonism was explicitly linked to the past and identified as a constituent element of national identity.

Harmonism rested on Confucian moral assumptions and was an attempt to reformulate traditional moral norms for use in the new industrial society. It was invoked first by the Kyōchōkai and increasingly by others within the government as a means of undermining what was seen as the adversarial relationship that was emerging in industrial relations. In numerous publications, lectures and schools the Kyōchōkai sought to inculcate Confucian values of harmony and organic unity as an antidote to the individualist or class-oriented values of the rising labour movement. The Kyōchōkai, therefore, was part of the generalized effort of ethics training (*shūshin*) pushed by numerous state and private groups. Thus it was one of several media through which community-oriented, nationalistic values were transmitted to popular society.

It would be wrong to argue, however, the Kyōchōkai's propagandizing was little more than an attempt at coercive social control. Successful programmes of ideological transvaluation and moral inculcation always involve some degree of mutuality between the assumptions and aspirations of the controller and the controlled.[1] Instead, in its indoctrination efforts the Kyōchōkai pursued what might be called positive moral conditioning. By manipulating traditional values and cultural symbols in the creation of its new industrial ideology, the Kyōchōkai created a model for modern society that was both familiar and resonant with a widely shared understanding of social and moral norms. As a result, harmonism was not an elite concoction distinct from the moral assumptions and attitudes of the larger society. Nor was it merely the residuum of traditional society. Harmonism, or a culture of harmony, was instead the fruition of a conscious reworking of traditionalist values to suit the new industrial world, an invention that was part of a transculturation process that was both aided by and contributed to national crisis.

As we have seen, the Kyōchōkai also advocated institutional and legal reforms as means of minimizing industrial conflict and encouraging labour–management harmony. This approach was rooted in Japanese leaders' belief in the need to act in accordance with world trends. With the victory of the allied powers in World War I, the establishment of the ILO, the growth of the Labour Party in Britain and growing labour activism throughout the world, the trends of the times seemed to demand reforms of labour conditions and the recognition of union rights. The Kyōchōkai and the social bureaucrats in the Home Ministry, therefore, put forth and saw enacted a strengthened Factory Law, health insurance legislation, a strike mediation law and related worker protection laws. They also supported and wrote drafts of labour union legislation that would have sanctioned sound unionism. Based on an Anglo-American model, the Kyōchōkai argued that a healthy union movement would lessen labour unrest by providing workers with responsible representatives to give voice to their grievances and demands. The Kyōchōkai and most other government leaders defined healthy unions more narrowly than did officials in Britain or even the United States. Ideally, they were little more than mutual-aid societies that implicitly and explicitly supported labour–management cooperation and harmony. To allow them to go further, to sanction Western-style trade unionism, would be to encourage a radical, class-based union movement. In this area, as in other reform programmes, therefore, the Kyōchōkai aimed at satisfying the most pressing demands of the labour movement without sacrificing the basic goal of achieving industrial harmony in the service of national objectives. The seemingly liberal social agenda of the 1920s was an instrumental tactic employed to further profoundly conservative social values. The crisis that began with the Great Depression and the failure of the labour law in 1931 brought an end to interest in the Anglo-American labour relations model. New trends of economic control and labour mobilization emanating from Germany and Italy became more attractive.

The reform impulse of the 1920s, however, was not merely an imitation of Western developments, nor was it only a response to the situational requirements of Japanese nationalism. Official efforts at reform can be characterized instead as an effort to domesticate capitalism, to build a Japanese-style capitalism supportive of and sustained by Japanese values and Japanese ideals. During the Meiji period the few proponents of free-market liberal capitalism that did express their views were quickly drowned out by a chorus of voices seeking social protection from the operation of an untrammelled capitalist economy. Similarly, the reform agenda of the 1920s sought to dilute the independence of market capitalism while building a communitarian based modern economy.

While the Kyōchōkai and its allies worked to re-establish the traditionalist ideals and moral values of the nation's past they were certainly not anti-modernists. Their larger purpose was to promote a distinctive kind of modern economy and to bring stability to modern society. They hoped to indigenize modernity not destroy it. The irony is that these groups shared the historical stage with a large and expanding number of individuals who genuinely were anti-modernist. Folklorists, agrarianists, imperial communists and numerous other ideological splinter groups also extolled communitarianism and traditionalist morality.[2] They, however, were less concerned with domesticating modern development than they were · with its elimination. The new culture of harmony and the ideological basis of conservative reformism dovetailed with the cultural exceptionalism of the anti-modernists and the more generalized ultra-nationalist movement. The Kyōchōkai and the numerous other supporters of conservative reform, therefore, were contributors to a climate supportive of the creation of an authoritarian social and economic system inimical to democracy and freedom.

At the same time, the Kyōchōkai's moral conditioning efforts helped to establish the culture of harmony as a normative value, an expression of Japanese identity. In the post-World War II period Japan's bureaucratic and business leaders have never tired of pointing to the uniqueness of Japan's industrial values or the importance of those values in fostering the nation's economic success. Those values, according to one observer, have led to the 'humanistic corporate system' that is the hallmark of contemporary Japan's economic and social arrangements and is its contribution to the modern world.[3] In one sense, of course, this kind of rhetoric is prescriptive. By repeatedly emphasizing what they believe Japanese to be (Japanese are cooperative, they live and work in harmony and prefer family-style relations) elites are implicitly specifying what Japanese ought to be (in order to be Japanese one must be cooperative, loyal and committed to the firm as a family member).[4] Therefore, one's very identity as a Japanese is seen to be bound to the culture of harmony as a normative social value. Thus, the moralist inculcation programme of the Kyōchōkai and its Meiji forebearers has not ceased. Traditionalist notions of communitarianism and industrial harmony continue to be propagated and extolled as core values of a living history.[5] The reproduction and recreation of the communitarian tradition is ongoing.

Yet it seems clear that elite rhetoric is not simply cynical propagandizing. To contemporary elites industrial harmony not only should be but indeed genuinely *is* part of the nation's core values. In his recently published autobiography Akio Morita, the founder of the Sony Corporation, stated that the emergence of a culture of harmony and family-centred values in Japan's post-World War II firms was a natural development. Entrepreneurs and managers emphasized those values so that their companies could restore their economic viability. This approach was inevitable, Morita claims, since 'after all, Japanese tend to feel that way almost instinctively about their Japanese-ness'.[6] The culture of harmony, therefore, is not simply an economic stratagem nor is it linked to or derived from institutional changes. Instead, to Morita, and countless others as well, such values are instinctive, part of the nation's cultural heritage and sense of Japanese-ness itself. What this study has shown, however, is that this tradition, this set of normative values, was consciously invented and propagated over the last century. It did not just emerge of itself. The Kyōchōkai and earlier Meiji reformers, seeking to meet the new situational needs of an emerging industrial society, were the agents of its creation.

Notes

Abbreviations

HTH   Hito to hito
KS   Kyōchōkai shi
MBZ   Meiji bunka zenshū
NRUS   Nihon rōdō undō shiryō
NSHZS   Nihon shakai hoshō zenshi shiryō
RGS   Rōdō gyōsei shi
SEDS   Shibusawa Eiichi denki shiryō
SSJ   Shakai seisaku jihō

Introduction

1 For two very different examples of this view see Ezra Vogel, *Comeback: Case by Case: Building the Resurgence of American Business*, New York, Simon & Schuster, 1985, and James Abegglen and G. Stalk, *Kaisha: The Japanese Corporation: The New Competitors in World Business*, New York, Basic Books, 1985.
2 This term is from Nishio Kanji, 'Japan's Parallel Path to Modernity,' *Japan Echo*, 1983, vol. 10, no. 1, p. 69.
3 Two varieties of this view may be found in James Abegglen, *The Japanese Factory: Aspects of its Social Organization*, Glencoe, The Free Press, 1958, and Ōkōchi Kazuo, *Nihon no rōdō kumiai*, Tokyo, Tōyō keizai shimpō sha, 1954.
4 Sumiya Mikio, *Nihon no rōdō mondai*, Tokyo, Tokyo daigaku shuppankai, 1967, *passim*, and Koji Taira, *Economic Development and the Labor Market in Japan*, New York, Columbia University Press, 1970. In a recent study, Andrew Gordon has revised this assessment by emphasizing the bi-directionality of the process. *The Evolution of Labor Relations in Japan: Heavy Industry, 1853–1955*, Cambridge, Mass., Council on East Asian Studies, Harvard University, 1985.
5 Chalmers Johnson, *MITI and the Japanese Miracle: The Growth of Industrial Policy, 1925-1975*, Stanford, Calif., Stanford University Press, 1982.

6 For a different view see Sheldon Garon, *The State and Labor in Modern Japan*, Berkeley, University of California Press, 1987.

7 Theodore C. Bestor, *Neighborhood Tokyo*, Stanford, Calif., Stanford University Press, 1989, p. 2, *passim*.

8 This issue is discussed in Eric Hobsbawm, 'Introduction: Inventing Traditions', in *The Invention of Tradition*, ed. Eric Hobsbawm and Terence Ranger, Cambridge, Cambridge University Press, 1983. Also see Robert J. Smith, 'Presidential Address: Something Old, Something New – Tradition and Culture in the Study of Japan', *The Journal of Asian Studies*, 1989, vol. 48, no. 4, and Marilyn Robinson Waldman, 'Tradition as a Modality of Change: Islamic Examples', *History of Religions*, 1986, vol. 25, no. 4.

9 On political myth-making in the Meiji period see Carol Gluck, *Japan's Modern Myths: Ideology in the Late Meiji Period*, Princeton, Princeton University Press, 1985.

10 Ernest Gellner, *Culture, Identity, and Politics*, Cambridge, Cambridge University Press, 1987, pp. 10, 16–18.

1 Society as moral community

1 Robert A. Rosenstone, *Mirror in the Shrine: American Encounters with Meiji Japan*, Cambridge, Mass., Harvard University Press, 1988, p. 234.

2 Keio Gijuku (ed.), *Fukuzawa Yukichi zenshū*, 21 vols, Tokyo, Iwanami shoten, 1958–64, vol. 15, 333–7.

3 Inoue Tomoichi, *Kyūsai seido yōgi*, Tokyo, Hakubunkan, 1909, p. 536.

4 For detailed discussions of premodern social welfare activities see Ikeda Yoshimasa, *Nihon shakai fukushi shi*, Kyoto, Hōritsu bunka sha, 1986, pp. 45–130; Tsuji Zennosuke (ed.), *Jizen kyūsai shiryō*, Tokyo, Kinkōdō shoseki kabushiki kaisha, 1932; Yoshida Kyūichi, *Nihon shakai jigyō no rekishi*, rev. edn., Tokyo, Keisō shobō, 1966, pp. 18–104.

5 Michio Umegaki, *After the Restoration: The Beginning of Japan's Modern State*, New York, New York University Press, 1988, p. 45.

6 For examples of such relief activities see Arne Kalland and Jon Pederson, 'Famine and Population in Fukuoka Domain During the Tokugawa Period', *Journal of Japanese Studies*, 1984, vol. 10, no. 1, pp. 63–9; William W. Kelly, *Deference and Defiance in Nineteenth-Century Japan*, Princeton, NJ, Princeton University Press, 1985, pp. 66–76; James L. McClain, 'Failed Expectations: Kaga Domain on the Eve of the Meiji Restoration', *Journal of Japanese Studies*, 1988, vol. 14, no. 2, p. 412; and Dana Morris and Thomas C. Smith, 'Fertility and Mortality in an Outcast Village in Japan, 1750–1869', in *Family and Population in East Asian History*, ed. Susan B. Hanley and Arthur P. Wolf, Stanford, Calif., Stanford University Press, 1985, p. 231.

7 Kelly, op. cit., pp. 66–76, 101–4, 139.

8 Umegaki, op. cit., p. 103.

9 Ikeda, op. cit., pp. 175–6.

10 Yoshida Kyūichi, 'Meiji isshin ni okeru hinkon no henshitsu', in *Nihon no kyūhin seido*, ed. Nihon shakai jigyō daigaku kyūhin seido kenkyūkai, Tokyo, Keisō shobō, 1960, pp. 4–5.

11 Taikakai (ed.), *Naimushō shi*, 4 vols, Tokyo, Chihō zaimu kyōkai, 1971–2, vol. 2, p. 466.

12 ibid., p. 467.

13 Ikeda, op. cit., pp. 179–81.

14 Osaka-shi, Shakai-bu, Shomuka, *Shakai jigyō shi*, Osaka, Osaka-shi, Shakai-bu, Shomuka, 1924, pp. 96–7; Tsuji Hidetake, *Ōita-ken no shakai fukushi jigyō shi*, Ōita, Ōita-ken shakai fukushi kyōgikai, 1973, pp. 67–72; Yoshida Kyūichi, 'Meiji isshin ni okeru kyūhin seido', in *Nihon no kyūhin seido*, ed. Nihon shakai jigyō daigaku kyūhin seido kenkyūkai, Tokyo, Keisō shobō, 1960, pp. 85–6.

15 *Dajō ruiten*, vol. 1, sect. 82, doc. 48.

16 ibid., doc. 56.

17 Umegaki, op. cit., pp. 97–105.

18 *Dajō ruiten*, vol. 1, sect. 83.

19 Andrew Fraser, 'Local Administration: The Example of Awa-Tokushima', in *Japan in Transition: From Tokugawa to Meiji*, ed. Marius B. Jansen and Gilbert Rozman, Princeton, NJ, Princeton University Press, 1986, p. 124.

20 Shakai hoshō kenkyū-jo (ed.), *Nihon shakai hoshō zenshi shiryō*, 7 vols., Tokyo, Shiseidō, 1982–3, vol. 5, p. 690 (hereafter cited as *NSHZS*).

21 Taikakai, op. cit., vol. 2, p. 467.

22 Ogawa Masaaki, 'Jukkyū kisoku no seiritsu – Meiji zettaishugi kyūhin hō no keisei katei', in *Koseki seido to 'ie' seido*, ed. Fukushima Masao, Tokyo, Tokyo daigaku shuppankai, 1959, pp. 280–8.

23 Text of the draft in Uda Kikue, Takasawa Takeji, and Furukawa Kōjun, *Shakai fukushi no rekishi: seisaku to undō no tenkai*, Tokyo, Yūhikaku, 1977, p. 328.

24 Among other places, the text of the Regulation may be found in ibid., p. 329, and *NSHZS*, vol. 4, p. 6. See also *Dajō ruiten*, vol. 2, sect. 137, doc. 11.

25 Inoue, op. cit., p. 168.

26 Ogawa, op. cit., p. 311.

27 Meiji bunka kenkyūkai, ed., *Meiji bunka zenshū*, vol. 6, Tokyo, Nihon hyōronsha, 1955, p. 559 (hereafter cited as *MBZ*).

28 Fukuzawa Yukichi, *An Encouragement of Learning*, trans. David A. Dilworth and Umeyo Hirano, Tokyo, Sofia University Press, 1969, p. 1.

29 *NSHZS*, op. cit., vol. 4, p. 6–7 (my emphasis).

30 Kimura Takeo, *Nihon kindai shakai jigyō shi*, Tokyo, Minerubua shobō, 1984, p. 18.

31 Ikeda, op. cit., p. 192. Annual expenditures under the Regulation can be found in Rōdō undō shiryō iinkai (ed.), *Nihon rōdō undō shiryō*, 10 vols, Tokyo, Rōdō undō shiryō kankō iinkai, 1959–68, vol. 10, p. 606 (hereafter cited as *NRUS*).

32 *NSHZS*, op. cit., vol. 4, p. 6.

33 Ogawa, op. cit., pp. 312–13.

34 ibid., p. 298.

35 This term is Inoue Tomoichi's. Inoue, op. cit., p. 167.

36 Abe Isoo, *Shakai mondai kaishaku hō*, Tokyo, Tokyo semmon gakkō shuppan-bu, 1901, pp. 50–7.

37 On this theme see my 'Japan's Discovery of Poverty: Poverty and Social Welfare in the Nineteenth Century', *Journal of Asian History*, 1988, vol. 22, no. 1, pp. 16–23.

38 William W. Lockwood, *The Economic Development of Japan*, exp. edn, Princeton, NJ, Princeton University Press, 1968, pp. 20–1, 135t.

39 E. Sydney Crawcour, 'Industrialization and Technological Change, 1885–1920', in *The Cambridge History of Japan*, vol. 6, *The Twentieth Century*, ed. Peter Duus, Cambridge, Cambridge University Press, 1988, p. 419.

40 Robert E. Cole and Ken'ichi Tominaga, 'Japan's Changing Occupational Structure and Its Significance', in *Japanese Industrialization and Its Social Consequences*, ed. Hugh Patrick, Berkeley, University of California Press, 1976, p. 59t.

41 Lockwood, op. cit., pp. 27–35.

42 Gary R. Saxonhouse, 'Country Girls and Communication among Competitors in the Japanese Cotton-Spinning Industry', in Patrick, op. cit., p. 99t.

43 Gail Lee Bernstein, 'Women in the Silk-Reeling Industry in Nineteenth Century Japan', in *Japan and the World: Essays in Japanese History and Politics*, ed. Gail Lee Bernstein and Haruhiko Fukui, New York, St Martin's Press, 1988, p. 61. See also Saxonhouse, op. cit., and Mikiso Hane, *Peasants, Rebels and Outcastes: The Underside of Modern Japan*, New York, Pantheon Books, 1982, pp. 172–204.

44 Andrew Gordon, *The Evolution of Labor Relations In Japan: Heavy Industry, 1853–1955*, Cambridge, Mass, Council on East Asian Studies, Harvard University, 1985, pp. 22–5, 33–8; Hyōdō Tsutomu, *Nihon ni okeru rōshi kankei no tenkai*, Tokyo, Tokyo daigaku shuppankai, 1971, pp. 305–11.

45 Centre for East Asian Cultural Studies, ed. *Meiji Japan Through Contemporary Sources*, 3 vols, Tokyo, Centre for East Asian Cultural Studies, 1969–72, vol. 3, p. 13.

46 This theme is developed in Byron Marshall, *Capitalism and Nationalism in Prewar Japan: The Ideology of the Business Elite, 1868–1941*, Stanford, Calif., Stanford University Press, 1967.

47 Most Japanese language biographies of Shibusawa (and some in Western languages as well) are little more than hagiography. The most useful works on him are Shibusawa Hideo, *Chichi, Shibusawa Eiichi*, 2 vols, Tokyo, Jitsugyō no Nihon sha, 1959, and Tsuchiya Takao, *Shibusawa Eiichi den*, Tokyo, Tōyō shokan, 1955. In English see Johannes Hirschmeier, 'Shibusawa Eiichi: Industrial Pioneer', in *The State and Economic Enterprise in Japan*, ed. William W. Lockwood, Princeton, NJ, Princeton University Press, 1965, and Kyugoro Obata, *An Outline of the Life of Viscount Shibusawa*, Tokyo, Daiyamondo kigyo kabushiki kaisha, 1937. Documents by and about Shibusawa have been collected in Shibusawa Seien kinen zaidan ryūmonsha (ed.), *Shibusawa Eiichi denki shiryō*, 58 vols and 10 appendix vols, Tokyo, Shibusawa Seien kinen zaidan ryūmonsha, 1955–71 (hereafter cited as *SEDS*).

48 *SEDS*, op. cit., vol. 3, p. 729.

49 ibid., appendix volume, 5, p. 61.

50 Shibusawa Eiichi, *Shosei no daidō*, Tokyo, Jitsugyō no sekaisha, 1954, pp. 235–7.

51 Tsuchiya Takao, *Nihon keieisha seishin*, Tokyo, Keizai ōraisha, 1959, p. 156.

52 Shibusawa Eiichi, *Keizai to dōtoku*, Tokyo, Shibusawa Ō shōtokukai, 1938, pp. 2–3.

53 Tsuchiya, 1955, op. cit., p. 270.

54 References to this ideal can be found throughout Shibusawa's writings. The most complete statement is in his *Rongo to soroban*, Tokyo, Tōadō shobō, 1916.

55 Tsuchiya, 1959, op. cit., pp. 228–31.

56 Mutō Sanji zenshū kankōkai (ed.), *Mutō Sanji zenshū*, 8 vols, and 1 supplemental vol., Tokyo, Shinjusha, 1963–6, vol. 2, pp. 6–12, 60–72, 188–93.

57 Hirschmeier, op. cit., pp. 238–9.

58 Toyohara Matao, *Sakuma Teiichi shoden*, Tokyo, Shūeisha, 1904, pp. 105–9.

59 Quoted in Ronald Dore, 'The Modernizer as a Special Case: Japanese Factory Legislation, 1882–1911', *Comparative Studies in Society and History*, 1969, vol. 11, no. 4, p. 437.

60 On the early concern over health issues see Taikakai, op. cit., vol. 2, p. 479. Health problems and the Factory Law are discussed in Kagoyama Takashi, 'Kōjōhō no seiritsu to jisshi ni okeru kanryō gun', in *Nihon kindaika no kenkyū*, vol. 2, ed. Takahashi Kōhachirō, Tokyo, Tokyo daigaku shuppankai, 1972; Sugaya Akira, *Nihon iryō seisaku shi*, Tokyo, Nihon hyōronsha, 1977, pp. 73–100.

61 Rōdōshō, *Rōdō gyōsei shi*, 2 vols, Tokyo, Rōdō hōrei kyōkai, 1961–9, vol. 1, p. 22 (hereafter cited as *RGS*).

62 Sheldon Garon, *The State and Labor in Modern Japan*, Berkeley, University of California Press, 1987, p. 19.

63 *RGS*, op. cit., vol. 1, p. 50.

64 Obama Ritei, *Meiji bunka shiryō soshō*, vol. 1, Tokyo, Fūkan shobō, 1961, pp. 44, 48, 89–91.

65 Dore, op. cit.

66 Obama, op. cit., p. 46.

67 Hazama Hiroshi (ed.), *Nihon rōmu kanrishi shiryō shū*, vol. 2, Tokyo, Gozandō shoten, 1987, p. 7 (each section of the volume has separate pagination; citation is from section on the Tokyo Chamber of Commerce).

68 Nihon shakai jigyō daigaku (ed.), *Kubota Shizutarō ronshū*, Tokyo, Nihon shakai jigyō daigaku, 1980, p. 51.

69 Hazama, op. cit., p. 20 (Tokyo Chamber of Commerce section).

70 Obama, op. cit., p. 93.

71 ibid., p. 104.

72 ibid., p. 54.

73 ibid., p. 93.

74 Ariga Nagafumi, 'Shokkō jōrei seitei no jiki ni tsuite', *Kokka gakkai zasshi*, 1897, no. 129, p. 918.

75 Obama, op. cit., p. 55.

76   Nihon shakai jigyō daigaku, op. cit., p. 51.
77   Oka Minoru, *Kōjōhō ron*, rev. edn., Tokyo, Yūhikaku, 1917, p. 142.
78   *NRUS*, op. cit., vol. 3, p. 208.
79   Shakai seisaku gakkai shiryō shūsei hensan iinkai, ed., *Shakai seisaku gakkai shiryō shūsei*, vol. 1, Tokyo, Ochanomizu shobō, 1977, p. 358.
80   ibid., p. 117.
81   On these themes see Kenneth B. Pyle, *The New Generation of Meiji Japan: Problems of Cultural Identity*, Stanford, Calif., Stanford University Press, 1969, and Carol Gluck, *Japan's Modern Myths: Ideology in the Meiji Period*, Princeton, NJ, Princeton University Press, 1985. In Japanese see especially Ishida Takeshi, *Meiji seiji shisōshi kenkyū*, Tokyo, Miraisha, 1954.
82   Sakai Yūzaburō, 'Shakai mondai', *Kokumin no tomo*, (3 May 1890), no. 81, p. 22.
83   'Kōgi no shakai mondai ni taisuru ikō', *Shakai zasshi*, 1897, vol. 1, no. 1, pp. 47–50.
84   Kōtoku Shūsui, 'Shakai mondai kenkyūkai ni tsuite', *Shakai zasshi*, 1897, vol. 1, no. 1, p. 60; Yamaji Aizan, 'Genji no shakai mondai oyobi shakaishugisha', *Dokuritsu hyōron*, 1908, no. 3, reprint in *MBZ*, op. cit., pp. 374–5.
85   On the emergence of social policy ideas in Japan see Kenneth B. Pyle, 'Advantages of Followership: German Economics and Japanese Bureaucrats, 1890–1925', *Journal of Japanese Studies*, 1974, vol. 1, no. 1; Chuhei Sugiyama, 'The Development of Economic Thought in Meiji Japan', *Modern Asian Studies*, 1968, vol. 2, no. 4; and Sumiya Etsuji, *Nihon keizaigaku*, Tokyo, Minerubua shobō, 1958.
86   Quoted in Sugiyama, op. cit., p. 337.
87   Kanai En, 'Boasonaddo-shi no keizai ron o hyōsu', *Hōgaku kyōkai zasshi*, 1892, vol. 10, no. 12, reprint in *MBZ*, op. cit., pp. 486–7.
88   'Shakai seisaku gakkai shuisho', *Kokka gakkai zasshi*, 1899, vol. 13, no. 150, reprint in Shakai seisaku gakkai shiryō shūsei hensan iinkai (ed.), *Shakai seisaku gakkai shiryō shūsei*, appendix vol. 1, Tokyo, Ochanomizu shobō, 1978, p. 38.
89   William Harbutt Dawson, *Bismark and State Socialism*, London, Swan Sonnenschein, 1891, p. v.

2 Founding of the Kyōchōkai

1   Hiroshi Hazama, 'Historical Changes in the Life Style of Industrial Workers', in *Japanese Industrialization and Its Social Consequences*, ed. Hugh Patrick, Berkeley, University of California Press, 1976, p. 29.
2   This term is Kozo Yamamura's, 'Then Came the Great Depression, Japan's Interwar Years', in *The Great Depression Revisited: Essays in the Economics of the Thirties*, ed. Herman van der Wee, The Hague, Netherlands, Martinus Nijohoff, 1972, p. 183.
3   Takamura Naosuke, 'Dokusen shihonshugi no kakuritsu to chūshō kigyō', in *Iwanami kōza: Nihon rekishi*, vol. 18, Tokyo, Iwanami shoten, 1975, p. 50; Kozo Yamamura, 'The Japanese Economy, 1911–1930: Concentration, Conflicts, and Crises', in *Japan in Crisis: Essays*

on Taishō Democracy, ed. Bernard S. Silberman and H.D. Harootunian, Princeton, NJ, Princeton University Press, 1974, p. 302.

4 Robert E. Cole and Ken'ichi Tominaga, 'Japan's Changing Occupational Structure and Its Significance', in Patrick, op. cit., pp. 57–8.

5 ibid., p. 65.

6 Yamamura, 1972, op. cit., p. 183.

7 For a sampling of profit rates in shipping, shipbuilding, and banking industries see Takamura, op. cit., p. 61.

8 Ikeda Makoto, *Nihon kikaikō kumiai setsuritsu shiron*, Tokyo, Nihon hyōronsha, 1970, p. 105.

9 ibid., pp. 101–5; Yamamura, 1974, op. cit., pp. 306–7; and idem, 1972, op. cit.

10 On strike demands see Rōdō undō shiryō iinkai (ed.), *Nihon rōdō undō shiryō*, 10 vols, Tokyo, Rōdō undō shiryō kankō iinkai, 1959–68, vol. 10, pp. 470–1 (hereafter cited as *NRUS*). It is, however, difficult to speak with assurance about wartime wage figures because of the very rapid entry of unskilled, low-paid rural workers into the workforce, Ikeda, op. cit., pp. 101–5.

11 Endō Yoshinobu, 'Taishō demokurashii ki no Nihon guntai no shisō dōkō', *Rekishigaku kenkyū*, 1981, no. 497, pp. 16–18.

12 Shimada Toshio, 'Jikyoku mondai kanken', *Seiyū*, 1918, no. 223, p. 3.

13 Usui Katsumi, 'Verusaiyu, Washington taisei to Nihon no shihaizō', in *Kindai Nihon seiji shisō shi*, vol. 2, ed. Hashikawa Bunzō and Matsumoto Sannosuke, *Kindai Nihon shisō shi taikei*, vol. 4, Tokyo, Yūhikaku, 1970, pp. 109–16.

14 Arahata Kanson, *Arahata Kanson chōsakushū*, 10 vols, Tokyo, Heibonsha, 1976–7, vol. 9, p. 352.

15 ibid., vol. 6, p. 441.

16 Gail L. Bernstein, 'The Russian Revolution, the Early Japanese Socialists and the Problem of Dogmatism', *Studies in Comparative Communism*, 1976, vol. 9, no. 4, pp. 330–5. See also Mitani Taichirō, *Taishō demokurashii ron*, Tokyo, Chūō kōronsha, 1974, pp. 93–100.

17 Stephen S. Large, *The Rise of Labor in Japan: The Yūaikai, 1912–1919*, Tokyo, Sophia University, 1972, pp. 95–7, 147–8.

18 Ivan Morris, *The Nobility of Failure: Tragic Heroes in the History of Japan*, New York, New American Library, 1976, pp. 185, 404n.

19 Matsuo Takayoshi, *Taishō demokurashii no kenkyū*, Tokyo, Aoki shoten, 1966), p. 207.

20 Watanabe Tōru, 'Rōdō mondai, rōdō undō e no ronhyō', in *Taishō-ki no kyūshinteki jiyūshugi: Tōyō keizai shimpō o chūshin toshite*, ed. Inoue Kiyoshi and Watanabe Tōru, Tokyo, Tōyō Keizai shimpōsha, 1972, p. 495.

21 Hashikawa Bunzō, 'Shōwa isshin no ronri to shinri', in *Kindai Nihon seiji shisō shi*, vol. 2, ed. Hashikawa Bunzō and Matsumoto Sannosuke, *Kindai Nihon shisō shi taikei*, vol. 4, Tokyo, Yūhikaku, 1970, p. 210; Oka Yoshitake and Hayashi Shigeru (eds), *Taishō demokurashii-ki no seiji: Matsumoto Gōkichi seiji nisshi*, Tokyo, Iwanami shoten, 1959, p. 35.

22 Mitani, op. cit., p. 25.

23 Quoted in Alan Atwood Stone, 'The Vanishing Village: The Ashio Copper Mine Pollution Case, 1890–1907', PhD diss., University of Washington, 1974, p. 138.

24 Quoted in Ishida Takeshi, 'Kawakami Hajime ni okeru itan e no michi', *Shisō*, 1979, no. 664, p. 8.

25 On the Relief Committee's organization, agenda and activities see Naimushō, shakai kyoku, *Kyūsai jigyō chōsakai hōkoku*, Tokyo, Naimushō, Shakai kyoku, n.d.

26 Ōshima Kiyoshi, *Takano Iwasaburō den*, Tokyo, Iwanami shoten, 1968, pp. 124–36; Byron K. Marshall, 'Academic Factionalism in Japan: The Case of the Todai Economics Department, 1919–1939', *Modern Asian Studies*, 1978, vol. 12, part 4, pp. 531–3. On the Tsukiji project see Sekiya Kōichi (ed.), *Seikatsu koten sōsho*, vol. 6, *Tsukijima chōsa*, Tokyo, Kōseikan, 1970.

27 Ōshima, op. cit. p. 113.

28 Naimushō, Shakai kyoku, op. cit., pp. 12–16.

29 Ōshima, op. cit. pp. 119–20.

30 Naimushō, Shakai kyoku, op. cit., p. 30.

31 Kushida Tamizō, *Kushida Tamizō zenshū*, 4 vols, Tokyo, Kaizōsha, 1949, vol. 4, pp. 221–7; Morita Tatsuo, 'Kyūsai jigyō chōsakai no setchi to waga shakai seisaku', *Kokka gakkai zasshi*, 1918, vol. 32, no. 8, pp. 133–41; Takano Iwasaburō, 'Kyūsai jigyō chōsakai no juyō ninmu', *Kokka gakkai zasshi*, 1918, vol. 32, no. 9, pp. 153–7. See also Ujihara Shōjirō, 'Dai-ichiji taisengo no rōdō chōsa to *Yoka seikatsu no kenkyū*', in *Seikatsu koten sōsho*, vol. 8, *Yoka seikatsu no kenkyū*, ed. Ujihara Shōjirō, Tokyo, Kōseikan, 1970, pp. 10–14.

32 Morito, op. cit., p. 136.

33 Kushida, op. cit., vol. 4, p. 224.

34 Maruyama Tsurukichi, 'Kyūsai jigyō no han-i', *Shimin*, 1919, vol. 14, no. 1, p. 13.

35 Miwa Ryōichi, 'Rōdō kumiahō seitei mondai no rekishiteki ichi', in *Ryōtaisenkan no Nihon shihonshugi*, ed. Andō Yoshio, Tokyo, Tokyo daigaku shuppankai, 1979, p. 239; Tsuchiana Fumito, 'Dai-ichiji taisengo no shakai seisaku no tenkai', *Takushoku daigaku ronshū*, 1978, no. 115, pp. 100–2.

36 Banno Junji, '"Taishō demokurashii-ki" no seiji', in *Nihon kindaishi yōsetsu*, ed. Takahashi Kōhachirō, Nagahara Keiji, and Ōishi Kaichirō, Tokyo, Tokyo daigaku shuppankai, 1980, pp. 251–2.

37 Nakano Seigō, 'Yatō no nanzo kekkisezaru', *Nihon oyobi Nihonjin*, 1916, no. 690, pp. 23–30.

38 Hara's 'realism' is a major theme in Mitani Taichirō, *Nihon seitō seiji no keisei*, Tokyo, Tokyo daigaku shuppankai, 1967; Tetsuo Najita, *Hara Kei in the Politics of Compromise, 1905–1915*, Cambridge, Mass., Harvard University Press, 1967.

39 Kamii Yoshihiko, 'Dai-ichiji taisen chokugo no rōdō seisaku', *Rōdō undō shi kenkyū*, 1979, no. 62, pp. 150–81.

40 Large, op. cit., pp. 81–106.

41 Sen Katayama, *The Labor Movement in Japan*, Chicago, Charles H. Kerr & Co., 1918, p. 6.

42 Mitani, 1967, op. cit., pp. 16–26.
43 Nakano, op. cit., pp. 26–7. Biographical details of Tokonami derived from Maeda Renzan, *Tokonami Takejirō den*, Tokyo, Tokonami Takejirō denki kankōkai, 1939; Taikakai (ed.), *Naimushō shi*, 4 vols, Tokyo, Chihō zaimu kyōkai, 1970–2, vol. 4, pp. 98–107. On the relationship between Hara and Tokonami see Mitani, 1967, op. cit., p. 20; Najita, op. cit., pp. 37–8.
44 Taikakai, op. cit., vol. 4, p. 104.
45 Mitani, 1967, op. cit., p. 20; Najita, op. cit., p. 37.
46 Kenneth B. Pyle, 'The Technology of Japanese Nationalism: The Local Improvement Movement, 1900–1918', *Journal of Asian Studies*, 1973, vol. 33, no. 1, p. 56.
47 'Tokonami naishō no kunji', *Seiyū*, 1918, no. 223, p. 48.
48 ibid.
49 *Nihon rōdō nenkan*, 1920, pp. 846–7.
50 Shibusawa Seien kinen zaidan ryūmonsha (ed.), *Shibusawa Eiichi denki shiryō*, 58 vols and 10 appendix vols, Tokyo, Shibusawa Seien kinen zaidan ryūmonsha, 1955–71 (hereafter cited as *SEDS*), vol. 31, p. 477.
51 ibid., vol. 31, pp. 615, 621, 641.
52 *Nihon rōdō nenkan*, 1920, p. 922. Various aspects of Kyōchōkai development are discussed in Fujino Yutaka, 'Kyōchō seisaku no suishin', in *Kindai Nihon no tōgō to teikō*, vol. 3, ed. Kano Masanao and Yui Masaomi, Tokyo, Nihon hyōronsha, 1982; Hamaguchi Haruhiko, 'Kyōchōkai to Dai-ichiji taisengo no rōshi kankei', *Shakai kagaku tōkyū*, 1970, vol. 15, no. 3,; Yonekawa Norio, 'Kyōchōkai no rōdō kumiai ron', *Keizai ronshū* (Niigata daigaku), 1979, no. 26–7; idem, 'Kyōchōkai no seiritsu katei', *Niigata daigaku keizaigaku nempō*, 1979, no. 3. The official history of the Kyōchōkai is 'Kyōchōkai' kaiwakai, *Kyōchōkai shi*, Tokyo, 'Kyōchōkai' kaiwakai, 1965 (hereafter cited as *KS*) which is a nearly complete published version of a 1947 ms. *Kyōchōkai shi* held by the Ōhara shakai mondai kenkyūjo. Pages 463–502 of the ms. are not included in *KS*.
53 Nihon kōgyō kurabu gojūnenshi hensan iinkai (ed.), *Zaikai kaisōroku*, 2 vols, Tokyo, Nihon kōgyō kurabu, 1967, vol. 1, p. 14.
54 Morita Yoshio, *Nihon keieisha dantai hatten shi*, Tokyo, Nikkan rōdō tsūshinsha, 1958, pp. 70–3; Nakamura Mototada, *Nihon kōgyō kurabu nijūgonenshi*, 2 vols, Tokyo, Nihon kōgyō kurabu, 1943, vol. 1, pp. 96–7, 130–2.
55 Text of the Prospectus in Nakamura, op. cit., vol. 1, pp. 134–5.
56 ibid., p. 135.
57 For the history and goals of the Association see Kikuchi Takenori, 'Shihon rōdō mondai kenkyūkai', in *Rōshi mondai sōsho*, vol. 1, ed. Shihon rōdō mondai kenkyūkai, Tokyo, Shihon rōdō mondai kenkyūkai, 1919.
58 *KS*, op. cit., p. 3.
59 Kikuchi, op. cit., p. 104.
60 ibid., p. 108.
61 Honda Seiichi, 'Naisei-jō oyobi kokusai-jō yori kantaru rōdō seisaku', *Rōshi mondai sōsho*, vol. 1, p. 182.
62 *SEDS*, op. cit., vol. 31, pp. 460–1.

63 *KS*, op. cit., pp. 6–9; *SEDS*, op. cit., vol. 31, p. 461–75.
64 Suzuki Bunji, *Rōdō undō nijūnen*, Tokyo, Ichigensha, 1931, pp. 191–5; Large, op. cit., pp. 175–7. Suzuki's version of this meeting and its aftermath is questionable at best. He was under great pressure from other union leaders over his relationship with Shibusawa and he clearly sought to distance himself from the Kyōchōkai. At the very least, his comment that his relationship with Shibusawa was severed as a result of the meeting is false. As early as 22 September 1919 the two men met together on the ILO representation issue and issued a joint statement. According to Shibusawa's appointment book they met at least fourteen times following the Kyōchōkai-related meeting. *Tokyo asahi shimbun*, 23 September 1919, p. 5; *Kokumin shimbun*, 24 September 1919, p. 5; *SEDS*, op. cit., vol. 31, pp. 455–6.
65 *SEDS*, op. cit., vol. 31, p. 441.
66 Hazama Hiroshi, *Nihon ni okeru rōshi kyōchō no teiryū*, Tokyo, Waseda daigaku shuppan-bu, 1978, pp. 231–3.
67 Hara Kei, *Hara Kei nikki*, 9 vols, ed. Hara Kei'ichirō, Tokyo, Kengensha, 1950, vol. 8, p. 298.
68 *KS*, op. cit., p. 9.
69 *SEDS*, op. cit., vol. 31, pp. 485–7.
70 For a complete list of contributors see *KS*, op. cit., pp. 151–4.
71 Suzuki Bunji, 'Rōdō kyōchōkai o hyōsu', *Rōdō oyobi sangyō*, 1919, vol. 8, no. 9, pp. 2–3.
72 ibid., p. 3.
73 Sheldon Garon, *The State and Labor in Modern Japan*, Berkeley, University of California Press, 1987, pp. 45–7.
74 Kazahaya Yasoji, *Nihon shakai seisaku shi*, 2nd edn, Tokyo, Nihon hyōronsha, 1947, p. 352.
75 *Osaka mainichi shimbun*, 16 August 1919, p. 5.
76 *Kyōchōkai shi*, ms., op. cit., p. 474; Yonekawa, 'Kyōchōkai no setsuritsu', op. cit., p. 67.
77 Nakamura, op. cit., vol. 1, p. 7; Nihon kōgyō kurabu gojūnenshi hensan iinkai, *Nihon kōgyō kurabu gojūnenshi*, Tokyo, Nihon kōgyō kurabu, 1972, pp. 129–30.
78 Wada Toyoji hensanjo, *Wada Toyoji den*, Tokyo, Wada Toyoji den hensanjo, 1926, p. 456.
79 ibid., pp. 456–9; Nakamura, op. cit., vol. 1, p. 137; Nihon kōgyō kurabu gojūnenshi hensan iinkai, 1967, op. cit., vol. 1, p. 15.

3 Kyōchōkai visions of industrial society

1 Tokutomi Iichirō, *Hakushaku Kiyoura Keigo den*, 2 vols, Tokyo, Hakushaku Kiyoura Keigo den kankōkai, 1932, vol. 1, p. 667.
2 Oka Yoshitake, 'Generational Conflict after the Russo-Japanese War', in *Conflict in Modern Japanese History: The Neglected Tradition*, eds Tetsuo Najita and J. Victor Koschmann, Princeton, NJ, Princeton University Press, 1982, p. 203.
3 Hyōdō Tsutomu, *Nihon ni okeru rōshi kankei no tenkai*, Tokyo, Tokyo daigaku shuppankai, 1971, p. 368.

4 The text of the Kyōchōkai Principles can be found in 'Kyōchōkai' kaiwakai, *Kyōchōkai shi*, Tokyo, 'Kyōchōkai' kaiwakai, 1965 (hereafter cited as *KS*), p. 6 and *Shakai seisaku jihō* (hereafter cited as *SSJ*), 1920, no. 1, pp. 171–2. The Act of Endowment is reproduced in *KS*, pp. 11–14. A third founding document, the Kyōchōkai Founding Prospectus (Kyōchōkai setsuritsu shuisho), which defined the organization's basic objectives, can be found in *KS*, p. 5; *SSJ*, 1920, no. 1, p. 171; and Kyōchōkai, *Saikin no shakai undō*, Tokyo, Kyōchōkai, 1929, p. 992.

5 Yoshio Iwamoto, 'Aspects of the Proletarian Literary Movement in Japan', in *Japan in Crisis: Essays on Taishō Democracy*, ed. Bernard S. Silberman and H.D. Harootunian, Princeton, NJ, Princeton University Press, 1974, pp. 157–9.

6 Tokonami Takejirō, *Rōdō mondai*, n.p., 1922, pp. 7, 23.

7 Tokonami Takejirō, 'Minryoku kanyō no shingi', *Shimin*, 1919, vol. 14, no. 6, p. 2.

8 ibid., p. 3.

9 'Tokonami naishō no kunji', *Seiyū*, 1921, no. 254, p. 3.

10 Tokonami, 1922, op. cit., pp. 2–3.

11 ibid., p. 6.

12 ibid., p. 4.

13 ibid., p. 6.

14 'Seimu chōsakai', *Seiyū*, 1918, no. 232, p. 49.

15 'Tokonami naishō no kunji', *Seiyū*, 1918, no. 223, p. 48.

16 The term *kyōchō*, which is the root word of Kyōchōkai and *kyōchōshugi*, was a coinage derived from the first syllables in the two words of the phrase *kyōdō chōwa* (harmony and cooperation), Shibusawa Seien kinen zaidan ryūmonsha (ed.), *Shibusawa Eiichi denki shiryō*, 58 vols and 10 appendix vols, Tokyo, Shibusawa Seien kinen zaidan ryūmonsha, 1955–71 (hereafter cited as *SEDS*), vol. 31, pp. 477, 479.

17 Tokonami, 1922, op. cit., p. 9.

18 'Seimu chōsakai', op. cit., p. 49.

19 Tokonami, 1919, op. cit., p. 2.

20 Maeda Renzan, *Tokonami Takejirō den*, Tokyo, Tokonami Takejirō denki kankōkai, 1939, p. 514.

21 Tokonami, 1922, op. cit., p. 22.

22 ibid., p. 13.

23 Kamii Yoshihiko, 'Dai-ichiji taisen chokugo no rōdō seisaku', *Rōdō undō shi kenkyū*, 1979, no. 62, p. 161.

24 'Seimu chōsakai', op. cit., p. 49.

25 Tokonami, 1922, op. cit., p. 12.

26 ibid., pp. 12–16.

27 'Rōdō mondai tokubetsu iinkai', *Seiyū*, 1919, no. 235, pp. 49–50; *Nihon rōdō nenkan*, 1920, p. 878.

28 'Rōdō mondai tokubetsu iinkai', op. cit. pp. 49–50; *Nihon rōdō nenkan*, 1920, p. 879. Tokonami made this statement in a speech on 25 October 1919. Although the exact wording of the statement differs substantially in these two sources, the basic meaning is consistent.

29 *SEDS*, op. cit., vol. 31, p. 464.
30 'Seimu chōsakai', op. cit., p. 49; *Nihon rōdō nenkan*, 1920, p. 449. See also Kawarada Kakichi, 'Iwayuru rōdō kumiai no kōnin to Chian keisatsuhō dai-jūshichi jo ni tsuite', in *Rōshi mondai sōsho*, vol. 1, ed. Shihon rōdō mondai kenkyūkai, Tokyo, Shihon rōdō mondai kenkyūkai, 1919, pp. 149–55.
31 Rōdōshō, *Rōdō gyōsei shi*, vol. 1, Tokyo, Rōdō hōrei kyōkai, 1961 (hereafter cited as *RGS*), p. 128.
32 Kawarada, op. cit., pp. 157–8.
33 Kamii, op. cit., p. 163.
34 'Tokonami naishō no kunji', op. cit., p. 48.
35 On the various interpretations of *kokutai* see Richard H. Minear, *Japanese Tradition and Western Law: Emperor, State and Law in the Thought of Hozumi Yatsuka*, Cambridge, Mass., Harvard University Press, 1970, pp. 64–8.
36 *SEDS*, op. cit., vol. 31, p. 478.
37 ibid., vol. 31, p. 460.
38 ibid., p. 605.
39 ibid., p. 612.
40 ibid., p. 621.
41 ibid., p. 630.
42 ibid., p. 622.
43 ibid., p. 613.
44 ibid., p. 476.
45 Shibusawa Eiichi, 'Rōdō mondai kaiketsu no konpongi', *SSJ*, 1920, no. 1, p. 3..
46 *SEDS*, op. cit., vol. 31, pp. 630–1.
47 Shibusawa Eiichi, 'Kyōchōkai', in *Rōshi mondai sōsho*, vol. 2, ed. Shihon rōdō mondai kenkyūkai, Tokyo, Shihon rōdō mondai kenkyūkai, 1919, p. 202.
48 *SEDS*, op. cit., vol. 31, p. 624.
49 ibid., vol. 31, p. 643.
50 ibid., vol. 31, pp. 646–7.
51 Shibusawa, 1920, op. cit., p. 5.
52 Kawazu Sen, *Shakai mondai ni tsuite*, Tokyo, Naimushō, Chihō kyoku, 1920, pp. 33–4.
53 Nakagawa Keiichirō, Chō Yukio and Kimbara Samon, 'Zaibatsu to kanryō: sono musubitsuki yuen', *Rekishi kōron*, 1982, no. 76, p. 55.
54 Shakai seisaku gakkai shiryō shūsei hensan iinkai, ed. *Shakai seisaku gakkai shiryō shūsei*, vol. 1, Tokyo, Ochanomizu shobō, 1977, p. 49.
55 *SEDS*, op. cit., vol. 31, p. 614.
56 ibid., p. 475.
57 Warren W. Smith Jr, *Confucianism in Modern Japan: A Study of Conservatism in Japanese Intellectual History*, 2nd edn, Tokyo, Hokuseido Press, 1973, pp. 103–45.
58 Ōki Tōkichi, 'Kangaku to shisō mondai', *Shibun*, 1920, vol. 2, no. 4, p. 3.
59 Kaneko Kentarō, 'Nihon no hatten to kangaku no seiryoku', *Shibun*, 1919, vol. 1, no. 1, p. 18.

60 Mizuno Rentarō, 'Kōfup¯shi no michi', *Shibun*, 1927, vol. 2, no. 12, p. 3.

61 Kyōchōkai, 1929, op. cit., pp. 283–5.

62 This letter is contained in an uncatalogued file entitled 'Sōgi, 1920', held in the Ōhara shakai mondai kenkyūjo.

63 'Kyōchōkai no taidō', *Rōdō*, 1920, vol. 9, no. 9, p. 1.

64 Suzuki Bunji, 'Kanryōshugi ka minponshugi ka', *Rōdō oyobi sangyō*, 1919, vol. 8, no. 11, pp. 2, 3.

65 *SEDS*, op. cit., vol. 31, p. 516.

66 Biographical details on Soeda may be found in Soeda Keiichirō kun kinenkai, *Soeda Keiichirō den*, Tokyo, Soeda Keiichirō kun kinenkai, 1955.

67 Nagai Tōru, 'Kyōchōkai no omoide', in *KS*, op. cit., p. 179. On Nagai's career see Hata Ikuhiko, *Senzen-ki Nihon kanryōsei no seido soshiki, jinji*, Tokyo, Tokyo daigaku shuppankai, 1981, p. 170.

68 Biographical details in Shimomura Kojin, *Kono hito o miyo*, Tokyo, Tazawa Yoshiharu kenshōkai, 1966; Tazawa Yoshiharu kinenkai, *Tazawa Yoshiharu*, Tokyo, Tazawa Yoshiharu kinenkai, 1954.

69 Soeda Keiichirō kun kinenkai, op. cit., p. 59.

70 Nagai Tōru, 'Kyōchōkai sengen ni tsuite', *SSJ*, 1921, no. 6, p. 1.

71 The text of the manifesto may be found, among other places, in *KS*, op. cit., pp. 21–2; Kyōchōkai, 1929, op. cit., p. 994.

72 Sumiya Mikio, *Katayama Sen*, Tokyo, Tokyo daigaku shuppankai, pp. 48–9.

73 Sumiya Etsuji et. al., *Taishō demokurashii no shisō*, Tokyo, Haga shoten, 1969, p. 260.

74 Matsusawa Hiroaki, *Nihon shakaishugi no shisō*, Tokyo, Chikuma shobō, 1973, p. 147.

75 For a sampling of union leaders' view on paternalism see Sōdōmei gojūnenshi kankō iinkai, *Sōdōmei gojūnenshi*, vol. 1, Tokyo, Sōdōmei gojūnenshi kankō iinkai, 1964, pp. 172–7; Tanaka Sōgorō (ed.), *Shiryō, Taishō shakai undō shi*, vol. 1, Tokyo, San'ichi shobō, 1970, p. 153.

76 Soeda Keiichirō, 'Kyōchōshugi no seishin narabi ni Kyōchōkai no jigyō', in *Shakai seisaku kōgiroku*, vol. 3, ed. Kyōchōkai, Tokyo, Kyōchōkai, 1923, p. 20.

77 Soeda Keiichirō, 'Rōshi kyōchō no konpongi', *Shimin*, 1920, vol. 15, no. 2, pp. 17–18.

78 Soeda Keiichirō, 'Rōdō mondai no kaiketsu', *SSJ*, 1921, no. 5, p. 2.

79 Soeda, 1923, op. cit., p. 22.

80 Soeda Keiichirō, 'Gojin no shimei', *Hito to hito* (hereafter cited as *HTH*), 1921, vol. 1, no. 1, p. 2.

81 Soeda, 1920, op. cit., p. 19.

82 This theme is developed in Matsuo Takayoshi, *Taishō demokurashii no kenkyū*, Tokyo, Aoki shoten, 1966, pp. 159–87; Matsusawa, op. cit., pp. 146–51; Sumiya Mikio, *Nihon no rōdō mondai*, Tokyo, Tokyo daigaku shuppankai, 1967, pp. 9–24; Yasuda Hiroshi, 'Nihon teikokushugi kakuritsu-ki no rōdō mondai', *Rekishigaku kenkyū*, 1980, no. 497, p. 129. In English see Thomas C. Smith, 'The Right to

Benevolence: Dignity and Japanese Workers, 1890–1920', *Comparative Studies in Society and History*, 1984, vol. 26, no. 4.

83 Hazama Hiroshi, *Nihon ni okeru rōshi kyōchō no teiryū*, Tokyo, Waseda daigaku shuppan-bu, 1978, pp. 193–4.

84 Matsunaga Shōzō, 'Shakai mondai no hassei', in *Iwanami Kōza: Nihon rekishi*, vol. 16, Tokyo, Iwanami shoten, 1976, pp. 251–5.

85 Hazama, 1978, op. cit., pp. 193–4.

86 Nihon kindai shiryō kenkyūkai (ed.), *Taishō goki Keiho kyoku kankō shakai undō shiryō*, Tokyo, Nihon kindai shiryō kenkyūkai, 1968, pp. 204–5.

87 Margit Maria Nagy, '"How Shall We Live?": Social Change, The Family Institution and Feminism in Prewar Japan', PhD diss., University of Washington, 1981, pp. 102–8; Yutaka Arase, 'Mass Communication between the Two World Wars', *The Developing Economies*, 1967, vol. 5, no. 4, pp. 752–62.

88 Sekiya Kōichi (ed.), *Seikatsu koten sōsho*, vol. 6, *Tsukijima chōsa*, Tokyo, Koseikan, 1970, p. 158.

89 Shiozawa Masatada, 'Rōdō mondai no honshitsu to sono kaiketsu hōshin', *SSJ*, 1920, no. 4, p. 15.

90 ibid.; Shiozawa Masatada, 'Jinkaku sonchōshugi', *Osaka mainichi shimbun*, 9 December 1919.

91 Kiga Kanjū, 'Rōshi kyōchō no hito hōhō', *SSJ*, 1920, no. 2, p. 5.

92 Tazawa Yoshiharu, 'Kyōchōshugi no dōtokuteki kisō', *SSJ*, 1921, no. 9, p. 2.

93 Kamishima Jirō, *Kindai Nihon no seishin kōzō*, Tokyo, Iwanami shoten, 1961, pp. 26–7.

94 Matsumoto Sannosuke, *Kindai Nihon no chiteki jōkyō*, Tokyo, Chūō kōronsha, 1974, p. 121.

95 ibid., pp. 121–2, 160.

96 ibid., pp. 328–9.

97 Peter Duus, 'Yoshino Sakuzō: The Christian as Political Critic', *Journal of Japanese Studies*, 1978, vol. 4, no. 2, pp. 316–18.

98 Nagai Tōru, 'Kyōchō to tōsō', *HTH*, vol. 1, no. 1, p. 50.

99 Kimbara Samon, *Taishō-ki no seitō to kokumin*, Tokyo, Hanawa shobō, 1973, pp. 182–3.

100 Shiozawa, 1920, op. cit., pp. 21–2.

101 Kuwata Kumazō, 'Ōshū taisen to rōdō mondai', in *Kuwata Kumazō ikōshū*, ed. Kuwata Kazuo, Tokyo, Seikōsha, 1934, p. 307.

102 Kuwata Kumazō, 'Rōdō mondai ni kansuru seikai no taisei', *SSJ*, 1920, no. 1, pp. 6–14; Soeda, 1921, op. cit., p. 4.

103 Kuwata, 1934, op. cit., p. 317.

104 Nagai, 1921, op. cit., pp. 49–50; Nishida Hirotarō, 'Shakai kaizō ni taisuru rōdōsha no sekimu', *HTH*, 1921, vol. 1, no. 1, pp. 10–13.

105 Nagai, 1921, op. cit., p. 50.

106 Soeda Keiichirō, 'Sōkan isshūnen ni saishite', *HTH*, 1922, vol. 2, no. 4, p. 3.

107 Soeda, 'Gojin no shimei', 1921, op. cit., pp. 4–5.

108 Soeda, 1923, op. cit., p. 16.

109 Soeda Keiichirō, 'Kyōchō ni taisuru nishu no hihan', *SSJ*, 1921, no. 7, p. 2.

4 To create society anew

1 Soeda Keiichirō, 'Kyōchō ni taisuru nishu no hihan', *SSJ*, 1921, no. 7, p. 2.

2 On the evolution of Tokyo's employment agency control legislation see Rōdōshō, *RGS*, vol. 1, Tokyo, Rōdō hōrei kyōkai, 1961, pp. 159–61.

3 Margit Maria Nagy, '"How Shall We Live?": Social Change, The Family Institution and Feminism in Prewar Japan', PhD diss., University of Washington, 1981, p. 134.

4 Abe Isoo, *Shitsugyō mondai*, Tokyo, Nihon hyōronsha, 1929, p. 119; Kyōchōkai, *Saikin no shakai undō*, Tokyo, Kyōchōkai, 1929, pp. 870–1.

5 Hugh T. Patrick, 'The Economic Muddle of the 1920's', in *Dilemmas of Growth in Prewar Japan*, ed. James W. Morley, Princeton, NJ, Princeton University Press, 1971, pp. 223–4.

6 Abe, op. cit., p. 59.

7 Kazahaya Yasoji, *Nihon shakai seisaku shi*, 2nd edn, Tokyo, Nihon hyōronsha, 1947, p. 286.

8 *Nihon rōdō nenkan*, 1920, p. 546.

9 Kazahaya, op. cit., pp. 292–3.

10 Naimushō, Shakai kyoku, *Kyūsai jigyō chōsakai hōkoku*, Tokyo, Naimushō, Shakai kyoku, 1919, p. 28.

11 Hisata Munenari, 'Zenkoku shokugyō shōkai-sho genkyō', *SSJ*, 1920, no. 2, p. 156; *RGS*, op. cit., p. 175. For a complete list of the existing exchanges on 10 September, see 'Zenkoku kōeki shokugyō shōkai-sho ichiran', *SSJ*, 1920, no. 2, pp. 157–60.

12 *RGS*, op. cit., p. 174.

13 Hisata Munenari, 'Chūō shokugyō shōkai-sho no setchi ni tsuite', *SSJ*, 1920, no. 1, p. 178.

14 'Kyōchōkai' kaiwakai, *KS*, Tokyo, 'Kyōchōkai' kaiwakai, 1965, pp. 29–31; Kyōchōkai, *Kyōchōkai jigyō ippan*, Tokyo, Kyōchōkai, 1923, pp. 117–23.

15 *KS*, op. cit., pp. 29–30; Hisata, 'Chūō shokugyō', 1920, op. cit., p. 179.

16 Yatsuhama Tokusaburō, 'Shokugyō shōkai jigyō no seishin', *SSJ*, 1920, no. 3, p. 67.

17 Hyman Kublin, *Asian Revolutionary: The Life of Sen Katayama*, Princeton, NJ, Princeton University Press, 1964, pp. 82–3, 96–101; Sumiya Mikio, *Katayama Sen*, Tokyo, Tokyo daigaku suppankai, 1960, pp. 40–1.

18 Kublin, op. cit., p. 98.

19 Sumiya, op. cit., p. 41.

20 Paul Boyer, *Urban Masses and Moral Order in America, 1820–1920*, Cambridge, Mass., Harvard University Press, 1978, pp. 155–8.

21 Yoshida Kyūichi, *Gendai shakai jigyō shi kenkyū*, Tokyo, Keisō shobō, 1979, pp. 137–8.

22 Soeda Keiichirō, 'Kyōchōshugi no seishin narabi ni Kyōchōkai no jigyō', in *Shakai seisaku kōgiroku*, vol. 3, ed. Kyōchōkai, Tokyo, Kyōchōkai, 1923, pp. 38–9.

23   *KS*, op. cit., p. 59; Kyōchōkai, 1923, op. cit., pp. 131–2; Yamada Yasuko, 'Rinpō jigyō to Kyōchōkai Zenrinkan ni tsuite', *HTH*, 1922, vol. 2, no. 6, pp. 24–7; *SSJ*, 1922, no. 23, pp. 191–8.
24   Yoshida, op. cit., p. 138.
25   On Tatsuno and his work at the Zenrinkan see Yamamoto Tsuneo, *Kindai Nihon toshi kyōka shi kenkyū*, Nagoya, Reimei shobō, 1972, pp. 64–7.
26   Thomas A. Stanley, *Ōsugi Sakae, Anarchist in Taishō Japan: The Creativity of the Ego*, Cambridge, Mass., Harvard University Press, 1982, p. 70.
27   Stephen S. Large, *The Rise of Labor in Japan: The Yūaikai, 1912–1919*, Tokyo, Sophia University Press, 1972, pp. 34–8.
28   Stephen S. Large, *Organized Workers and Socialist Politics in Interwar Japan*, Cambridge, Cambridge University Press, 1981, pp. 88–9, 257.
29   Kenneth B. Pyle, 'Advantages of Followership: German Economics and Japanese Bureaucrats, 1890–1925', *Journal of Japanese Studies*, 1974, vol. 1, no. 1, p. 159.
30   Nagai Tōru, 'Kyōchōkai wa donna jigyō o shite iru ka', *HTH*, 1921, vol. 1, no. 3, p. 11.
31   Nagai Tōru, 'Kyōchōkai no mokuteki oyobi jigyō ni tsuite', *SSJ*, 1921, no. 8, pp. 3–4.
32   ibid., pp. 4–7; Nagai, 'Kyōchōkai no omoide', in *KS*, op. cit., pp. 179–80.
33   Nagai Tōru, *Rōdō mondai to rōdō undō*, Tokyo, Ganshōdō, 1922, pp. 3, 47.
34   ibid., p. 27.
35   ibid., pp. 62–3.
36   ibid., pp. 1–2.
37   A. Morgan Young, *Japan under Taishō Tenno, 1912–1926*, London, George Allen & Unwin Ltd, 1928, p. 150.
38   Kyōchōkai, 1923, op. cit., p. 70.
39   A bibliography of the Kyōchōkai's most important publications can be found in *KS*, op. cit., pp. 169–78.
40   Soeda, 1923, op. cit., p. 32.
41   Tazawa Yoshiharu, *Tazawa Yoshiharu senshū*, Tokyo, Tazawa Yoshiharu kinenkai, 1967, p. 544.
42   Kyōchōkai, 1923, op. cit., p. 133.
43   ibid., pp. 133–5.
44   Yamamoto, op. cit., pp. 66, 73.
45   Solomon B. Levine and Hisashi Kuwada, *Human Resources in Japanese Industrial Development*, Princeton, NJ, Princeton University Press, 1980, pp. 100–1.
46   Nakamura Hideo, 'Kyōchōkai jigyō keika', *SSJ*, 1921, no. 7, p. 203.
47   Tazawa, 1967, op. cit., p. 544; Kyōchōkai, 1923, op. cit., p. 102.
48   Tazawa, 1967, op. cit., p. 544.
49   Tazawa Yoshiharu kinenkai, *Tazawa Yoshiharu*, Tokyo, Tazawa Yoshiharu kinenkai, 1954, p. 109.
50   Shimomura Kojin, *Kono hito o miyo*, Tokyo, Tazawa Yoshiharu kenshōkai, 1966, p. 96.
51   Tazawa, 1967, op. cit., p. 545.

52 Details on courses up to 1923 may be found in Kyōchōkai, 1923, op. cit., pp. 104–9.

53 Kyōchōkai, *Saikin no shakai undō*, Tokyo, Kyōchōkai, 1929, p. 946.

54 Tazawa Yoshiharu, 'Kagai kōen', in *Kōmin kyōiku kōenshū*, vol. 1, ed. Mombushō, Jitsugyō gakumu kyoku, Tokyo, Mombushō kōnai, Jitsugyō hoshū kyōiku kenkyūkai, 1923, p. 3.

55 Kyōchōkai, 1929, op. cit., p. 945.

56 *KS*, op. cit., pp. 27–9; Kyōchōkai, 1923, op. cit., pp. 78–84, 112–16; Soeda, 1923, op. cit., p. 35. On the vocational and technical training programmes, see e.g. 'Kurumae kōgyō senshū gakkō gaikyō', *SSJ*, 1922, no. 27, pp. 231–8.

57 'Kyōchōkai Ōsaka shijo kinkyō', *SSJ*, 1922, no. 27, pp. 239–40. On the establishment of the Osaka branch see *KS*, op. cit., pp. 37–8.

58 'Hoshū kyōiku no shinkō ni tsutomeyo', *HTH*, 1921, vol. 1, no. 5, p. 3.

59 Nagai, 1922, op. cit., p. 38.

60 ibid., p. 18.

61 Soeda Keiichirō, 'Rōdō mondai no kaiketsu', *SSJ*, 1921, no. 5, p. 4.

62 On the development of scientific management as an international phenomenon see Judith A. Merkle, *Management and Ideology: The Legacy of the International Scientific Management Movement*, Berkeley and Los Angeles, University of California Press, 1980.

63 Hiroshi Hazama and Jacqueline Kaminski, 'Japanese Labor–Management Relations and Uno Riemon', *Journal of Japanese Studies*, 1979, vol. 5, no. 1, p. 99; Okuda Kenji, *Hito to keiei*, Tokyo, Manejimento sha, 1985, pp. 54–9. A variety of key documents on scientific management have been collected and reproduced in Hazama Hiroshi, ed., *Nihon rōmu kanrishi shiryō shū*, vol. 8, Tokyo, Gozandō shoten, 1987.

64 Inagaki Tomomi, 'Taishō narabi ni Shōwa shoki sōsetsu shiritsu gakkō no kengaku seishin', in *Kindai Nihon no shigaku*, ed. Nihon kyōiku kagaku kenkyūjo, Tokyo, Yūshindō, 1972, p. 403.

65 Kyōchōkai, 1923, op. cit., pp. 126–7.

66 Machida Tatsujirō, 'Keite iku chū-rō-i no tatemono o shinonde', *Chūō rōdō jihō*, 1965, no. 423, p. 4.

67 Inagaki, op. cit., pp. 402–6.

68 Robert E. Cole, *Work, Mobility, and Participation: A Comparative Study of American and Japanese Industry*, Berkeley and Los Angeles, University of California Press, 1979, pp. 105–11.

69 Tazawa Yoshiharu, 'Kyōchōshugi no dōtokuteki kisō', *SSJ*, 1921, no. 9, pp. 3–4.

70 *KS*, op. cit., p. 22.

71 Nishi Minoru, *Wagakuni rōshi chōsei kikō no hattatsu*, Tokyo, Sakai shoten, 1940, pp. 79–80.

72 Kiga Kanjū, 'Rōshi kyōchō no hito hōhō', *SSJ*, 1920, no. 2, p. 7.

73 George O. Totten, 'Japanese Industrial Relations at the Crossroads: The Great Noda Strike of 1927–1928', in *Japan in Crisis: Essays on Taishō Democracy*, ed. Bernard S. Silberman and H.D. Harootunian, Princeton, NJ, Princeton University Press, 1974, pp. 424–5.

74 Kyōchōkai, Rōdō ka, 'Noda rōdō sōgi no temmatsu', part 2, *SSJ*, 1928, no. 94, pp. 8–11.

75 ibid., p. 13.

76 Kyōchōkai, 1929, op. cit., pp. 354–6; Yatsugi Kazuo, *Mukashi no rōdō sōgi no omoide*, Tokyo, Kokusaku kenkyūkai shuppanbu, 1956, pp. 57–9.

77 John Owen Haley, 'The Myth of the Reluctant Litigant', *Journal of Japanese Studies*, 1978, vol. 4, no. 2, pp. 371–8.

78 This argument is based on John Owen Haley, 'The Politics of Informal Justice: The Japanese Experience, 1922–1942', in *The Politics of Informal Justice*, vol. 2, ed. Richard L. Abel, New York, Academic Press, 1982.

79 League of Nations Union, *Towards Industrial Peace*, London, P.S. King & Son Ltd, 1927, p. 112, also pp. 119–26.

80 William Leavitt Stoddard, *The Shop Committee, A Handbook for Employer and Employee*, New York, The MacMillan Company, 1919, pp. 6–20.

81 ibid., p. 100.

82 John Raphael Staude, 'German Socialists and Russian Soviets: The Transfer of Workers' Councils from Russia to Germany in 1918', in *The Transfer of Ideas: Historical Essays*, ed. C.D.W. Goodwin and I.B. Holley, Jr., Durham, NC, The South Atlantic Quarterly, 1968, p. 104.

83 Philip Taft, 'Germany', in *Comparative Labor Movements*, ed. Walter Galenson, New York, Russell & Russell, 1952, pp. 278–84.

84 Ikeda Makoto, *Nihon kikaikō kumiai seiritsu shiron*, Tokyo, Nihon hyōronsha, 1970, pp. 170–98.

85 Suzuki Bunji, 'Kanryōshugi ka minponshugi ka', *Rōdō oyobi sangyō*, 1919, vol. 8, no. 11, pp. 4–5.

86 Kagawa Toyohiko, *Kagawa Toyohiko zenshū*, vol. 9, Tokyo, Kirisuto shimbunsha, 1962, p. 70.

87 Kyōchōkai, 1929, op. cit., p. 523; George O. Totten, 'Collective Bargaining and Works Councils as Innovations in Industrial Relations in Japan during the 1920s', in *Aspects of Social Change in Modern Japan*, ed. R.P. Dore, Princeton, NJ, Princeton University Press, 1970, p. 218.

88 Fujiwara Sōsuke, 'Senzen ni okeru Kokutetsu rōdō seisaku no hensen', *Chōsa kenkyū shiryō*, 1960, no. 26, pp. 6–26.

89 Ikeda, op. cit., pp. 85–90.

90 Kyōchōkai, 1929, op. cit., p. 526.

91 These examples are discussed in Endō Yoshinobu, 'Taishō demokurashii ki no Nihon guntai no shisō dōkō', *Rekishigaku kenkyū*, 1981, no. 497, p. 19; Fujiwara, op. cit., pp. 33–50; and Shakai kyoku, Rōdōbu, *Wagakuni ni okeru rōdō iinkai no gaikyō*, Tokyo, Shakai kyoku, Rōdōbu, 1937, pp. 25–37, 228.

92 Kyōchōkai, 1929, op. cit., p. 528.

93 Hyōdō Tsutomo, *Nihon ni okeru rōshi kankei no tenkai*, Tokyo, Tokyo daigaku shuppankai, 1971, pp. 367–72; Totten, 1970, op. cit.

94 'Rōdō iinkaihō seitei ni kansuru kengian', *SSJ*, 1921, no. 15, p. 7.

95 Kohashi Ichita, 'Wagakuni rōdō mondai', ms., *Kohashi Ichita kankei*

monjo. This document is housed in the Bungaku-bu, Tokyo University.

96 Soeda Keiichirō, 'Rōdō iinkai seido', *Chikuhō sekitan kōgyō kumiai geppō*, 1926, no. 259, p. 41.
97 Maeda Renzan, *Tokonami Takejirō den*, Tokyo, Tokonami Takejirō denki kankōkai, 1939, p. 527.
98 Soeda, 1926, op. cit., p. 41.
99 e.g. see Ikeda, op. cit., pp. 188–91.
100 Text of the draft is reproduced in *RGS*, op. cit., pp. 146–50.
101 Text in ibid., pp. 151–3; Shakai kyoku, Rōdōbu, op. cit., pp. 41–2; Soeda Keiichirō, 'Rōdō iinkaihō seitei no hitsuyō', *SSJ*, 1921, no. 15, pp. 8–10.
102 The new, revised draft is in Shakai kyoku, Rōdōbu, op. cit., pp. 42–4.
103 *RGS*, op. cit., p. 145.
104 Soeda, 'Rōdō iinkaihō', 1921, op. cit., p. 5.
105 Ōkōchi Kazuo, 'Nihonteki rōshi kankei to sono dentō', *Keizaigaku ronshū*, 1963, vol. 20, no. 1, p. 10.
106 Soeda, 'Rōdō iinkaihō', 1921, op. cit., pp. 2–3.
107 Ōkōchi Kazuo, 'Nihonteki rōshi kankei no genkei: Dai-ichiji taisengo no "kōjō iinkai" o megutte', in *Nihon rōshi kankei no kenkyū*, ed. Ariizumi Tōru, Tokyo, Tokyo daigaku shuppankai, 1963, pp. 14–15; Nihon kōgyō kurabu gojūnenshi, *Nihon kōgyō kurabu gojūnenshi*, Tokyo, Nihon kōgyō kurabu, 1972, pp. 152–3.
108 'Rōdō iinkaihō seitei ni kansuru kengian', op. cit., p. 7.
109 Kawazu Sen, 'Shakai seisaku no seishin to rōdō iin seido', *SSJ*, 1922, no. 17, p. 5.
110 'Rōdō iinkaihō seitei ni kansuru kengian', op. cit., p. 7.
111 Kawazu, op. cit., p. 5.
112 'Rōdō iinkaihō seitei ni kansuru kengian', op. cit., pp. 11, 17.
113 Soeda, 'Rōdō iinkaihō', 1921, op. cit., p. 4.
114 Shiozawa Masatada, 'Dōmei higyō oyobi sono yobōsaku', *Taiyō*, 1912, vol. 18, no. 6, p. 87.
115 Shiozawa Masatada, 'Rōdō mondai no honshitsu to sono kaiketsu hōshin', *SSJ*, 1920, no. 4, p. 18.
116 See Ikeda Makoto, 'Rōshi kyōchō seisaku no keisei: Naimushō shakai kyoku (gaikyoku) setchi no igi ni tsuite', *Nihon rōdō kyōkai zasshi*, 1978, no. 226, p. 20; Machida Tatsujirō, *Rōdō sōgi no kaibō*, Tokyo, Dai'ichi shuppansha, 1929, p. 221; Soeda, 'Rōdō iinkaihō', 1921, op. cit., p. 4.
117 Itō Takashi, *Shōwa shoki seiji shi kenkyū*, Tokyo, Tokyo daigaku shuppankai, 1969, p. 61.
118 *KS*, op. cit., pp. 44–8; Soeda Keiichirō kun kinenkai, *Soeda Keiichirō den*, Tokyo, Soeda Keiichirō kun kinenkai, 1955, p. 71.
119 Soeda Keiichirō, 'Sangyō heiwa to rōdō kumiaihō', *SSJ*, 1930, no. 120, p. 3.
120 Quoted in Large, 1981, op. cit., p. 146. Yoshida's views are fully developed in Yoshida Shigeru, *Rōdō kumiaihō no seitei ni tsuite*, n.p., 1930.
121 On businessmen in the House of Peers, see Arthur E. Tiedemann, 'The Hamaguchi Cabinet: First Phase July 1929–February 1930: A

Study in Japanese Parliamentary Government', PhD diss., Columbia University, 1959, p. 254. An excellent study of the debate over labour union legislation may be found in Sheldon Garon, *The State and Labor in Modern Japan*, Berkeley, University of California Press, 1987, pp. 157–86.

122 Kitaoka Juitsu, 'Kyū-shakai kyoku no omoide', in *Rōdō gyōsei shi yoroku*, ed. Rōdōshō, Tokyo, Rōdō hōrei kyōkai, 1961, pp. 7–9.

5 The moral community in crisis

1 US Department of State, *The Paris Peace Conference*, 5 vols, in *Papers Relating to the Foreign Relations of the United States*, 77th Congress, 2nd Session, 1943, vol. 4, p. 538.

2 ibid. ⁄

3 Ehud Harari, *The Politics of Labor Legislation in Japan*, Berkeley and Los Angeles, University of California Press, 1973, p. 24.

4 Kobayashi Hideo and Sasaki Ryūji, '"Fuyu no jidai" kara no dakkyaku', *Rekishigaku kenkyū*, 1983, no. 515, pp. 40–1.

5 Kitaoka Juitsu, 'Kyū-shakai kyoku no omoide', in *Rōdō gyōsei shi yoroku*, ed. Rōdōshō, Tokyo, Rōdō hōrei kyōkai, 1961, p. 1.

6. Nagai Tōru, 'Kyōchōkai no omoide', in 'Kyōchōkai' kaiwakai, *KS*, Tokyo, 'Kyōchōkai' kaiwakai, 1965, p. 180.

7 *KS*, op. cit., pp. 49–50.

8 On the organization and responsibilities of the Social Bureau see Rōdōshō, *RGS*, vol. 1, Tokyo, Rōdō hōrei kyōkai, 1961, pp. 193–201.

9 *KS*, op. cit., p. 49.

10 The essential provisions of the bill may be found in *RGS*, op. cit., pp. 209–13.

11 Yoshida Shigeru, 'Shūnin no kotoba', *SSJ*, 1931, no. 129, p. 4.

12 Yoshida Shigeru forward to a *Shakai seisaku jihō* special number on 'A Re-examination of Social Policy', *SSJ*, 1932, no. 146, p. 3.

13 Soeda Keiichirō kun kinenkai, *Soeda Keiichirō den*, Tokyo, Soeda Keiichirō kun kinenkai, 1955, pp. 72–3.

14 Hugh Byas, *Government by Assassination*, New York, Alfred A. Knopf, 1942.

15 *KS*, op. cit., p. 70.

16 'Kyōchōkai, Jikyoku taisaku iinkai keika gaikyō, *SSJ*, 1932, no. 144, p. 2.

17 The complete proposal may be found in ibid., pp. 2–3.

18 Yoshida Shigeru denki kankō henshū iinkai, *Yoshida Shigeru*, Tokyo, Yoshida Shigeru denki kankō henshū iinkai, 1969, pp. 65–6.

19 These efforts are discussed in *KS*, op. cit., pp. 68–9, 74–5.

20 Machida Tatsujirō, 'Sangyō heiwa ni taisuru shiken', *Shakai undō ōrai*, 1932, vol. 4, no. 10, p. 18.

21 Chalmers Johnson, *MITI and the Japanese Miracle: The Growth of Industrial Policy, 1925–1975*, Stanford, Calif., Stanford University Press, 1982, p. 109.

22 ibid., p. 108.

23 George O. Totten, 'Collective Bargaining and Works Councils as

Innovations in Industrial Relations in Japan during the 1920s', in *Aspects of Social Change in Modern Japan*, ed. R.P. Dore, Princeton, NJ, Princeton University Press, 1970, p. 212.
24 *RGS*, op. cit., p. 527.
25 ibid., p. 531.
26 Miwa Yasushi, 'Nihon fuashizumu keiseki ni okeru shin-kanryō to keisatsu', *Nihon shi kenkyū*, 1983, no. 252, p. 17.
27 Stephen S. Large, *Organized Workers and Socialist Politics in Interwar Japan*, Cambridge, Cambridge University Press, 1981, p. 181.
28 Rōdō undō shiryō iinkai (ed.), *NRUS*, 10 vols, Tokyo, Rōdō undō shiryō kankō iinkai, 1959–68, vol. 10, p. 440.
29 *RGS*, op. cit., p. 509.
30 Sakurabayashi Makoto, 'Senji Nihon no rōshi kyōgisei: sangyō hōkokukai no kondankai o chūshin toshite', *Jōchi keizai ronshū*, 1972, vol. 18, no. 3, p. 41.
31 *RGS*, op. cit., pp. 509–10.
32 Shakai kyoku, Rōdōbu, *Wagakuni ni okeru rōdō iinkai no gaikyō*, Tokyo, Shakai kyoku, Rōdōbu, 1937, p. 4.
33 Ujihara Shōjirō and Hagiwara Susumu, 'Sangyō hōkoku undō no haikei', in *Fuashizumu-ki no kokka to shakai*, vol. 6, ed. Tokyo daigaku shakai kagaku kenkyūjo, Tokyo, Tokyo daigaku shuppankai, 1979, p. 221.
34 Sakurabayashi, op. cit., pp. 41–2; and Ujihara and Hagiwara, op. cit., pp. 224–7.
35 Ujihara and Hagiwara, op. cit., pp. 224–5.
36 Kawarada Kakichi, 'Shūnin no kotoba', *SSJ*, 1935, no. 182, p. 2.
37 *KS*, op. cit., p. 77.
38 Quoted in Soeda Keiichirō kun kinenkai, op. cit., p. 74.
39 Machida Tatsujirō, 'Kokumin seishin undō to sangyō heiwa undō', *Kyōchō*, 15 September 1937, no. 4, p. 1.
40 Machida Tatsujirō, 'Sangyō heiwa ni taisuru shiken', *Shakai undō ōrai*, 1932, no. 4, pp. 16–23.
41 Ujihara and Hagiwara, op. cit., p. 225.
42 Sakurabayashi, op. cit., p. 42.
43 *Kyōchō*, 15 October 1937, no. 5, p. 10.
44 ibid.
45 ibid., p. 11; *Kyōchō*, 15 November 1937, no. 6, pp. 8–10.
46 Large, op. cit., pp. 202–8.
47 *KS*, op. cit., pp. 88–9; Sakurabayashi, op. cit., p. 43.
48 *Kyōchō*, 15 April 1938, no. 11, p. 7.
49 *KS*, op. cit., p. 90; Sakurabayashi, op. cit., p. 44.
50 *KS*, op. cit., p. 87; *Kyōchō*, 15 February 1938, no. 9, p. 3.
51 Kyōchōkai, Jikyoku taisaku iinkai, *Shōi gunjin taisaku*, Tokyo, Kyōchōkai, 1938, p. 3.
52 Morita Yoshio, *Nihon keieisha dantai hatten shi*, Tokyo, Nikkan rōdō tsūshinsha, 1958, p. 260.
53 ibid.
54 The most complete discussion of these meetings in either English or Japanese may be found in Ernest James Notar, 'Labor Unions and the *Sangyō Hōkoku* movement, 1930–1945: A Japanese Model for

Industrial Relations', PhD diss., University of California, Berkeley, 1979, pp. 233–43.

55 The text of the plan may be found, among other places, in *KS*, op. cit., pp. 92–5; Morita, op. cit., pp. 262–5.

56 *Kyōchō*, 15 June 1938, no. 13, pp. 2–6.

57 Yoshii Yukiko, 'Sangyō hōkoku undō: sono seiritsu o megutte', *Hitotsubashi ronsō*, 1975, vol. 73, no. 2, pp. 48–51.

58 *KS*, op. cit., p. 104.

59 On the sectional divisions in wartime Japan see Johnson, op. cit., pp. 116–56; Richard Rice, 'Economic Mobilization in Wartime Japan: Business, Bureaucracy, and Military in Conflict', *Journal of Asian Studies*, 1979, vol. 38, no. 4.

60 Quoted in Ujihara and Hagiwara, op. cit., p. 209.

Afterword

1. This point is made in John Paul Scott, 'Science and Social Control', *Social Control and Social Change*, ed. John Paul Scott and Sarah F. Scott, Chicago, University of Chicago Press, 1971, pp. 1–8.

2 See Tetsuo Najita and H.D. Harootunian, 'Japanese Revolt Against the West: Political and Cultural Criticism in the Twentieth Century', in *The Cambridge History of Japan*, vol. 6, *The Twentieth Century*, ed. Peter Duus, Cambridge, Cambridge University Press, 1988, pp. 711–74.

3 Itami Hiroyuki, 'The Humanistic Corporation – An Exportable Concept?', *Japan Echo*, 1986, vol. 13, no. 4, p. 57.

4 This point is made by Winston Davis, 'Religion and Development: Weber and the East Asian Experience', in *Understanding Political Development*, ed. Myron Weiner and Samuel P. Huntington, Boston, Little, Brown & Company, 1987, p. 263.

5 For a description of contemporary 'spiritual education' (*seishin kyōiku*) see Thomas P. Rohlen, *For Harmony and Strength: Japanese White-Collar Organization in Anthropological Perspective*, Berkeley, University of California Press, 1974, pp. 192–211.

6 Akio Morita, with Edwin M. Reingold and Mitsuko Shimomura, *Made in Japan: Akio Morita and Sony*, New York, E.P. Dutton, 1986, p. 181.

Bibliography

Unpublished sources

Kohashi Ichita kankei monjo, Bungaku-bu, Tokyo University, Tokyo.
'Dajō ruiten', microfilm courtesy of Center for Research Libraries, Chicago
'Kyōchōkai shi', 1947, Ōhara shakai mondai kenkyūjo, Tokyo.
'Nihon gakki kaisha sogi', Ōhara shakai mondai kenkyūjo, Tokyo.
'Sōgi', 1920, Ōhara shakai mondai kenkyūjo, Tokyo.

Major periodicals and newspapers

Hito to hito
Kokumin shimbun
Kyōchō
Nihon rōdō nenkan
Seiyū
Shakai seisaku jihō
Shibun
Shimin
Tokyo asahi shimbun

Works cited

Abe Isoo, *Shakai mondai kaishaku hō*, Tokyo: Tokyo semmon gakkō shuppan-bu, 1901.
—— *Shitsugyō mondai*, Tokyo: Nihon hyōronsha, 1929.
Abegglen, James, *The Japanese Factory: Aspects of its Social Organization*, Glencoe, Illinois: The Free Press, 1958.
Abegglen, James and Stalk, G., *Kaisha: The Japanese Corporation: The New Competitors in World Business*, New York: Basic Books, 1985.
Arahata Kanson, *Arahata kanson chosakushū*, 10 vols, Tokyo: Heibonsha, 1976–7.
Arase, Yutaka, 'Mass Communication between the Two World Wars', *The Developing Economies* 5 (1967): 748–66.
Ariga Nagafumi, 'Shokkō jōrei seitei no jiki ni tsuite', *Kokka gakkai zasshi* 129 (1897): 917–39.

Banno Junji, '"Taishō demokurashii" ki no seiji', in Takahashi Kōhachirō, Nagahara Keiji, and Ōishi Kaichirō (eds) *Nihon kindaishi yōsetsu*, Tokyo: Tokyo daigaku shuppankai, 1980.

Bernstein, Gail L., 'The Russian Revolution, the Early Japanese Socialists and the Problem of Dogmatism', *Studies in Comparative Communism* 9 (1976): 327–48.

—— 'Women in the Silk-reeling Industry in Nineteenth Century Japan', in Gail Lee Bernstein and Haruhiko Fukui (eds) *Japan and the World: Essays in Japanese History and Politics*, New York: St Martin's Press, 1988.

Bestor, Theodore C., *Neighborhood Tokyo*, Stanford, Calif.: Stanford University Press, 1989.

Boyer, Paul, *Urban Masses and Moral Order in America, 1820–1920*, Cambridge, Mass.: Harvard University Press, 1978.

Byas, Hugh, *Government by Assassination*, New York: Alfred A. Knopf, 1942.

Centre for East Asian Cultural Studies (eds), *Meiji Japan Through Contemporary Sources*, 3 vols, Tokyo: Centre for East Asian Cultural Studies, 1969–72.

Cole, Robert E., *Work, Mobility, and Participation: A Comparative Study of American and Japanese Industry*, Berkeley: University of California Press, 1979.

Cole, Robert E. and Tominaga, Ken'ichi, 'Japan's Changing Occupational Structure and Its Significance', in Hugh Patrick (ed.) *Japanese Industrialization and Its Social Consequences*, Berkeley: University of California Press, 1976.

Crawcour, E. Sydney, 'Industrialization and Technological Change, 1885–1920', in Peter Duus (ed.) *The Cambridge History of Japan*, vol. 6, *The Twentieth Century*, Cambridge: Cambridge University Press, 1988.

Davis, Winston, 'Religion and Development: Weber and the East Asian Experience', in Myron Weiner and Samuel P. Huntington (eds) *Understanding Political Development*, Boston: Little, Brown & Company, 1987.

Dawson, William Harbutt, *Bismarck and State Socialism*, London: Swan Sonnenschein & Co., 1891.

Dore, Ronald, 'The Modernizer as a Special Case: Japanese Factory Legislation, 1882–1911', *Comparative Studies in Society and History* 11 (1969): 433–50.

Duus, Peter, *Party Rivalry and Political Change in Taishō Japan*, Cambridge, Mass.: Harvard University Press, 1968.

—— 'Yoshino Sakuzō: The Christian as Political Critic', *Journal of Japanese Studies* 4, 2 (1978): 301–26.

Endō Yoshinobu, 'Taishō demokurashii ki no Nihon guntai no shisō dōkō', *Rekishigaku kenkyū* 497 (1981): 15–29.

Fraser, Andrew, 'Local Administration: The Example of Awa-Tokushima', in Marius B. Jansen and Gilbert Rozman (eds) *Japan in Transition: From Tokugawa to Meiji*, Princeton, NJ: Princeton University Press, 1986.

Fujino Yutaka, 'Kyōchō seisaku no suishin', in Kano Masanao and Yui Masaomi (eds) *Kindai Nihon no tōgō to teiko*, vol. 3, *1911–1931*, Tokyo: Nihon hyōronsha, 1982.

Fujiwara Sōsuke, 'Senzen ni okeru Kokutetsu rōdō seisaku no hensen', *Chōsa kenkyū shiryō* 26 (1960): 1–52.

Fukaya Susumu, 'Kyōchōkaiteki "rōdōsha kyōiku" no hihan', *Musansha kyōiku* 1 (1929): 21–4.

Fukuzawa Yukichi, *An Encouragement of Learning*, trans. David A. Dilworth and Umeyo Hirano, Tokyo: Sophia University Press, 1969.

Garon, Sheldon, *The State and Labor in Modern Japan*, Berkeley: University of California Press, 1987.

Gellner, Ernest, *Culture, Identity, and Politics*, Cambridge: Cambridge University Press, 1987.

Gluck, Carol, *Japan's Modern Myths: Ideology in the Late Meiji Period*, Princeton, NJ: Princeton University Press, 1985.

Gordon, Andrew, *The Evolution of Labor Relations in Japan: Heavy Industry, 1853–1955*, Cambridge, Mass.: Council on East Asian Studies, Harvard University, 1985.

Haley, John Owen, 'The Myth of the Reluctant Litigant', *Journal of Japanese Studies* 4 (1978): 359–90.

—— 'The Politics of Informal Justice: The Japanese Experience, 1922–1942', in Richard L. Abel (ed.) *The Politics of Informal Justice*, vol. 2, New York: Academic Press, 1982.

Hamaguchi Haruhiko, 'Kyōchōkai to Dai-ichiji taisengo no rōshi kankei', *Shakai kagaku tōkyū* 15 (1970): 525-54. .

Hane, Mikiso, *Peasants, Rebels and Outcastes: The Underside of Modern Japan*, New York: Pantheon Books, 1982.

Hara Kei, *Hara Kei nikki*, 9 vols, ed. Hara Kei'ichirō, Tokyo: Kengensha, 1950.

—— 'Shinshun shokan', *Seiyū* 237 (1920): 26–8.

Harari, Ehud, *The Politics of Labor Legislation in Japan*, Berkeley: University of California Press, 1973.

Hashikawa Bunzō, 'Shōwa isshin no ronri to shinri', in Hashikawa Bunzō and Matsumoto Sannosuke (eds) *Kindai Nihon seiji shisō shi*, vol. 2, of Oka Yoshitake and Hayashi Shigeru (eds) *Kindai Nihon shisō shi taikei*, vol. 4, Tokyo: Yūhikaku, 1970.

Hata Ikuhiko, *Senzen-ki Nihon kanryōsei no seido, soshiki, jinji*, Tokyo: Tokyo daigaku shuppankai, 1981.

Hazama Hiroshi, *Nihon rōmu kanrishi kenkyū*, Tokyo: Daiyamondosha, 1964.

—— 'Historical Changes in the Life Style of Industrial Workers', in Hugh Patrick (ed.) *Japanese Industrialization and Its Social Consequences*, Berkeley: University of California Press, 1976.

—— *Nihon ni okeru rōshi kyōchō no teiryū*, Tokyo: Waseda daigaku shuppanbu, 1978.

—— (ed.), *Nihon rōmu kanrishi shiryō*, 8 vols, Tokyo: Gozandō shoten, 1987.

Hazama, Hiroshi and Kaminski, Jacqueline, 'Japanese Labor–Management Relations and Uno Riemon', *Journal of Japanese Studies* 5 (1979): 71–106.

Hirschmeier, Johannes, S.V.D., 'Shibusawa Eiichi: Industrial Pioneer', in William W. Lockwood (ed.) *The State and Economic Enterprise in Japan*, Princeton, NJ: Princeton University Press, 1965.

Hisata Munenari, 'Chūō shokugyō shokai-sho genkyō', *Shakai seisaku jihō* 1 (1920): 178–9.

—— 'Zenkoku shokugyō shōkai-sho genkyō', *Shakai seisaku jihō* 2 (1920): 156–7.

Hobsbawm, Eric, 'Introduction: Inventing Traditions', in Eric Hobsbawm and Terence Ranger (eds) *The Invention of Tradition*, Cambridge: Cambridge University Press, 1983.

Honda Seiichi, 'Naisei-jō oyobi kokusai-jō yori kantaru rōdō seisaku', in Shihon rōdō mondai kenkyūkai (ed.) *Rōshi mondai sōsho*, vol. 1, Tokyo: Shihon rōdō mondai kenkyūkai, 1919.

'Hoshū kyōiku no shinkō ni tsutomeyo', *Hito to hito* 1, 5 (1921): 3.

Hyōdō Tsutomu, *Nihon ni okeru rōshi kankei no tenkai*, Tokyo: Tokyo daigaku shuppankai, 1971.

Ikeda Makoto, *Nihon kikaikō kumiai seiritsu shiron*, Tokyo: Nihon hyōronsha, 1970.

—— 'Rōshi kyōchō seisaku no keisei: Naimushō shakai kyoku (gaikyoku) setchi no igi ni tsuite', *Nihon rōdō kyōkai zasshi* 226 (1978): 14–23.

Ikeda Yoshimasa, *Nihon shakai fukushi shi*, Kyoto: Hōritsu bunka sha, 1986.

Inagaki Tomomi, 'Taishō narabi ni Shōwa shoki sōsetsu shiritsu gakkō no kengaku seishin', in Nihon kyōiku kagaku kenkyūjo (ed.) *Kindai Nihon no shigaku*, Tokyo: Yūshindo, 1972.

Inoue Tomoichi, *Kyūsai seido yōgi*, Tokyo: Hakubunkan, 1909.

Ishida Takeshi, *Meiji seiji shisoshi kenkyū*, Tokyo: Miraisha, 1954.

—— 'Kawakami Hajime ni okeru itan e no michi', *Shisō* 664 (1979): 1–18.

—— 'Kindai Nihon ni okeru "shakai fukushi" kanren kannen no hensen', *Shakai kagaku kenkyū* 32 (1981): 1–57.

Itami Hiroyuki, 'The Humanistic Corporation: An Exportable Concept?', *Japan Echo* 13, 4 (1986): 56–60.

Itō Takashi, *Shōwa shoki seiji shi kenkyū*, Tokyo: Tokyo daigaku shuppankai, 1969.

Iwamoto Yoshio, 'Aspects of the Proletarian Literary Movement in Japan', in Bernard S. Silberman and H.D. Harootunian (eds) *Japan in Crisis: Essays on Taishō Democracy*, Princeton, NJ: Princeton University Press, 1974.

Johnson, Chalmers, *MITI and the Japanese Miracle: The Growth of Industrial Policy, 1925–1975*, Stanford, Calif.: Stanford University Press, 1982.

Kagawa Toyohiko, *Kagawa Toyohiko zenshū*, 24 vols., Tokyo: Kirisuto shimbunsha, 1962–4.

Kagoyama Takashi, 'Kōjōhō no seiritsu to jisshi ni okeru kanryō gun', in Takahashi Kōhachirō (ed.) *Nihon kindaika no kenkyū*, vol. 2, Tokyo: Tokyo daigaku shuppankai, 1972.

Kalland, Arne and Pederson, Jon, 'Famine and Population in Fukuoka Domain During the Tokugawa Period', *Journal of Japanese Studies* 10, 1 (1984): 31–72.

Kamii Yoshihiko, 'Dai-ichiji taisen chokugo no rōdō seisaku', *Rōdō undō shi kenkyū* 62 (1979): 150–81.

Kamishima, Jirō, *Kindai Nihon no seishin kōzō*, Tokyo: Iwanami shoten, 1961.

Kanai En, 'Boasonaddo-shi no keizai ron o hyōsu', *Hōgaku kyōkai zasshi* 10 (1892), reprint in Yoshino Sakuzō (ed.) *Meiji bunka zenshū*, vol. 21, Tokyo: Nihon hyōronsha, 1929.

Kaneko Kentarō, 'Nihon no hatten to kangaku no seiryoku', *Shibun* 1, 1 (1919): 5–18.

Kano Masanao, *Shihonshugi keiseiki no chitsujo ishiki*, Tokyo: Chikuma shobō, 1969.

Katayama, Sen, *The Labor Movement in Japan*, Chicago: Charles H. Kerr & Co., 1918.

Kawarada Kakichi, 'Iwayuru rōdō kumiai no kōnin to Chian keisatsuhō daijūshichi jō ni tsuite', in Shihon rōdō mondai kenkyūkai (ed.) *Rōshi mondai sōsho*, vol. 1, Tokyo: Shihon rōdō mondai kenkyūkai, 1919.

—— 'Wagakuni no rōdō mondai', *Shimin* 14 (1919): 10–13.

—— 'Shūnin no kotoba', *Shakai seisaku jihō* 182 (1935): 1–4.

Kawazu Sen, *Shakai mondai ni tsuite*, Tokyo: Naimushō, Chihō kyoku, 1920.

—— 'Shakai seisaku no seishin to rōdō iin seido', *Shakai seisaku jihō* 17 (1922): 2–7.

Kazahaya Yasoji, *Nihon shakai seisaku shi*, 2nd edn, Tokyo: Nihon hyōronsha, 1947.

Keio gijuku (ed.), *Fukuzawa Yukichi zenshū*, 21 vols., Tokyo: Iwanami shoten, 1958–64.

Kelly, William W., *Deference and Defiance in Nineteenth-century Japan*, Princeton, NJ: Princeton University Press, 1985.

Kiga Kanjū, 'Rōshi kyōchō no hito hōhō', *Shakai seisaku jihō* 2 (1920): 1–19.

Kikuchi Takenori, 'Shihon rōdō mondai kenkyūkai', in Shihon rōdō mondai kenkyūkai (ed.) *Rōshi mondai sōsho*, vol. 1, Tokyo: Shihon rōdō mondai kenkyūkai, 1919.

Kimbara Samon, *Taishō-ki no seitō to kokumin*, Tokyo: Hanawa shobō, 1973.

Kimura Takeo, *Nihon kindai shakai jigyō shi*, Tokyo: Minerubua shobō, 1984.

Kinmonth, Earl H., *The Self-Made Man in Meiji Japanese Thought: From Samurai to Salary Man*, Berkeley: University of California Press, 1981.

Kinzley, W. Dean, 'Japan's Discovery of Poverty: Poverty and Social Welfare in the Nineteenth Century', *Journal of Asian History* 22, 1, (1988): 1–24.

Kitaoka Juitsu, 'Kyū-shakai kyoku no omoide', in Rōdōshō (ed.) *Rōdō gyōsei shi yoroku*, Tokyo: Rōdō hōrei kyōkai, 1961.

Kobayashi Gorō, '"Kyōchōkai" ron', *Shakai undō ōrai* 3 (1931): 11–15.

—— 'Ese-kyōchōshugi o haigekisu', *Shakai ōrai* 7 (1935): 6–20.

Kobayashi Hideo and Sasaki Ryūji, '"Fuyu no jidai" kara no dakkyaku', *Rekishigaku kenkyū* 515 (1983): 34–49.

'Kōgi no shakai mondai ni taisuru', *Shakai zasshi* 1 (1897): 47–50.

Kōtoku Shūsui, 'Shakai mondai kenkyūkai ni tsuite', *Shakai zasshi* 1 (1897): 60.

Kublin, Hyman, *Asian Revolutionary: The Life of Sen Katayama*, Princeton, NJ: Princeton University Press, 1964.

'Kurumae kōgyō senshū gakkō gaikyō', *Shakai seisaku jihō* 27 (1922): 231–8.

Kushida Tamizō, *Kushida Tamizō zenshū*, 4 vols, Tokyo: Kaizōsha, 1949.

Kuwata Kumazō, 'Rōdō mondai ni kansuru sekai no taisei', *Shakai seisaku jihō* 1 (1920): 6–14.

——— 'Ōshū taisen to rōdō mondai', in Kuwata Kazuo (ed.) *Kuwata Kumazō ikōshū*, Tokyo: Seikōsha, 1934.

Kyōchōkai, *Kyōchōkai jigyō ippan*, Tokyo: Kyōchōkai, 1923.

——— *Wagakuni ni okeru rōdō iinkai seido*, Tokyo: Kyōchōkai, 1923.

——— *Saikin no shakai undō*, Tokyo: Kyōchōkai, 1929.

Kyōchōkai, Jikyoku taisaku iinkai, *Shōi gunjin taisaku*, Tokyo: Kyōchōkai, 1938.

'Kyōchōkai' kaiwakai, *Kyōchōkai shi: Kyōchōkai sanjūnen no ayumi*, Tokyo: 'Kyōchōkai' kaiwakai, 1965.

'Kyōchōkai no taidō', *Rōdō* 9 (1920): 1.

'Kyōchōkai Osaka shijo kinkyō', *Shakai seisaku jihō* 27 (1922): 239–40.

Large, Stephen S., *The Rise of Labor in Japan: The Yūaikai, 1912–1919*, Tokyo: Sophia University Press, 1972.

——— *Organized Workers and Socialist Politics in Interwar Japan*, Cambridge: Cambridge University Press, 1981.

League of Nations Union, *Towards Industrial Peace*, London: P.S. King & Son Ltd, 1927.

Levine, Solomon B. and Kawada Hisashi, *Human Resources in Japanese Industrial Development*, Princeton, NJ: Princeton University Press, 1980.

Lockwood, William W., *The Economic Development of Japan*, exp. edn, Princeton, NJ: Princeton University Press, 1968.

Machida Tatsujirō, *Rōdō sōgi no kaibō*, Tokyo: Dai-ichi shuppansha, 1929

——— 'Sangyō heiwa ni taisuru shiken', *Shakai undō ōrai* 4 (1932): 16–32.

——— 'Kokumin seishin undō to sangyō heiwa undō', *Kyōchō* 4 (1937): 1.

——— 'Keite iku chū-rō-i no tatemono o shinonde', *Chūō rōdō johō* 423 (1965): 3–4.

McClain, James L., 'Failed Expectations: Kaga Domain on the Eve of the Meiji Restoration', *Journal of Japanese Studies* 14, 2 (1988): 403–47.

Maeda Renzan, *Tokonami Takejirō den*, Tokyo: Tokonami Takejirō denki kankōkai, 1939.

Marshall, Byron K., *Capitalism and Nationalism in Prewar Japan: The Ideology of the Business Elite, 1868–1941*, Stanford, Calif.: Stanford University Press, 1967.

——— 'Academic Factionalism in Japan: The Case of the Tōdai Economics Department, 1919–1939', *Modern Asian Studies* 12 (1978): 529–51.

Maruyama Tsurukichi, 'Kyūsai jigyō no han-i', *Shimin* 14 (1919): 13–18.

Matsumoto Sannosuke, *Kindai Nihon no chiteki jōkyō*, Tokyo: Chūō kōronsha, 1974.

Matsunaga Shōzō, 'Shakai mondai no hassei', in *Iwanami kōza: Nihon rekishi*, vol. 16, Tokyo: Iwanami shoten, 1976.

Matsuo Takayoshi, *Taishō demokurashii no kenkyū*, Tokyo: Aoki shoten, 1966.

Matsuzawa Hiroaki, *Nihon shakaishugi no shisō*, Tokyo: Chikuma shobō, 1973.

Meiji bunka kenkyūkai (ed.), *Meiji bunka zenshū*, vol. 6, Tokyo: Nihon hyōronsha, 1955.

Merkle, Judith A., *Management and Ideology: The Legacy of the International Scientific Management Movement*, Berkeley: University of California Press, 1980.

Minear, Richard H., *Japanese Tradition and Western Law: Emperor, State and Law in the Thought of Hozumi Yatsuka*, Cambridge, Mass.: Harvard University Press, 1970.

Mitani Taichirō, *Nihon seitō seiji no keisei*, Tokyo: Tokyo daigaku shuppankai, 1967

—— *Taishō demokurashii ron*, Tokyo: Chūō kōronsha, 1974.

Miwa Ryōichi, 'Rōdō kumiaihō seitei mondai no rekishiteki ichi', in Andō Yoshio (ed.) *Ryōtaisen aida no Nihon shihonshugi*, Tokyo: Tokyo daigaku shuppankai, 1979.

Miwa Yasushi, 'Nihon fuashizumu keiseiki ni okeru shin-kanryō to keisatsu', *Nihon shi kenkyū* 252 (1983): 1–31.

Miyachi Masato, *Nichi-Ro sengo seiji shi no kenkyū*, Tokyo: Tokyo daigaku shuppankai, 1973.

Mizuno Rentarō, 'Kōfūshi no michi', *Shibun* 2, 12 (1927): 1–6.

Morita, Akio with Reingold, Edwin M. and Shimomura, Mitsuko, *Made in Japan: Akio Morita and Sony*, New York: E.P. Dutton, 1986.

Morita Yoshio, *Nihon keieisha dantai hatten shi*, Tokyo: Nikkan rōdō tsushinsha, 1958.

Morito Tatsuo, 'Kyūsai jigyō chōsakai no setchi to waga shakai seisaku', *Kokka gakkai zasshi* 32 (1918): 133–41.

Morris, Dana and Smith, Thomas C., 'Fertility and Mortality in an Outcast Village in Japan, 1750–1869', in Susan B. Hanley and Arthur P. Wolf (eds) *Family and Population in East Asian History*, Stanford, Calif.: Stanford University Press, 1985.

Morris, Ivan, *The Nobility of Failure: Tragic Heroes in the History of Japan*, New York: New American Library, A Meridian Book, 1976.

Mutō Sanji zenshū kankōkai (eds), *Mutō Sanji zenshū*, 8 vols and 1 supplemental vol., Tokyo: Shinjusha, 1963–6.

Nagai Tōru, 'Kyōchō to tōsō,' *Hito to Hito* 1, 1 (1921): 47–50.

—— 'Kyōchōkai no mokuteki oyobi jigyō ni tsuite', *Shakai seisaku jihō* 8 (1921): 1–8.

—— 'Kyōchōkai wa donna jigyō o shite iru ka', *Hito to hito* 1, 1 (1921): 5–7.

—— 'Sangyōjō ni okeru kyōchō', *Shakai seisaku jihō* 11 (1921): 1–5.

—— *Rōdō mondai to rōdō undō*, Tokyo: Ganshōdō, 1922.

—— *Sangyō rikken to sangyō fukuri*, rev. edn, Tokyo: Ganshōdō, 1924.

—— 'Shin-bunka no kensetsu', *Rōdō bunka* 1 (1924): 9–14.

—— 'Shakai shisō no kenkyū oyobi shutei', *Shakai seisaku jihō* 70 (1926): 1–9.

—— 'Kyōchōkai no omoide', in 'Kyōchōkai' kaiwakai (ed.) *Kyōchōkai shi: Kyōchōkai sanjūnen no ayumi*, Tokyo: 'Kyōchōkai' kaiwakai, 1965.

Nagy, Margit Maria, '"How Shall We Live?": Social Change, The Family Institution and Feminism in Prewar Japan', Ph.D. dissertation, University of Washington, 1981.

Naimushō, Shakai kyoku, *Kyūsai jigyō chōsakai hōkoku*, Tokyo: Naimushō, Shakai kyoku, 1919.

Najita, Tetsuo, *Hara Kei in the Politics of Compromise, 1905–1915*, Cambridge, Mass.: Harvard University Press, 1967.

Najita, Tetsuo and H.D. Harootunian, 'Japanese Revolt Against the West: Political and Cultural Criticism in the Twentieth Century', in Peter Duus (ed.) *The Cambridge History of Japan*, vol. 6, *The Twentieth Century*, Cambridge: Cambridge University Press, 1988.

Nakagawa Keiichirō, Chō Yukio, and Kimbara Samon, 'Zaibatsu to kanryō: sono musubitsuki yuen', *Rekishi kōron* 76 (1982): 37–56.

Nakajima Kumakichi, *Seikai zaikai gojūnen*, Tokyo: Dai-Nippon yūbenkai kōdansha, 1951.

Nakamura Hideo, 'Kyōchōkai jigyō keika', *Shakai seisaku jihō* 7 (1921): 203–4.

Nakamura Mototada, *Nihon kōgyō kurabu nijūgonenshi*, 2 vols, Tokyo: Nihon kōgyō kurabu, 1943.

Nakamura Takafusa, Itō Takashi and Hara Akira (eds), *Gendai shi o tsukuru hitobito*, 4 vols, Tokyo: Mainichi shimbunsha, 1971–2.

Nakano Seigō, 'Yatō no nanzo kekkisezaru', *Nihon oyobi Nihonjin* 690 (1916): 23–30.

Nihon kindai shiryō kenkyūkai (ed.), *Taishō goki Keiho kyoku kankō shakai undō shiryō*, Tokyo: Nihon kindai shiryō kenkyūkai, 1968.

Nihon kōgyō kurabu gojūnenshi hensan iinkai, *Nihon kōgyō kurabu gojūnenshi*, Tokyo: Nihon kōgyō kurabu, 1972.

—— *Zaikai kaisoroku*, 2 vols, Tokyo: Nihon kōgyō kurabu, 1967.

Nihon shakai jigyō daigaku (ed.), *Kubota Shizutarō ronshū*, Tokyo: Nihon shakai jigyō daigaku, 1980.

Nishi Minoru, *Wagakuni rōshi chōsei kikō no hattatsu*, Tokyo: Sakai shoten, 1940.

Nishida Hirotarō, 'Shakai kaizō ni taisuru rōdōsha no sekimu', *Hito to hito* 1, 1 (1921): 10–13.

Nishio Kanji, 'Japan's Parallel Path to Modernity', *Japan Echo* 10, 1 (1983): 65–72.

Notar, Ernest James, 'Labor Unions and the *Sangyō Hōkoku* Movement, 1930–1945: A Japanese Model for Industrial Relations', Ph.D. dissertation, University of California, Berkeley: 1979.

Obama Ritei, *Meiji bunka shiryō soshō*, vol. 1, Tokyo: Fukan shobō, 1961.

Obata Kyugoro, *An Interpretation of the Life of Viscount Shibusawa*, Tokyo: Daiyamondo Jigyo Kabushiki Kaisha, 1937.

Ogawa Masaaki, 'Jukkyū kisoku no seiritsu – Meiji zettaishugi kyūhin hō no keisei katei', in Fukushima Masao (ed.) *Koseki seido to 'ie' seido*, Tokyo: Tokyo daigaku shuppankai, 1959.

Ohkawa, Kazushi and Rosovsky, Henry, 'A Century of Japanese Economic Growth', in William W. Lockwood (ed.) *The State and Economic Enterprise*, Princeton, NJ: Princeton University Press, 1965.

Oka Minoru, *Kōjōhō ron*, rev. edn, Tokyo: Yūhikaku, 1917.

Oka Yoshitake, 'Generational Conflict after the Russo-Japanese War', in Tetsuo Najita and J. Victor Koschmann (eds) *Conflict in Modern Japanese History: The Neglected Tradition*, Princeton, NJ: Princeton University Press, 1982.

Oka Yoshitake and Hayashi Shigeru (eds), *Taishō demokurashii ki no seiji: Matsumoto Gōkichi seiji nisshi*, Tokyo: Iwanami shoten, 1959.

Ōki Tōkichi, 'Kangaku to shisō mondai', *Shibun* 2, 4 (1920): 1–8.

Ōkōchi Kazuo, *Nihon no rōdō kumiai*, Tokyo: Tōyō keizai shimpō sha, 1954.

—— 'Nihonteki rōshi kankei no genkei: Dai-ichiji taisengo no "kōjō iinkai" o megutte', in Ariizumi Tōru (ed.) *Nihon rōshi kankei no kenkyū*, Tokyo: Tokyo daigaku shuppankai, 1963.

—— 'Nihonteki rōshi kankei to sono dentō', *Keizaigaku ronshū* 29 (1963): 1–13.

Okuda Kenji, *Hito to keiei*, Tokyo: Manejimento sha, 1985.

Osaka-shi, Shakai-bu, Shomuka, *Shakai jigyō shi*, Osaka, Osaka-shi, Shakai-bu, Shomuka, 1924.

Ōshima Kiyoshi, *Takano Iwasaburō den*, Tokyo: Iwanami shoten, 1968.

Patrick, Hugh T., 'The Economic Muddle of the 1920's', in James W. Morley (ed.) *Dilemmas of Growth in Prewar Japan*, Princeton, NJ: Princeton University Press, 1971.

Pyle, Kenneth B., *The New Generation in Meiji Japan: Problems of Cultural Identity, 1885–1895*, Stanford, Calif.: Stanford University Press, 1969.

—— 'The Technology of Japanese Nationalism: The Local Improvement Movement, 1900–1918', *Journal of Asian Studies* 33 (1973): 51–65.

—— 'Advantages of Followership: German Economics and Japanese Bureaucrats, 1890–1925', *Journal of Japanese Studies* 1, 1 (1974): 127–64.

Rice, Richard, 'Economic Mobilization in Wartime Japan: Business, Bureaucracy, and Military in Conflict', *Journal of Asian Studies* 38 (1979): 689–706.

'Rōdō mondai tokubetsu iinkai', *Seiyū* 235 (1919): 49–50.

Rōdōshō, *Rōdō gyōsei shi*, vol. 1, Tokyo: Rōdō hōrei kyōkai, 1961.

Rōdō undō shiryō iinkai (ed.), *Nihon rōdō undō shiryō*, 10 vols, Tokyo: Rōdō undō shiryō kankō iinkai, 1959–68.

Rohlen, Thomas P., *For Harmony and Strength: Japanese White-Collar Organization in Anthropological Perspective*, Berkeley: University of California Press, 1974.

Rosenstone, Robert A., *Mirror in the Shrine: American Encounters with Meiji Japan*, Cambridge, Mass.: Harvard University Press, 1988.

Sakurabayashi Makoto, 'Senji Nihon no rōshi kyōgisei: sangyō hōkokukai no kondankai o chūshin toshite', *Jōchi keizai ronshū* 18 (1972): 37–84.

Sakai Yūzaburō, 'Shakai mondai', *Kokumin no tomo* 81, 82, and 83 (1890): 21–7, 23–8, 15–20.

Saxonhouse, Gary R., 'Country Girls and Communication among Competitors in the Japanese Cotton-Spinning Industry', in Hugh Patrick (ed.) *Japanese Industrialization and Its Social Consequences*, Berkeley: University of California Press, 1976.

Scott, John Paul, 'Science and Social Control', in John Paul Scott and Sarah F. Scott (eds) *Social Control and Social Change*, Chicago: University of Chicago Press, 1971.

'Seimu chōsakai', *Seiyū* 232 (1918): 49.

Sekiya Kōichi (ed.), *Seikatsu koten sōsho*, vol. 6, *Tsukijima chōsa*, Tokyo: Kōseikan, 1970.

Shakai hoshō kenkyū-jo (ed.) *Nihon shakai hoshō zenshi shiryō*, 7 vols, Tokyo: Shiseidō, 1982–3.

Shakai kyoku, Rōdōbu, *Wagakuni ni okeru rōdō iinkai no gaikyō*, Tokyo: Shakai kyoku, Rōdōbu, 1937.

Shakai seisaku gakkai shiryō shūsei hensan iinkai (ed.), *Shakai seisaku gakkai shiryō shūsei*, vol. 1, *Kōjōhō to rōdō mondai*, Tokyo: Ochanomizu shobō, 1977.

—— *Shakai seisaku gakkai shiryō shūsei*, appendix vol. 1, Tokyo: Ochanomizu shobō, 1978.

Shibusawa Eiichi, *Rongo to soroban*, Tokyo: Tōadō shobō, 1916.

—— 'Kyōchōkai', in Shihon rōdō mondai kenkyūkai (ed.) *Rōshi mondai sōsho*, vol. 2, Tokyo: Shihon rōdō mondai kenkyūkai, 1919.

—— 'Rōdō mondai kaiketsu no konpongi', *Shakai seisaku jihō* 1 (1920): 1–5.

—— 'Sameyo rōshi aitazuaete', *Hito to hito* 1, 1 (1921): 6–9.

—— *Keizai to dōtoku*, Tokyo: Shibusawa Ō shōtokukai, 1938.

—— *Shosei no daidō*, Tokyo: Jitsugyō no sekaisha, 1954.

Shibusawa Hideo, *Chichi, Shibusawa Eiichi*, 2 vols, Tokyo: Jitsugyō no Nihon sha, 1959.

Shibusawa Seien kinen zaidan ryūmonsha (ed.), *Shibusawa Eiichi denki shiryō*, 58 vols and 10 appendix vols, Tokyo: Shibusawa Seien kinen zaidan ryūmonsha, 1955–71.

Shimada Tosho, 'Jikyoku mondai kanken', *Seiyū* 223 (1918): 2–7.

Shimomura Kojin, *Kono hito o miyo*, Tokyo: Tazawa Yoshiharu ken-shōkai, 1966.

Shiozawa Masatada, 'Dōmei higyō oyobi sono yobōsaku', *Taiyō* 18 (1912): 78–90.

—— 'Rōdō mondai no honshitsu to sono kaiketsu hōshin', *Shakai seisaku jihō* 4 (1920): 1–22.

Smith, Robert J., 'Presidential Address: Something Old, Something New: Tradition and Culture in the Study of Japan', *Journal of Asian Studies* 48, 4 (1989): 715–23.

Smith, Thomas C., 'The Right to Benevolence: Dignity and Japanese Workers, 1890–1920', *Comparative Studies in Society and History* 26, 4 (1984): 587–613.

Smith, Warren W. Jr, *Confucianism in Modern Japan: A Study of Conservatism in Japanese Intellectual History*, 2nd edn, Tokyo: Hokuseido Press, 1973.

Sōdōmei gojūnenshi kankō iinkai, *Sōdōmei gojūnenshi*, vol. 1, Tokyo: Sōdōmei gojūnenshi kankō iinkai, 1964.

Soeda Keiichirō, 'Rōshi kyōchō no konpongi', *Shimin* 15 (1920): 15–19.

—— 'Gojin no shimei', *Hito to hito* 1, 1 (1921): 2–5.

—— 'Kyōchō ni taisuru nishu no hihan', *Shakai seisaku jihō* 7 (1921): 1–3.

—— 'Rōdō iinkaihō seitei no hitsuyō', *Shakai seisaku jihō* 15 (1921): 1–6.

—— 'Rōdō mondai no kaiketsu', *Shakai seisaku jihō* 5 (1921): 1–5.

—— 'Sōkan isshūnen ni saishite', *Hito to hito* 2, 4 (1922): 2–4.

—— 'Kyōchōshugi no seishin narabi ni Kyōchōkai no jigyō', in Kyōchōkai (ed.) *Shakai seisaku kōgiroku*, vol. 3, Tokyo: Kyōchōkai, 1923.

—— 'Rōdō iinkai seido', *Chikuhō sekitan kōgyō kumiai geppō* 22 (1926): 33–42.

—— 'Sangyō heiwa to rōdō kumiaihō', *Shakai seisaku jihō* 120 (1930): 1–8.

Soeda Keiichirō kun kinenkai, *Soeda Keiichirō den*, Tokyo: Soeda Keiichirō kun kinenkai, 1955.

Stanley, Thomas A., *Ōsugi Sakae, Anarchist in Taishō Japan: The Creativity of the Ego*, Cambridge, Mass.: Harvard University Press, 1982.

Staude, John Raphael, 'German Socialists and Russian Soviets: The Transfer of Workers' Councils from Russia to Germany in 1918', in C.D.W. Goodwin and I.B. Holley, Jr (eds) *The Transfer of Ideas: Historical Essays*, Durham, NC: The South Atlantic Quarterly, 1968

Stoddard, William Leavitt, *The Shop Committee, A Handbook for Employer and Employee*, New York: The MacMillan Company, 1919.

Stone, Alan Atwood, 'The Vanishing Village: The Ashio Copper Mine Pollution Case, 1890–1907', PhD dissertation, University of Washington, 1974.

Sugaya Akira, *Nihon iryō seisaku shi*, Tokyo: Nihon hyōronsha, 1977.

Sugiyama, Chuhei, 'The Development of Economic Thought in Meiji Japan', *Modern Asian Studies* 2 (1968): 325–41.

Sumiya Etsuji, *Nihon keizaigaku shi*, Tokyo: Minerubua shobō, 1958.

Sumiya Etsuji, Yamaguchi Kōsaku, Koyama Hitoshi, Asada Mitsuteru and Koyama Hirotake, *Taishō demokurashii no shisō*, Tokyo: Haga shoten, 1969.

Sumiya Mikio, *Nihon chinrōdō shiron*, Tokyo: Tokyo daigaku shuppankai, 1955.

—— *Katayama Sen*, Tokyo: Tokyo daigaku shuppankai, 1960.

—— *Nihon no rōdō mondai*, Tokyo: Tokyo daigaku shuppankai, 1967.

Suzuki Bunji, 'Kanryōshugi ka minponshugi ka', *Rōdō oyobi sangyō* 8, 11 (1919): 1–8.

—— 'Rōdō kyōchōkai o hyōsu', *Rōdō oyobi sangyō* 8, 9 (1919): 1–8.

—— *Rōdō undō nijūnen*, Tokyo: Ichigensha, 1931.

Taft, Philip, 'Germany', in Walter Galenson (ed.) *Comparative Labor Movements*, New York: Russell & Russell, 1952.

Taikakai, *Naimushō shi*, 4 vols, Tokyo: Chihō zaimu kyōkai, 1970.

Taira, Koji, *Economic Development and the Labor Market in Japan*, New York: Columbia University Press, 1970.

Takamura Naosuke, 'Dokusen shihonshugi no kakuritsu to chūshō kigyō', in *Iwanami kōza: Nihon rekishi*, vol. 18, Tokyo: Iwanami shoten, 1975.

Takano Iwasaburō, 'Kyūsai jigyō chōsakai no juyō ninmu', *Kokka gakkai zasshi* 32 (1918): 153–7.

Tanaka Sōgorō, *Shiryō: Taishō shakai undō shi*, vol. 1, Tokyo: San'ichi shobō, 1970.

Tazawa Yoshiharu, 'Kyōchōshugi no dōtokuteki kisō', *Shakai seisaku jihō* 9 (1921): 1–6.

—— 'Kagai kōen', in Mombushō, Jitsugyō gakumu kyoku (ed.) *Kōmin kyōiku kōenshu*, vol. 1, Tokyo: Mombushō kōnai, Jitsugyō hoshū kyōiku kenkyūkai, 1923.

—— *Tazawa Yoshiharu senshū*, Tokyo: Tazawa Yoshiharu kinenkai, 1967.

Tiedemann, Arthur E., 'The Hamaguchi Cabinet: First Phase July 1929–February 1930: A Study in Japanese Parliamentary Government', PhD dissertation, Columbia University, 1959.

'Tokonami naishō no kunji', *Seiyū* 254 (1918): 3.

Tokonami Takejirō, 'Minryoku kanyō no shingi', *Shimin* 14 (1919): 1–3.
—— *Rōdō mondai*, n.p., 1922.
Tokutomi Iichirō, *Hakushaku Kiyoura Keigo den*, 2 vols, Tokyo: Hakushaku Kiyoura Keigo den kankōkai, 1932.
Totten, George O., 'Collective Bargaining and Works Councils as Innovations in Industrial Relations in Japan during the 1920s', in R.P. Dore (ed.) *Aspects of Social Change in Modern Japan*, Princeton, NJ: Princeton University Press, 1970.
—— 'Japanese Industrial Relations at the Crossroads: The Great Noda Strike of 1927–1928', in Bernard S. Silberman and H.D. Harootunian (eds) *Japan in Crisis: Essays on Taishō Democracy*, Princeton, NJ: Princeton University Press, 1974.
Toyohara Matao, *Sakuma Teiichi shoden*, Tokyo: Shūeisha, 1904.
Tsuchiya Takao, *Shibusawa Eiichi den*, Tokyo: Tōyō shokan, 1955.
—— *Nihon keieisha seishin*, Tokyo: Keizai ōraisha, 1959.
Tsuchiana Fumito, 'Dai-ichiji taisengo no shakai seisaku no tenkai', *Takushoku daigaku ronshū* 115 (1978): 63–134.
Tsuji Hidetake, *Ōita-ken no shakai fukushi jigyō shi*, Ōita: Ōita-ken shakai fukushi kyōgikai, 1973.
Tsuji Zennosuke (ed.) *Jizen kyūsai shiryō*, Tokyo: Kinkōdō shoseki kabushiki kaisha, 1932.
Uda Kikue, Takasawa Takeji and Furukawa Kōjun, *Shakai fukushi no rekishi: seisaku to undō no tenkai*, Tokyo: Yūhikaku, 1977.
Ujihara Shōjirō, 'Dai-ichiji taisengo no rōdō chōsa to *Yoka seikatsu no kenkyū*', in Ujihara Shōjirō (ed.) *Seikatsu koten sōsho*, vol. 8, *Yoka seikatsu no kenkyū*, Tokyo: Kōseikan, 1970.
Ujihara Shōjirō and Hagiwara Susumu, 'Sangyō hōkoku undō no haikei', in Tokyo daigaku shakai kagaku kenkyūjo (ed.) *Fuashizumu-ki no kokka to shakai*, vol. 6, Tokyo: Tokyo daigaku shuppankai, 1979.
Umegaki, Michio, *After the Restoration: The Beginning of Japan's Modern State*, New York: New York University Press, 1988.
US Department of State. *The Paris Peace Conference, 1919*, 5 vols, *Papers Relating to the Foreign Relations of the United States*, 77th Congress, 2nd Session, Washington, DC, Government Printing Office, 1943.
Usui Katsumi, 'Verusaiyu, Washington taisei to Nihon no shihaizō', in Hashikawa Bunzō and Matsumoto Sannosuke (eds) *Kindai Nihon seiji shisō shi*, vol. 2, of Oka Yoshitake and Hayashi Shigeru (eds) *Kindai Nihon shisō shi taikei*, vol. 4, Tokyo: Yūhikaku, 1970.
Vogel, Ezra, *Comeback: Case by Case: Building the Resurgence of American Business*, New York: Simon & Schuster, 1985.
Wada Toyoji den hensanjo (ed.) *Wada Toyoji den*, Tokyo: Wada Toyoji den hensanjo, 1926.
Waldman, Marilyn Robinson, 'Tradition as a Modality of Change: Islamic Examples', *History of Religions* 25, 4 (1986): 318–40.
Watanabe Tōru, 'Rōdō mondai, rōdō undō e no ronhyō', in Inoue Kiyoshi and Watanabe Tōru (eds) *Taishō-ki no kyūshinteki jiyūshugi: Tōyō keizai shimpō o chūshin toshite*, Tokyo: Tōyō keizai shimpōsha, 1972.
Yamada Yasuko, 'Rinpō jigyō to Kyōchōkai zenrinkan ni tsuite', *Hito to hito* 2, 6 (1922): 24–7.
Yamaji Aizan, 'Genji no shakai mondai oyobi shakaishugisha', *Dokuritsu*

hyōron 3 (1908), reprint in Yoshino Sakuzō (ed.) *Meiji bunka zenshū*, vol. 21, Tokyo: Nihon hyōronsha, 1929.

Yamamoto Tsuneo, *Kindai Nihon toshi kyōka shi kenkyū*, Nagoya, Reimei shobō, 1972.

Yamamura, Kozo, 'Then Came the Great Depression, Japan's Interwar Years', in Herman van der Wee (ed.) *The Great Depression Revisited: Essays on the Economics of the Thirties*, The Hague: Netherlands, Martinus Nijhoff, 1972.

—— 'The Japanese Economy, 1911–1930: Concentration, Conflicts, and Crises', in Bernard S. Silberman and H.D. Harootunian (eds) *Japan in Crisis: Essays on Taishō Democracy*, Princeton, NJ: Princeton University Press, 1974.

Yasuda Hiroshi, 'Seitō seiji taiseika no rōdō seisaku', *Rekishigaku kenkyū* 420 (1975): 15–28.

—— 'Nihon teikokushugi kakuritsu-ki no rōdō mondai', *Rekishigaku kenkyū* 497 (1980): 124–37.

Yatsugi Kazuo, *Mukashi no rōdō sōgi no omoide*, Tokyo: Kokusaku kenkyūkai shuppanbu, 1956.

Yatsuhama Tokusaburō, 'Shokugyō shōkai jigyō no seishin', *Shakai seisaku jihō* 3 (1920): 62–8.

Yonekawa Norio, 'Kyōchōkai no rōdō kumiai ron', *Keizai ronshū* (Niigata daigaku) 26–7 (1979): 81–108.

—— 'Kyōchōkai no seiritsu katei', *Niigata daigaku keizaigaku nempō* 3 (1979): 55–77.

Yoshida Kyūichi, 'Meiji isshin ni okeru hinkon no henshitsu', in Nihon shakai jigyō daigaku kyūhin seido kenkyūkai (ed.) *Nihon no kyūhin seido*, Tokyo: Keisō shobō, 1960.

—— 'Meiji isshin ni okeru kyūhin seido', in Nihon shakai jigyō daigaku kyūhin seido kenkyūkai (ed.) *Nihon no kyūhin seido*, Tokyo: Keisō shobō, 1960.

—— *Nihon shakai jigyō no rekishi*, rev. edn, Tokyo: Keisō shobō, 1966.

—— *Gendai shakai jigyō shi kenkyu*, Tokyo: Keisō shobō, 1979.

Yoshida Shigeru, *Rōdō kumiaihō no seitei ni tsuite*, n.p., 1930.

—— 'Shūnin no kotoba', *Shakai seisaku jihō* 129 (1931): 1–4.

Yoshida Shigeru denki kankō henshū iinkai (ed.) *Yoshida Shigeru*, Tokyo: Yoshida Shigeru denki kankō henshū iinkai, 1969.

Yoshii Yukiko, 'Sangyō hōkoku undō: sono seiritsu o megutte', *Hitotsubashi ronsō* 73 (1975): 35–52.

Young, A. Morgan, *Japan Under Taisho Tenno, 1912–1926*, London: George Allen & Unwin Ltd, 1928.

Index